MIT Lincoln Laboratory

Technology in the National Interest

Edited by Eva C. Freeman

Lincoln Laboratory
Massachusetts Institute of Technology
Lexington, Massachusetts

Right: Lincoln Laboratory in 1956, after the completion of Building F and the cafeteria.

Contents

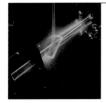
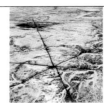

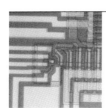

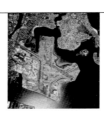

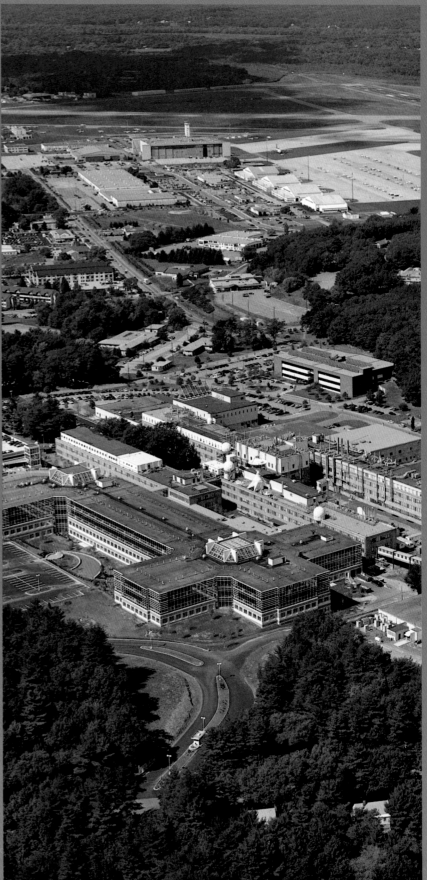

Foreword

President Charles M. Vest, standing, and Provost Mark S. Wrighton, Massachusetts Institute of Technology

Since Lincoln Laboratory's founding in 1951, it has been an integral part of the Massachusetts Institute of Technology. We are proud to operate a laboratory that has accomplished so much in support of the missions of the Department of Defense and other federal agencies. The Laboratory has made significant contributions to the science and technology base underlying the strength of the United States as a world leader. Many remarkable achievements of Lincoln Laboratory are detailed in this book, in which we review our history and capabilities as we prepare to assist the nation into the twenty-first century.

Several attributes have characterized the staff of Lincoln Laboratory throughout its history. Whether we are referring to the successes in developing air defense technology, improving the air traffic control system, contributing to the educational development of scientists and engineers or transferring know-how and show-how to small and large companies, the Laboratory staff has exemplified enduring qualities in executing its tasks. These qualities include responsiveness, dedication, commitment to excellence and a spirit of partnership with our sponsors.

The Laboratory's *responsiveness* has been evident since its founding. The U.S. Air Force called on MIT to establish Lincoln Laboratory to provide technical assistance in addressing the threat posed by the Soviet Union. In the ensuing years, the Laboratory's size and scope of activities have changed in response to national needs.

Dedication distinguishes the staff of the Laboratory. The work of Lincoln Laboratory is often at the cutting edge of technology; indeed, the development of new technologies at the Laboratory — including lasers, communications systems and computers — is a source of pride. These achievements stem from hard, innovative work by a dedicated staff. For example, hundreds of MIT Lincoln Laboratory employees have worked at the missile test range facility on the tiny atoll of Kwajalein in the Pacific, supporting efforts to develop missile defense systems.

A commitment to excellence is found in all facets of the Laboratory's activity. This excellence is achieved by the selection of world-class scientists and engineers to join the Laboratory staff and a rigorous annual performance review process. The result is an organization committed to doing the best work most efficiently and most creatively. The widely held view of Lincoln Laboratory as a premier research and development organization stems from its exceptional efforts to build quality by attracting and retaining the best people. The partnership with MIT helps provide a setting that nurtures and encourages this excellence.

Lincoln Laboratory is a national resource with a rich history of achievements that have been *attained in a spirit of partnership with our sponsors*. Problems are addressed, and their solutions identified and developed, in close collaboration with the Department of Defense and other agencies of the federal government, including the Federal Aviation Administration. This tradition of partnership must be sustained as we continue to serve the nation in the decades ahead. MIT and its Lincoln Laboratory look forward to a future of scientific and technological leadership in the national interest.

Charles M. Vest
President

Mark S. Wrighton
Provost

Acknowledgments

This book would not have been possible without the contributions of numerous past and current Lincoln Laboratory staff members. I am most grateful to the individuals who wrote or coordinated portions of the book: Allan Anderson, John Andrews, Bob Bergemann, Sid Borison, Barry Burke, Bill Delaney, John Evans, Alan Grometstein, Dennis Hall, Hal Heggestad, Lenny Johnson, Bill Keicher, Israel Kupiec, Ben Lax, Jack Lifsitz, Richard Lippmann, Ted Lyszczarz, Alan McWhorter, Ivars Melngailis, Walter Morrow, Ed Muehe, Al Murphy, Burt Nichols, Chuck Primmerman, Charles Rader, Richard Ralston, Bob Richardson, Mordy Rothschild, Ed Schwartz, Dave Spears, Ernie Stern, Mel Stone, Leo Sullivan, Bor-Yeu Tsaur, Bill Ward, Steve Weiner, Cliff Weinstein and Jerry Welch. To each of you, many thanks.

I would like to express my profound appreciation to Walter Morrow, Director of Lincoln Laboratory, who conceived of this project and gave it his steady support, and to three Assistants to the Director: Alan Grometstein, who initiated the effort, Walter Wells, who oversaw the compilation of the work, and Roger Sudbury, who brought it to completion. It has been a joy to work for each of you.

Leslie Spiro enhanced the text through her careful review and skillful editing, and dedicated many hours to expediting the production of this book. Karen Challberg copyedited and proofread the text under enormous time pressure, and helped to ensure that no errors crept in during the final stages of production. Archivist Mary Murphy, who seems able to track down every Lincoln Laboratory document ever written, has been an invaluable resource. Thanks also to the following members of the Lincoln Laboratory Publications Group: Jonathan Barron, who took the cover photograph; Susan Dionne, who scanned the artwork; Richard Doubleday, who produced the line art; and Phoebe Wang, who organized the photographs. I would like to express my profound gratitude to Celia Metcalf, who created the innovative design of this book, and to Randall Warniers, who added his own flair for the visual element and who maintained the design integrity of each page. I am particularly indebted to Jack Nolan, who did an outstanding job in the massive task of collecting the photographs.

If there is one individual without whom this book would never have been completed, it certainly is Bill Ward. Bill collected artwork, checked the text, pursued authors and wrote three chapters. Bill put in an extraordinary number of hours into seeing that all the pieces came together.

I would also like to acknowledge the efforts of earlier Lincoln Laboratory historians, Joe Mindel and Lucy Nedzel, whose work provided a strong foundation for this book.

My most heartfelt thanks go to the management of Lincoln Laboratory and the Massachusetts Institute of Technology for their enlightened view of the needs of the modern family. The outstanding care provided by the staff of the Lincoln Laboratory Child Care Center meant that my younger daughter was actually better off than if I had stayed home. I must also express my gratitude to my immediate supervisors for giving me the most valuable gift of all — time to be with my children. For allowing me flexibility in my work hours, my husband, Jerry Black, my beautiful daughters, Holly and Laurel Black, and I cannot express our thanks sufficiently.

It is this sensitivity to the needs of real people that is the essence of Lincoln Laboratory, and that will maintain the Laboratory's strength into the next century.

Eva C. Freeman
Editor

Introduction

The end of the Cold War in the 1990s has ushered in an era of astonishing political shifts and regional conflicts. The world has changed, and so too has Lincoln Laboratory. For Lincoln Laboratory these changes are marking the beginning of a new era, one requiring a refocusing of many efforts and a redirection of talents. And thus the time is right to document Lincoln Laboratory's contributions during the Cold War years, to review the Laboratory's many achievements and to plan its future activities in developing technology in the national interest.

A history of Lincoln Laboratory must begin with the nation's need for air defense, for that is why the Laboratory was brought into being. By the end of the 1940s, the Union of Soviet Socialist Republics had developed both the atomic bomb and the long-range bombers that could deliver a bomb to the United States. The possibility that the Soviet Union might be able to send aircraft to drop atomic bombs on the United States suddenly became a terrible reality, and the Truman administration asked the U.S. Air Force to develop a system to defend the nation against that threat. The Air Force called on the Massachusetts Institute of Technology for technical assistance, and in 1951 MIT founded Lincoln Laboratory as a "Laboratory for Air Defense." Its mission: to develop an air defense system that could detect, identify, intercept and direct resources against hostile aircraft.

Lincoln Laboratory met that challenge.

The design of the air defense system known as the Semiautomatic Ground Environment (SAGE) called for widely ranging scientific and engineering advances: digital communications, a real-time software system, networking and, most difficult of all, a completely reliable computer. None of these existed in 1951, but Lincoln Laboratory took on the job and, through a combination of hard work and inspiration, successfully developed the technology and worked with industry to demonstrate and complete the SAGE design. The SAGE program had an extraordinary impact on the high-technology industry throughout the United States and especially in eastern Massachusetts. It is no exaggeration to say that SAGE created the computer industry and digital communications. International Business Machines, the prime contractor for SAGE computers, utilized the expertise it developed during the SAGE program to become the world's largest commercial computer manufacturer. Kenneth Olsen built on his experience working on SAGE at Lincoln Laboratory to found, with fellow Laboratory staff member Harlan Anderson, the Digital Equipment Corporation. Indeed, much of the eastern Massachusetts high-technology electronics industry originated in the engineering talent and financial resources that flowed from the SAGE program.

In 1952 Lincoln Laboratory hosted a Summer Study that undertook an assessment of the vulnerability of the United States to surprise air attack and the need for early warning of an approaching attack. This study led to the creation of the Distant Early Warning (DEW) Line, a network of radars stretching from Alaska to Greenland. Lincoln Laboratory assisted the Air Force in the development of radars and long-range communication systems for the DEW Line and for the Ballistic Missile Early Warning System (BMEWS), which led to the Laboratory's subsequent participation in the development of radar systems for ballistic missile defense and satellites for military communications.

The Laboratory's role as an MIT research and development organization did not extend to system implementation. Therefore, in 1958 the MITRE Corporation was formed from part of Lincoln Laboratory to complete the engineering task of SAGE deployment, and the early air defense era came to an end. This was a critical moment in Lincoln Laboratory's history. Its mission was accomplished, and the question came up whether the Laboratory should continue operations. In 1951 the assumption had been that the Laboratory would close once the air defense program was completed. The personnel office had even made a practice of informing new employees that their moving expenses would be covered when the program ended.

Figure 1-6
Building 22 at MIT, constructed to house the Radiation Laboratory during World War II, was the site of early work on Project Lincoln.

Figure 1-7
The Barta Building, home of Whirlwind.

Killian emphasized that the current Lincoln budget figures were "firm conclusions" and that the time had come when "we must squarely face the question as to whether budgetary arrangements can be made which can assure the necessary continuity of the project."

MIT's own policies caused some of the financial problems. Internal regulations prohibited the transfer of funds from MIT's endowment to Project Lincoln — even if the funds had already been allotted. Because MIT could not give Project Lincoln a financial cushion, Killian asked Finletter for reassurance that it should be managing the program:

"The Institute would welcome objective and outside judgment as to the advisability (1) of the project itself being carried through and (2) as to whether MIT is the best agency to do it." [12]

The reply from Finletter on February 5, 1952, emphatically assured Killian of MIT's suitability as a contractor for air defense research.[13] However, his letter begged the question of how the Air Force could meet all its financial responsibilities. Finletter promised that 1952 funds would be forthcoming, but he did not offer any reassurance for 1953.

Finletter's letter notwithstanding, Brigadier General Donald Yates, director of Air Force research and development and chairman of the Joint Advisory Committee (JAC), instructed Loomis to cut $4 million from his 1953 budget of $18.2 million. Yates also warned Loomis that further cuts were likely, and he requested a detailed breakdown of the program budget.

Loomis was mastering the skills for working with the government. He submitted a twenty-five-page budget proposal, divided into two sections: itemized expenses for each division and project, and detailed descriptions of the projects. A one-page analysis summarized the status of the six-month-old Project Lincoln.

A JAC meeting was held on February 11, 1952, to review the proposed technical program and budget for 1953. At this landmark meeting General Yates stated that the Air Force was looking to Project Lincoln "as the focal point for Air Defense Research and Development." [14] Upon his recommendation, the committee approved an $18.2 million budget for 1953.

With staff coming on board and the funding secure, Loomis now turned his attention to the construction of buildings. The space on the MIT campus was already inadequate, and hundreds of employees were joining the project.

The sole site available on campus for classified work was Building 22 (Figure 1-6). Unclassified research was carried out in Building 20, and administrative offices of Project Lincoln were located in the Sloan Building at MIT. Temporary housing for the motor pool, the electronics shops and the publications office was found in a two-story commercial building on Vassar Street.

Although the MIT Digital Computer Laboratory (originally part of the Servomechanisms Laboratory) became part of Project Lincoln, work on Whirlwind continued to be carried out in the Barta Building on Massachusetts Avenue (Figure 1-7) and in the Whittemore Building on Albany Street.

Space was not the only issue. President Killian believed that MIT should not be carrying out classified research on the Cambridge campus. He thought that MIT had an obligation to disseminate its research results throughout the academic community and that classified research was inherently incompatible with this obligation. Therefore, Killian wanted MIT to maintain its integrity by conducting Project Lincoln off campus. The Bedford-Lincoln-Lexington area mentioned in the Charter for the Operation of Project Lincoln had space for new construction, and it was a comfortable distance from Cambridge.

Notes

12 Killian in *Project Lincoln Case History, Vol II*, pp. 3–4.

13 T.K. Finletter in *Project Lincoln Case History, Vol II*, p. 68.

14 Meeting notes recorded by J.G. Perry, in *Project Lincoln Case History, Vol. II*, p. 71.

This site was the Laurence G. Hanscom Field, now Hanscom Air Force Base and still the home of Lincoln Laboratory. Hanscom Field became a Commonwealth of Massachusetts facility in May 1941, when the state legislature acquired 509 acres for the construction of an airport. It was located in part in each of the towns of Concord, Lincoln, Lexington and Bedford, on a flat area between the Concord and Shawsheen Rivers. The official groundbreaking ceremony for the airfield, then known simply as the Boston Auxiliary Airport at Bedford, was held on June 26, 1941.

On February 11, 1943, the site was named the Laurence G. Hanscom Field, Boston Auxiliary Airport at Bedford, in memory of a *Worcester Telegraph* State House reporter who had died in an aircraft accident in 1941. Hanscom had been an aviation enthusiast and had served as the first commander of the Massachusetts Wing of the Civilian Air Reserve.

Following the United States' entry into World War II, Hanscom Field was pressed into service for national defense. The Army Corps of Engineers signed a lease with the Massachusetts Department of Public Works, and Army Air Forces units began to operate out of the airfield. Squadrons from Hanscom engaged in combat in both the Mediterranean and the European theaters of combat. After the war, control over the airfield, now expanded by about 600 acres, passed to the Commonwealth of Massachusetts, but military activity continued.

On October 12, 1951, as a result of the AFCRL's requirement for increased facilities, the Secretary of the Air Force informed the governor of Massachusetts of a military need for the airfield. The Commonwealth preferred to continue to lease the facility, and several months of negotiations ensued. On May 7, 1952, the federal and state governments reached a compromise: 396 acres were deeded to the United States, 641 acres were leased to the United States and 83 acres were retained by the Commonwealth.

A major construction project was carried out from 1952 to 1953. Taxiways, hangars, offices and military residences were constructed. The Shawsheen River was relocated, swamps were drained, hills were leveled and woodlands were cleared.

Groundbreaking for Project Lincoln began in 1951 at the foot of Katahdin Hill in Lexington. The site lay directly below 47 acres of farmland that had been acquired by MIT in 1948 as a site for cosmic-ray research. Twenty-six acres were transferred to the Army, and the remaining 21 acres were assigned to Project Lincoln.

The new buildings were laid out in an open-wing configuration, with alternate wings along a central axis. The plans called for four wings (Buildings A, B, C and D) plus a concrete block utility structure (Building E).

The Boston firm of Cram and Ferguson was chosen as the architect. Although the firm was among the oldest and largest of its kind in the United States, it was not generally associated with laboratory construction. In fact, the firm was better known for Gothic and art deco architecture, such as the Cathedral of St. John the Divine in New York City and the 1948 John Hancock building in Boston.

Cram and Ferguson came up with a modular design for the buildings, with each staff member allotted 9×9 sq ft. The main corridor of each building was 400 ft long, which yielded 44 modules along each side. Supporting columns were spaced 18 ft apart, and movable partitions were used for the internal walls.

Buildings were 60 ft wide, with 15-ft-wide corridors. Because laboratories required more space than offices, modules were 18 ft deep on one side of the corridor and 27 ft deep on the other. Buildings B and C each had four stories, three above and one below ground level. Buildings A and D had three stories, and the lowest levels were only partially below ground. Building E had a single story and a small basement. It held the receiving room, stockroom, storage area, shops and garage.

The Army Corps of Engineers contracted with the Volpe Construction Company to erect Building B on a cost-plus basis. Predictably, the bill was extremely high. After this experience, the Corps insisted on fixed-price bids for the remainder of the construction. Building B was completed on March 31, 1952, followed by Buildings D, A, C and E (Figure 1–8).

Building B was completed barely two years after the first meeting of ADSEC and less than a year after the Project Charles Final Report. The scientists and engineers working on Project Lincoln were talented indeed, as are so many working at Lincoln Laboratory today. But the MIT Radiation Laboratory had instituted procedures that were remarkably free of red tape, and this was its legacy to Project Lincoln.

Fear of nuclear holocaust pervaded the thinking of Americans in the 1950s, and the government of the United States was committed to protecting the country against this threat. Because Project Lincoln's mission was vital to the security of the nation, red tape was eliminated at all stages.

The Air Force had put its resources at the disposal of Project Lincoln. The staff had only one more problem to solve — they had to deliver a reliable air defense system for North America. And they would succeed.

Figure 1-8
Original Lincoln Laboratory building complex in Lexington.

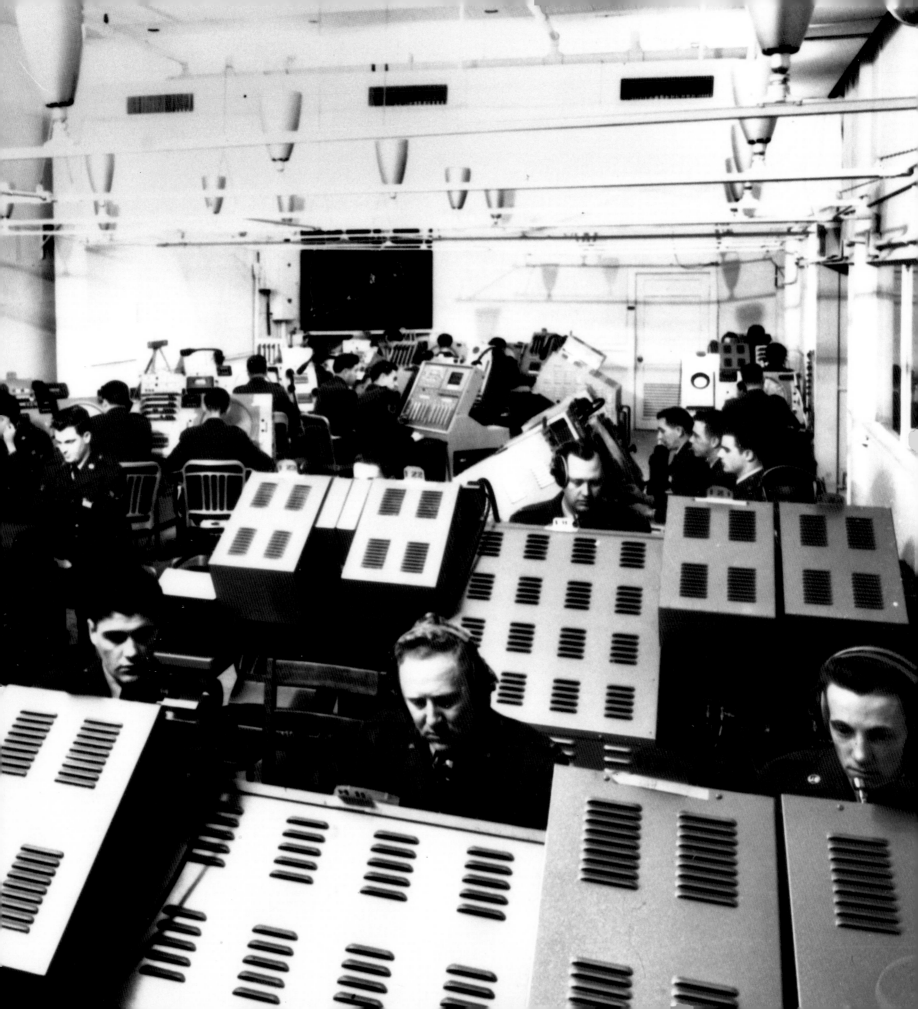

2   The SAGE Air Defense System

With the establishment of Lincoln
Laboratory, efforts turned from
validation of air defense concepts to
system implementation and testing.
Over a period of seven years the
Laboratory broke new ground in a
wide range of technologies, developed
the digital computer as a real-time
control system and successfully
completed the design of the SAGE air
defense system.

Left: Cape Cod System direction
center in the Barta Building.
The operators in the foreground are
intercept monitors.

By the spring of 1952 Project Lincoln had become a
major activity at MIT. Within only one year its personnel
had grown from zero to 550. It was time to give the program a greater sense of permanence.

The transition from Project Lincoln to Lincoln Laboratory was remarkably informal. F. Wheeler Loomis, the
director of Project Lincoln, simply decided that the name
Project Lincoln was obsolete and changed it. Loomis
made the name Lincoln Laboratory official in a letter to
MIT President James Killian on April 17, 1952:

"The Lincoln Steering Committee is inclined to be rather
dissatisfied with the appellation 'Project Lincoln' because
the word 'Project' seems to us to convey unnecessary
implications of impermanence and probably also to be
inappropriate to an organization of the scale of Lincoln.

"We propose, with your approval, to begin at once using
the name 'Lincoln Laboratory' for the *organization*.

"I believe that this change can be instituted without
higher approval, and without amendment of the Lincoln
Charter since, in that instrument, it is the *program* which is
denominated 'Project Lincoln.'"[1]

Loomis resigned his position as director on July 9, 1952.
When he originally agreed to become Lincoln Laboratory's first director, he had made it clear that he would be
willing to serve in that capacity for no more than a year.
And so, almost exactly one year after the signing of the
Charter for the Operation of Project Lincoln, Loomis
resumed his teaching duties at the University of Illinois.

Albert Hill became Lincoln Laboratory's second director,
a position he held until May 5, 1955. George Valley
continued to serve as associate director.

By 1952 the air defense program was already approaching a degree of maturity. A radar network had been
assembled, and Lincoln Laboratory was ready to begin
operational tests. The reliability of the computer, however, still posed a problem. Before plans for a nationwide
air defense system could be taken seriously, the computer
would have to become much more reliable.

Magnetic-Core Memory

Storage-tube memories, used for internal memory up to
the early 1950s, were large and slow. Worst of all, they
were unreliable.

The greatest breakthrough in the development of
Whirlwind was the invention of magnetic-core memory
(Figure 2-1). That invention was the key development
leading to the widespread adoption of computers for
industrial applications, because, unlike computers with
storage-tube memories, computers with magnetic-core
memories were reliable.

In 1947, while working on Whirlwind in the MIT
Servomechanisms Laboratory, Jay Forrester began to
think about developing a new type of memory. He conceived of a new way of configuring memory units — in
a three-dimensional structure. Although Forrester initially
thought of using glow-discharge tubes, preliminary tests
indicated that the emission process was too unreliable.

Lacking a good way to implement a three-dimensional
memory, Forrester dropped work on his concept for a
couple of years. Then in the spring of 1949 he saw an
advertisement from the Arnold Engineering Company
for a reversibly magnetizable material called Deltamax.
Forrester immediately recognized that this was the
material he needed for the three-dimensional memory
structure.

Forrester directed one of his students, William Papian, to
study combinations of small toroidal-shaped cores made
of ferromagnetic materials possessing rectangular hysteresis
loop characteristics. Papian's master's thesis, "A Coinci-
dent-Current Magnetic Memory Unit," completed in
August 1950, described the concept of magnetic-core
memories and showed how the cores could be combined
in planar arrays, which could in turn be connected into
three-dimensional assemblies.

Papian fabricated the first magnetic-core memory, a 2×2
array, in October 1950. The early results were encouraging, and by the end of 1951 a 16×16 array of metallic
cores was completed.

Figure 2-1
Magnetic-core-memory array.

Figure 2-2
Whirlwind core-memory banks.

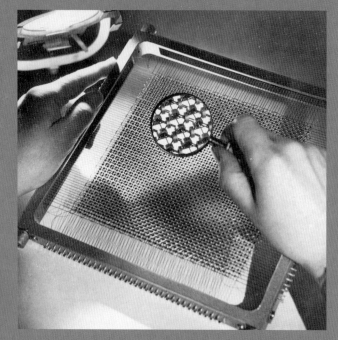

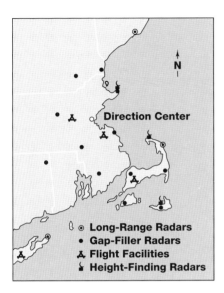

Figure 2-3
Map of the Cape Cod System.

Direction Center

◎ Long-Range Radars
• Gap-Filler Radars
⚓ Flight Facilities
⚑ Height-Finding Radars

Notes

1 Loomis in *Project Lincoln Case History, Vol. II*, p. 125.

2 This section has been taken largely from C.R. Wieser, "The Cape Cod System," *Ann. Hist. Comput.* **5**, 362 (1983).

The organization and direction of Project Whirlwind now went through a major change. The task of developing a flight simulator was abandoned, and the focus of the program shifted to air defense. In September 1951 all members of the Servomechanisms Laboratory who were working on Whirlwind were assigned to a new laboratory — the MIT Digital Computer Laboratory, headed by Jay Forrester. Six months later, the Digital Computer Laboratory was absorbed by Lincoln Laboratory as the Digital Computer Division. Lincoln Laboratory took over the development of magnetic-core memories.

Operation of the early metallic magnetic-core memories was still unsatisfactory — switching times were 30 μsec or longer. Therefore, in cooperation with the Solid State and Transistor Group, Forrester began an investigation of ferrites. These nonconducting magnetic materials had weaker output signals than the metallic cores, but their switching times were at least ten times faster.

In May 1952 a 16×16 array of ferrite cores was operated as a memory, with an adequate signal and a switching time of less than a microsecond. So promising was the performance of the new array that the Digital Computer Division began construction of a $32 \times 32 \times 6$ memory, the first three-dimensional memory.

Whirlwind was by this time in considerable demand, so a new machine called the Memory Test Computer was built to evaluate the 16,384-bit core memory. When the Memory Test Computer went into operation in May 1953, the magnetic-core memory, in sharp contrast to the electrostatic-storage-tube memory in Whirlwind, was highly reliable.

Forrester promptly removed the core memory from the Memory Test Computer and installed it in Whirlwind. The first bank of core storage was wired into Whirlwind on August 8, 1953 (Figure 2-2). A month later a second bank went in. A different memory was subsequently installed in the Memory Test Computer, enabling that machine to be used in other applications. The improvement

in Whirlwind's performance was dramatic. Operating speed doubled; the input data rate quadrupled. Maintenance time on the memory dropped from four hours per day to two hours per week, and the mean time between memory failures jumped from two hours to two weeks.

The invention of core memory was a watershed in the development of commercial computers. The technology was quickly adopted by International Business Machines (IBM), and the first nonmilitary system to use magnetic-core memories, the IBM 704, went on the market in 1955. Magnetic cores were used in virtually all computers until 1974, when they were superseded by semiconductor integrated-circuit memories.

The Cape Cod System
While the Digital Computer Division wrestled with Whirlwind, the Aircraft Control and Warning Division concentrated its efforts on verifying the underlying concepts of air defense.[2] A key recommendation in the Project Charles *Final Report* was that a small air defense system should be constructed and evaluated before work on a more extensive system began. The report proposed that the experimental network be established in eastern Massachusetts, that it include ten to fifteen radars and that all radars be connected to Whirlwind.

As soon as the air defense program began, Lincoln Laboratory started to set up an experimental system and named it, for its location, the Cape Cod System (Figure 2-3). It was functionally complete; all air defense functions could be demonstrated, tested and modified. The Cape Cod System was a model air defense system, scaled down in size but realistically embodying all operational functions.

Cape Cod, which was chosen because of its convenience to the Laboratory, was a good test site. It covered an area large enough for realistic testing of air defense functions. In addition, its location was challenging — hilly and bounded on two sides by the ocean, with highly variable weather and a considerable amount of air traffic.

Every aspect of the Cape Cod System called for innovation. Not only did it require radar netting, but radar data filtering was also needed to remove clutter that was not canceled by the moving-target indicator (MTI). Phone-line noise also had to be held within acceptable limits.

A long-range AN/FPS-3 radar, the workhorse of the operational air defense net, was installed at South Truro, Massachusetts, near the tip of Cape Cod, and equipped with an improved digital radar relay. Less powerful radars, known as gap fillers, were installed to enhance the coverage provided by the long-range system (Figure 2-4). Because near-total coverage was required, the beams of the radars in the network would have to overlap, which meant that they could be separated by no more than twenty-five miles.

Initially, two SCR-584 radars that had been developed during World War II by the MIT Radiation Laboratory were installed as gap fillers at Scituate and Rockport, Massachusetts. Early tests of these radars showed much shorter ranges than expected. Improvements in the components and the test equipment not only resolved the problem but also helped to establish an important policy: to activate sites well before the start of data acquisition.

As new radars became operational, each included a Mark-X identification, friend or foe (IFF) system, and reports were multiplexed with the radar data. Dedicated telephone circuits to the Barta Building in Cambridge were leased and tested.

Buffer storage had to be added to Whirlwind I to handle the insertion of data from the asynchronous radar network, and the software had to be expanded considerably. A direction center needed to be designed and constructed to permit Air Force personnel to operate the system: to control the radar data filtering, initiate and monitor tracks, identify aircraft and assign and monitor interceptors.

A high priority was to develop a radar mapper to filter data at the direction center. The radar MTI of the early 1950s was analog and provided limited subclutter visibil-

ity, especially at short range. Since targets could not be detected in dense clutter, insertion of dense clutter data into the computer wasted its capacity. A simple, ingenious solution was devised. It consisted of a polar plan position indicator (PPI) display of the incoming data for each radar. A single photocell was mounted above the horizontal cathode-ray-tube (CRT) face, and the photocell response to the bright blue initial flash from displayed position reports controlled a gate that passed the data into the computer. Consequently, any area of the tube face that was masked (opaque to blue light) resulted in rejection of the radar data. The mask material, a paint that could be applied or removed manually, transmitted the afterglow on the tube face so that data under the mask were visible to the operator but not to the photocell. Changes in clutter patterns were relatively slow, since they were caused by changes in weather. Another key problem was solved.

Construction of a realistic direction center depended heavily on the development of an interactive display console. Nothing comparable had ever been done before, and the technology was primitive. What was needed was a computer-generated PPI display that would include alphanumeric characters (for labels on aircraft tracks) and a separate electronic tote-board status display. Then the console operator could select display categories of information (for example, hostile aircraft tracks) without being distracted by all of the information available.

The Cape Cod display console was developed around the Stromberg-Carlson Charactron CRT. The tube contained an alphanumeric mask in the path of the electron beam. The beam was deflected to pass through the desired character on the mask, refocused and then deflected a second time to the desired location on the tube face — this was electronically complex, but it worked.

The console operator had a keyboard for data input and a light-sensing gun, which was used to recognize positional information and enter it into the computer (Figure 2-5). This novel means of control for high-speed computers was invented at the Laboratory by Robert Everett.

Notes

3 Lincoln Laboratory, *Joint Progress Report* JPR-2, 1 Dec. 1953, p. 4.

Figure 2-4, top
Gap-filler radar.

Figure 2-5, bottom
**An Air Force airman uses a light gun
to select tracks for identification and
display.**

A large part of the Cape Cod System effort was devoted to software development. For example, integration of the external storage drum was a software problem as well as a hardware problem. The scarcity of internal memory capacity required that much of the software be stored on the drum and transferred into the central computer when needed. The radar network data, also stored on a drum, had to be read into the computer and transformed into a common coordinate system for proper registration.

The software task was to develop quickly the largest real-time control program ever coded, and to do all the coding in machine language, since higher-order languages did not yet exist. Furthermore, the code had to be assembled, checked and realistically tested on a one-of-a-kind computer that was a shared test bed for software development, hardware development, demonstrations for visiting officials and training of the first crew of Air Force operators.

Even though radars were a critical element in the air defense system, Lincoln Laboratory did not contribute to the SAGE radar hardware because the Laboratory was forbidden to get involved in the design of the radars, which was the responsibility of the Air Defense Command (ADC). Lincoln Laboratory's assignment was to integrate the radars into an operational system. However, the Laboratory did perform field tests on various radars, and ADC based its specifications and procurements on those tests.

All these complex engineering tasks were carried out in parallel, on schedule and with little reworking. By September 1953, just two years and five months after the go-ahead, the Cape Cod System was fully operational. The radar network consisted of gap-filler radars, height-finding radars and long-range radars.

The software program could handle, in abbreviated form, most of the air defense tasks of an operational system. Facilities were in place to initiate and track forty-eight aircraft, identify and find the height of targets, control ten simultaneous interceptions from two air bases and give early warning and transmit data on twelve tracks to an antiaircraft operations center.[3]

Early-Warning Systems

In the summer of 1952 a group of scientists, engineers and military personnel met at Lincoln Laboratory to consider ways to improve the air defense of North America.[1] Headed by Jerrold Zacharias, the group included Albert Hill, director of Lincoln Laboratory, Herbert Weiss and Malcolm Hubbard, among others from the Laboratory, and a number of distinguished scientists including J. Robert Oppenheimer, Isidor Rabi and Robert Pound.

The 1952 Summer Study undertook the task of assessing the vulnerability of the United States to surprise air attack and recommending ways to lessen that vulnerability. Since the greatest threat appeared to be an air attack by the Soviet Union via the North Pole, the study group focused its attention on the airspace above the 55th parallel, where Soviet bombers, having passed over the Pole, could fly undetected nearly to the border of the United States.

The plan for SAGE, already under way, was to detect, identify, track and intercept just such aircraft. However, without early warning of an approaching attack, the readiness of interceptors and depth of airspace in which interception could take place would be drastically limited.

The Summer Study concluded it would be feasible to install a network of surveillance radars and communication links across northernmost North America from Alaska to Greenland that could give three to six hours' early warning against the threat envisioned. The results and recommendations of the study were briefed to key personnel of the DoD in late August 1952 and were well received.

The DEW Line

The DoD approved the 1952 Summer Study configuration for what would soon be known as the Distant Early Warning (DEW) Line, and directed the Air Force to take immediate implementing action. By December the Air Force had awarded a contract to Western Electric for the construction and operation of a radar and communications network across northern Canada. The difficulties of installing, operating and maintaining radars in the Arctic environment were immense, and the DEW Line, which became operational in 1957, remains an extraordinary feat of engineering (Figure 3-1).

In addition to hosting the Summer Study, Lincoln Laboratory provided numerous technical contributions to the DEW Line. One of the first issues the Summer Study had to resolve concerned the feasibility of long-distance communications in the Arctic. The frequent occurrence of solar disturbances in the far north ruled out the then standard forms of ionospheric-reflection HF communications. Fortunately, however, researchers at Lincoln Laboratory and MIT had already developed a better form of long-range communication — VHF ionospheric-scatter propagation, which was not susceptible to solar disturbances.

VHF scatter propagation used the inhomogeneities of the ionosphere to provide a reliable method of long-distance communications, even in the Arctic. Solar disturbances did not disrupt this form of communications; in fact, they often improved it. Moreover, VHF scatter propagation required only moderate-power transmitters — 10 to 50 kW. Until the advent of satellite communications, therefore, VHF scatter communications was able to provide a reliable method of rearward communications for the DEW Line. In addition, tropospheric-scatter propagation, also investigated in large part by Lincoln Laboratory, was adopted for multichannel lateral communication between stations along the DEW Line.

Another issue discussed at meetings of the Summer Study was the staffing of the installations. It was clearly desirable to post as few technicians as possible at each site, and the automatic alerting radar developed by Lincoln Laboratory provided a way to reduce personnel requirements. An automatic alerting radar sounds an alarm whenever an aircraft enters the area of surveillance, thus freeing site technicians from twenty-four-hour PPI scope vigilance. This radar was especially useful in the far northern regions, because the PPI scope was generally empty. With reasonably well-trained personnel, a typical site could be maintained with fewer than twenty technicians.

The X-1 automatic alerting radar was designed and fabricated in a five-month crash program at Lincoln Laboratory. Following the completion of this program, models X-2 through X-6 were designed and assembled in rapid succession for installation by Western Electric at test sites in Illinois and the Arctic. The design of the X-3 automatic alerting radar was turned over to Raytheon for engineering as a modification of the AN/TPS-1D, and production models were installed along the DEW Line. This radar was designated the AN/FPS-19. Lincoln Laboratory also had a hand in developing a continuous-wave bistatic fence radar that was used as a gap filler between AN/FPS-19 radars to detect low-flying aircraft. In the design of these radars, later designated AN/FPS-23, and in the improvement of large search radars, new techniques and components were introduced to decrease false-alarm rates and enhance automatic operation.

Yet another radar, the Sentinel (AN/FPS-30), was designed for the DEW Line East, an extension of the original line. This radar was built specifically for early-warning operation in the far north, and was characterized by improved high-altitude coverage, increased reliability, transistorized automatic alarm circuits and velocity filtering to minimize false alarms.

Lincoln Laboratory's efforts in radar design focused primarily on electrical engineering issues, but the high winds and extreme temperatures of the Arctic environment compelled Lincoln Laboratory to advance the mechanical engineering aspects of radars as well. Antenna shelters had to offer sufficient structural strength to withstand Arctic windstorms and still cause minimal attenuation of the radar beam. Before the development of the DEW Line, inflatable radomes had been occasionally used as antenna shelters, but inflatable radomes had great difficulty surviving Arctic conditions. Lincoln Laboratory solved this problem by developing rigid, electromagnetically transparent radomes. These radomes made possible not only uninterrupted operation of the DEW Line, but also a new generation of very large, precisely steerable antennas for long-range surveillance. This kind of rigid radome continues to be manufactured for many purposes.

Personnel in the newly formed Engineering Group approached Buckminster Fuller, inventor of the geodesic dome, and asked him for assistance in designing a rigid radome. Fuller suggested a three-quarter-sphere design and recommended polyester-bonded fiberglass, which offered a high strength-to-weight ratio, excellent weather resistance and reasonable cost.

The concept of the geodesic dome seemed feasible, so the Engineering Group at Lincoln Laboratory procured a series of prototype rigid radomes. The first one (31-ft equatorial diameter) was erected on the roof of Building C. It was unexpectedly pummeled by Hurricane Carol in August 1954, with winds estimated up to 110 mph, and no damage was inflicted. The radome was then disassembled and erected on Mount Washington in New Hampshire, and it successfully survived that mountain's fierce environment. A second 31-ft-diameter radome was erected over an AN/FPS-8 antenna on the roof of Building C. Tests demonstrated that the radome's effect on radar performance was negligible.

Lincoln Laboratory designed and procured a series of 50-ft-diameter rigid radomes that were installed in Thule, Greenland; Saglek Bay, Newfoundland; and Truro, Massachusetts. A second radome was also erected on the roof of Building C, where it sheltered the Sentinel antenna. The program culminated with the installation of a 150-ft-diameter radome at the Haystack Observatory (see chapter 7, "Space Science").

Western Electric carried out the immense and highly successful project of installing the DEW Line radars. The DEW Line was completed in October 1962 with an extension to Iceland, giving the Air Force a 6000-mi radar surveillance chain from the Aleutians to Iceland.

UHF Airborne Early-Warning Radar

Construction of the DEW Line resolved concerns about the security of the northern perimeter of the United States.[2] But, as was recognized both during the 1952 Summer Study and subsequently, the DEW Line did nothing to reduce the vulnerability of the east and west coast to an attack over the ocean.

With no land to the east or west of the United States, the logical counterpart to the DEW Line was airborne radar. The members of the Summer Study discussed the need for airborne early warning (AEW) radar and identified the most important requirements.

Notes

1 Material for this section was contributed by Daniel Dustin.

2 Material for this section was provided by William Ward.

Figure 3-1
One of the DEW Line radar sites.

Figure 3-2
Navy blimp installation of the
UHF AEW radar.

In particular, they observed that it was more important to alert SAGE of distant aircraft intrusion than to control interceptors. Range resolution, azimuth resolution and height-finding capability were, therefore, less important characteristics for AEW radars than sheer range. The need for the greatest possible range mandated the use of a relatively low operating frequency.

As radar wavelength increases (and frequency decreases), the effect of ripples and waves at the surface of the sea becomes progressively less noticeable. The sea is more mirrorlike at longer wavelengths, reflecting more incident radar energy and scattering less. Thus a double benefit was to be gained by changing from S-band (3000 MHz, the operating frequency of the AN/APS-20 AEW radar developed by the MIT Radiation Laboratory during World War II) to UHF (300 to 600 MHz). Sea-clutter returns received by the radar were reduced and the detection range was increased. In addition, since the Doppler shift of a sea-clutter return was smaller at lower frequencies, the airborne moving-target indicator (AMTI) circuit of a UHF AEW radar would cancel most of the sea-clutter spectrum (narrower by the ratio of the wavelengths) without also canceling a significant fraction of the high-speed airborne targets of interest.

The Summer Study concluded that UHF AEW radar looked like a winner, and it proved to be just that. A program began at Lincoln Laboratory in the summer of 1952 to study existing radars and to test the feasibility of UHF radar. The first goal was to set up a UHF search radar, to see if the hoped-for benefits were real. The frequency chosen for the first radar was 425 MHz, primarily because a few dozen war-surplus Western Electric 7C22 dual-cavity triodes were available. Their limited mechanical tuning range covered that frequency. The experiments were successful and 425 MHz became the frequency of choice for Lincoln Laboratory radars. In fact, Lincoln Laboratory's use of 425 MHz for numerous subsequent radars followed directly from the availability of 7C22s in 1952.

In 1953, recognizing the importance of flight-test support for the development of AEW radars, the Navy established a unit at South Weymouth Naval Air Station, Massachusetts, to support several Lincoln Laboratory programs. The Air Force based an RC-121D and a B-29 at Hanscom Air Force Base for the same purpose.

An early demonstration of UHF AEW radar was on a Navy blimp (Figure 3-2). Its operating altitude was limited to a few thousand feet, but its comparatively low velocity made AMTI easier.

Lincoln Laboratory modified a standard AN/APS-20 transmitter to accommodate the UHF triode operating as an oscillator. The maximum unambiguous range was 500 km.

Flight testing commenced in March 1954. Side-by-side tests with a low-power UHF AEW radar in one blimp and an AN/APS-20 S-band AEW radar in another proved the advantage of lower-frequency operation.

Despite some advantages, blimps failed as AEW-radar platforms because their operation was restricted to low altitudes. However, heartened by successful flight tests in the blimp, Lincoln Laboratory set out to install an AEW radar in a Super Constellation–class aircraft and to increase the transmitted power.

The new radar, the AN/APS-70, was fielded in three experimental development (XD) versions. Two AN/APS-70(XD-1) radars were built at Lincoln Laboratory. Two each of the AN/APS-70(XD-2) and AN/APS-70(XD-3) radars were built by Hazeltine Electronics and by General Electric (GE), respectively. The broadband 425-MHz antennas with IFF provisions for the AN/APS-70(XD-2) and the AN/APS-70(XD-3) were supplied by Hughes. All three firms carried out production under contract to Lincoln Laboratory, and the technology was thus transferred to industry.

J.R. Zacharias

H.G. Weiss

M.M. Hubbard

Lincoln Laboratory had demonstrated in 1954 that UHF AEW radar gave better results than S-band systems, but the Air Force felt that independent testing was warranted. Therefore, it carried out a series of flight-test comparisons of S-band and UHF AEW radars in 1956. In these tests, called Project Gray Wheel, an RC-121D aircraft was equipped with the AN/APS-20E (the most advanced configuration) S-band AEW radar, and another RC-121D aircraft was outfitted with Lincoln Laboratory's AN/APS-70(XD-1) UHF AEW radar.

The tests proved the superiority of the UHF system in detecting bombers. Moreover, they demonstrated the capability of the UHF system to direct interceptors to the bombers. The success of the AN/APS-70-equipped aircraft helped convince the Air Force to outfit its fleet of RC-121 Super Constellations with UHF aircraft early-warning and control (AEW&C) radar.

The Laboratory produced an improved UHF AEW radar prototype of the AN/APS-95 that featured single-knob tuning and other features not included in the AN/APS-70. Hazeltine produced the production AN/APS-95 UHF AEW radar for the Air Force and GE produced an advanced version, the AN/APS-96 UHF AEW radar, for the Navy.

Even though UHF operation helped remove some sea clutter, a way to remove more of it without losing low-flying targets was badly needed. By 1952 long-range ground-based air-surveillance radars could discriminate between targets that were moving radially and those that were not by pulse-to-pulse subtraction of successive received signals after detection. However, the radar transmitter could not be counted on to produce the exact same frequency and starting phase each time it was pulsed, so the CW reference signal had to be coherently locked to the transmitted signal for every pulse.

Lincoln Laboratory developed a two-part solution to the problem of AMTI. First, the CW reference signal was locked to a sample of the clutter return from surface scatterers at close range. This technique was called time-averaged clutter-coherent airborne radar (TACCAR).

For moderate levels of sea clutter, TACCAR worked well. As the radar antenna scanned through 360° in azimuth, TACCAR automatically took care of the problem of when the radar was looking forward or backward. The implementation of TACCAR at a radar's IF was an early application of the phase-locked loop.

The second part of the solution was the displaced-phase-center antenna (DPCA), first suggested by engineers at GE. DPCA compensated for the translation of an aircraft by comparing successive received pulses for AMTI; by contrast, without DPCA, the sea-clutter spectrum became wider as the airborne antenna looked away in azimuth from the airplane's ground track. GE's demonstration of DPCA used an X-band (9375 MHz) radar with dual antenna feeds offset in azimuth. A hybrid junction provided sum-pattern transmission and monopulse sum- and difference-pattern reception. Radar echoes received through the sum pattern both ahead and behind the central axis of the scanning beam were simultaneously adjusted in phase by vector addition with the radar echoes received through the difference pattern. The resulting signals were processed by noncoherent AMTI circuitry.

The Laboratory's existing UHF AEW-radar antennas were easily adapted to DPCA operation. The conventional pattern resulting from uniform in-phase illumination of the horizontal aperture for transmission and reception was supplemented on reception by a difference pattern corresponding to illumination of the right and left halves 180° out of phase. The received signals were then combined to provide the DPCA function. The sea-clutter spectrum narrowed accordingly, and the full clutter-cancellation capabilities of the IF TACCAR AMTI system were achieved at all azimuths.

First geodesic radome

AEW&C Super Constellation

Figure 3-6
The Texas Tower radar stations
provided early warning against hostile
aircraft arriving over water.

Figure 3-7
AN/FPS-17 radar antenna in Laredo, Texas.

Notes

4 Material for this section was provided by William Ward and Robert Lerner.

The first Texas Tower, located on Georges Shoal about 100 miles from Truro, Massachusetts, went into operation a year later. A total of five platforms were eventually built.

Standing on 10-ft-diameter steel caissons driven into the sea floor, each Texas Tower was a half-acre steel island elevated 67 ft above the sea (Figure 3-6). The uppermost of the four decks carried three radomes, housing an AN/FPS-3 search radar and two AN/FPS-6 height-finding radars. The deck also held IFF equipment, a Mark X beacon and four AN/FST-2 digital-data transmitters. The remaining three decks housed the personnel and maintenance equipment, control equipment, water and fuel. Fifty Air Force personnel, two meteorologists and twenty civilians operated each station.

The AN/FPS-17 Coded-Pulse Radar
In 1954 the United States learned that the Soviet Union was making rapid progress in the development of ballistic missiles.[4] But information about the Soviet ballistic missile program was scanty. What the U.S. government needed was a way to observe Soviet missile tests from a site outside the Soviet Union. And, once again, they called on Lincoln Laboratory.

GE had been approached first by the Air Force to produce a radar that could monitor Soviet missile tests, and had produced an initial design employing TV transmitters and an array of six 60-ft-diameter paraboloids. However, because the scheme used long pulses to obtain sufficient power at a 1000-km range, the range resolution was inadequate.

Lincoln Laboratory was then asked to improve on the design, which it did by developing the AN/FPS-17 coded-pulse radar, with a 200-MHz parabolic antenna and a pulse-compression system that provided the necessary range resolution. The Laboratory conceived, designed, tested, installed and operated the AN/FPS-17 coded-pulse radar within less than two years after the go-ahead in November 1954. It was the first radar built for tracking targets at very long ranges (Figure 3-7). In almost every aspect — transmitter, antenna, feed system, transmitted-signal generation, received-signal processing — the AN/FPS-17 concepts pushed hard on the existing state of the art.

The nearest site available for tracking Soviet missile tests was in northeastern Turkey, more than 1000 km from the testing area at Krasnyy Yar in central Asia. To track small targets at such a range, the radar had to have a large antenna and a powerful transmitter.

A study of technology trade-offs led to the selection of a radar frequency of 200 MHz. The antenna was designed to be as large as possible without exceeding the coherence limits for atmospheric propagation at that frequency. The resulting beam was narrow and thus imposed stringent requirements on scanning. The beam also needed a feed arrangement that could handle high peak and high average transmitted powers, while having low noise characteristics. The distance to the targets called for a low pulse-repetition rate, which, when used with mechanical scanning of the beam, allowed only a few pulses to be transmitted in each beam position.

The ballistic missile targets of interest to the AN/FPS-17 were small and distant; they could be detected only if an immense amount of energy was transmitted in each pulse. The peak power of the available transmitter, however, was limited. The solution was to transmit very long pulses.

Once a target was detected, the AN/FPS-17 was used as a tracker. And tracking a target is a completely different task from detecting it. For detection, the optimal pulse is simply a long one to obtain power aperture; for improved tracking performance, the pulse needs to have a structure.

To establish a precise track on a target, the radar had to measure the target's position and its velocity simultaneously. But accurate range and velocity measurements call for exactly opposite types of measurements. Precise range measurements need a wide bandwidth, which generally means short transmitted pulses. Precise velocity measurements require long transmitted pulses, with correspondingly narrow signal bandwidths. The solution was to construct a long pulse from short pulses. The short pulses were separated by giving them 180° phase shifts with respect to a reference signal. To prevent jamming, the phase shifts followed a linear-shift-register pseudo-noise sequence.

For the AN/FPS-17, a target echo from its 2-msec transmitted coded-phase pulse was compressed to a 20-μsec spike at the receiver output. The peak signal-to-noise power ratio at the wideband receiver output was equal to the ratio that could have been achieved by a narrowband receiver matched to a simple CW transmitted pulse.

The AN/FPS-17's circuitry for generating the coded pulse and for compressing the received echoes from a target was based on acoustic delay lines. Lincoln Laboratory built eight sets of receiver/exciter systems. The central cabinet contained a 2-msec Invar acoustic delay line, 10 m long, which formed the transmitted pulse. An index of equipment complexity is the vacuum-tube count of the systems — each set contained 331 tubes.

A single 20-μsec pulse of a 200-kHz sinusoidal wave was launched by a piezoelectric transducer and propagated along the rod. Small fractions of the wave were picked off by magnetostrictive sensors at 100 points, 20 μsec apart. The 100 sinusoidal pulses, adjacent in time, were weighted in a summing network to form the 2-msec phase-coded pulse. The expanded pulse was translated in frequency to about 200 MHz for high-power amplification and transmission. Since returning echo signals could not be received until the transmitted pulse ended, the same acoustic delay line could be used to compress them.

Doppler-shifted target echoes had to be detected separately. The AN/FPS-17 had eighteen frequency bins, which covered the likely spread of Doppler shifts. The bins were processed simultaneously by using a matrix of eighteen different resistive networks to add up the signals from the tapped Invar delay line. The data-recording arrangement allowed the range rate of the target (observed in as many as three adjacent frequency bins) to be estimated more accurately than to within a single bin, depending on the signal-to-noise ratio of the radar echo.

The phase-coded-pulse technique conceived for the AN/FPS-17 shared many features with the linear-frequency-modulation (chirp) technique of pulse compression. However, unlike the chirp technique, the AN/FPS-17 technique provided simultaneous measurements of range and of range rate on each pulse.

The antenna system for the AN/FPS-17 was designed by Lincoln Laboratory and was fabricated in old shipyard facilities, under rush orders, by the D.S. Kennedy Company of Hingham, Massachusetts. The reflector occupied almost half an acre.

In 1956 the AN/FPS-17 was installed at Laredo Air Force Base, Texas. Its scanning beam was aimed in a generally northwest direction, toward the White Sands Missile Range in New Mexico, several hundred miles away. In July, sounding rockets launched from Holloman Air Force Base (adjacent to White Sands) were observed by the radar. The tests demonstrated that the newly developed coded-pulse technique could simultaneously measure the range and velocity of a target.

The real-world checkout of the radar revealed a surprising problem: echoes from ionized meteor trails activated the automatic target-detection circuitry. The system was modified to eliminate unacceptable background of false alarms.

The site chosen for the operational installation of the AN/FPS-17 was Pirinclik, near Diyarbakir in northeastern Turkey. GE set up and managed the radar site, which was selected with convenience to a railhead as a consideration. Material had to be brought in, buildings and the antenna had to be erected and equipment had to be installed — all in an undeveloped rural environment.

Notes

5 "How U.S. Taps Soviet Missile Secrets," *Aviation Week,* October 21, 1957, p. 26.

6 W.M. Siebert, "The Development of AN/FPS-17 Coded-Pulse Radar at Lincoln Laboratory," *IEEE Trans. Aerosp. Electron. Syst.* **24,** 833 (1988).

BMEWS tracker antenna, Trinidad

Prince Albert Radar Laboratory, Saskatchewan

A key factor in the choice of Pirinclik was that the site had elevated terrain between it and the USSR, so that the radar could not be jammed by a transmitter within the Soviet Union's borders. Jamming was further discouraged because the transmitter frequency had been chosen within a band being used for navigation on the Black Sea.

In 1957 the Soviets launched Sputnik I from the Baikonur Cosmodrome near Tyuratam (several hundred miles north and slightly east of Pirinclik). The AN/FPS-17 radar had good coverage of that launch, as it did of numerous subsequent launches.

The AN/FPS-17 turned out to be a successful radar, yielding much valuable data. The installation at Pirinclik later became part of the U.S. SPACETRACK network.

Although the initial installation of the AN/FPS-17 in Turkey was classified, rumors of the system spread and a partial description of the system was noted in 1957 in *Aviation Week*.[5] A similar account appeared in a Czech book on military applications of electronics and in a German article. The most complete report of the AN/FPS-17 was given by William Siebert upon receiving the 1988 IEEE Aerospace and Electronic Systems Society's Pioneer Award for the development of coded-pulse radar.[6]

The motivations for the AN/FPS-17 project were straightforward — to replace speculations with facts and to avoid surprise. By 1954 the understanding of the fundamentals of radar theory had advanced far enough that Lincoln Laboratory and GE could build this extraordinary radar and help to stabilize the global balance of power.

The Ballistic Missile Early Warning System

During 1953 and 1954, Lincoln Laboratory carried out several preliminary studies of the properties of ballistic missile trajectories, the problems of radar systems for detection and tracking of long-range ballistic missiles and the effects of meteors on such radar detection systems. By then it had become clear from intelligence sources that the Soviet Union was rapidly developing intercontinental ballistic missiles (ICBM). These early studies suggested that radar was the only sensor technology that offered the near-term possibility of developing a warning system against these missiles.

The development of ICBMs armed with nuclear weapons compelled the DoD to rethink its approach to strategic defense. The underlying assumption for SAGE — that an approaching bomber could be detected, tracked and intercepted — did not apply. Based on the premise that it would be virtually impossible to intercept incoming missiles, a new concept came into vogue: mutual assured destruction. According to this concept, the only practical defense was to develop such a forbidding counterstrike capability of bombers and missiles that no sane individual or nation would launch an attack on the United States; the citizens of any country that did so would be assuring themselves of their own destruction.

Mutual assured destruction thus called for the development of a robust counterstrike capability, a key element of which was the assured capability to detect an attack as soon as it commenced. Reliable early warning of even a few minutes was critical, perhaps even more so than it had been for air defense.

The success of the DEW Line led the Air Force to approach the Laboratory for support in designing and developing a new radar system to provide warning of a Soviet ICBM attack against North America. Beginning in 1955, this became a major Laboratory activity and remained so until the Ballistic Missile Early Warning System (BMEWS) was well into production in the early 1960s. Lincoln Laboratory's role was its usual one — to provide solid technical advice to the Air Force sponsor and to the contractors that would ultimately build BMEWS.

BMEWS search radars, Thule, Greenland

1960

Figure 3-8
Antenna and supporting structure of the long-range UHF tracking radar on Millstone Hill in Westford, Massachusetts.

Notes

7 G.H. Pettengill and D.E. Dustin, "A Comparison of Selected ICBM Warning Radar Configurations," *Lincoln Laboratory Technical Report No. 127,* Lexington, Mass.: MIT Lincoln Laboratory, 13 August 1956.

8 M.I. Skolnik, "A Long Range Radar Warning System for the Detection of ICBMs," *Lincoln Laboratory Technical Report No. 128,* Lexington, Mass.: MIT Lincoln Laboratory, 15 August 1956.

The Laboratory formed the Systems Research Group in 1955 to study problems that would have to be understood in designing a reliable warning system. Problems such as the radar reflection properties of ICBMs, effects of propagation, meteor trials and aurora effects and the optimization of prediction methods for estimating missile impacts from radar observations were to be dealt with.

The Systems Research Group compared various radar warning-system configurations[7] and the most promising one, which consisted of detection radars scanning several pencil beams in azimuth at fixed elevations and an associated pencil-beam tracking radar, was studied extensively.[8] This warning system was recommended by the Laboratory and adopted by the Air Force and the DoD as the basic configuration for BMEWS.

The Air Force awarded the prime contract for BMEWS to the Radio Corporation of America in January 1958. Four objectives were defined for the system: (1) a fifteen-minute warning of a mass ICBM attack directed against North America; (2) a reliability of 0.9999; (3) a maximum false-alarm rate of one during a three-month period; and (4) an inherent flexibility and growth potential.

The Laboratory supported BMEWS with research, development and engineering programs. The Millstone radar was the model for the BMEWS tracking radar (AN/FPS-49). The model for the AN/FPS-50 BMEWS surveillance radar was assembled by GE at Trinidad, British West Indies. This large scanning-beam radar used a large parabolic-torus reflector (165 ft high and 400 ft wide) with an organ-pipe feed and incorporated many components and specifications developed and tested at Lincoln Laboratory.

The operational BMEWS network consisted of three radar sites — Clear, Alaska; Thule, Greenland; and Fylingsdale Moor, Yorkshire, England — and a data processing center in the Cheyenne Mountain complex near Colorado Springs, Colorado.

The BMEWS radar effort at Lincoln Laboratory began with the design and construction of a prototype UHF tracking radar on Millstone Hill in Westford, Massachusetts. The radar served as a test bed for the components and techniques of BMEWS, including the data processing and display equipment. It went into operation in the fall of 1957, just in time to observe returns from Sputnik I. Since then, the Millstone radar has observed virtually every space vehicle that has risen above its horizon.

The original Millstone radar was unusual in many respects, among them its high power at 440 MHz and its agile 84-ft antenna system (Figure 3-8). The transmitter produced a peak power of 1 MW and an average power of 60 kW, feeding an antenna with a rotating conical feed horn.

It was the first radar to use a digital computer as an integral part of the radar system for real-time data processing and control. The CG-24 computer, designed and built at Lincoln Laboratory for this purpose and installed at Millstone in 1958, was also the first completely solid state computer.

In addition to demonstrating the value of automatic pointing and tracking of radar antennas, the CG-24 was a major factor in the development of real-time signal processing techniques that were essential to the evolution of modern space-tracking and measurement radars.

As with so many of Lincoln Laboratory's programs, a number of groups were able to contribute to the eventual success of the Millstone radar. The sensitivity of the radar was increased by reducing the system noise through the use of the cooled parametric amplifier and the maser amplifier, developed in the Laboratory's Solid State Division.

The first evaluation of the noise temperature of an operating maser amplifier was made at Lincoln Laboratory in 1957. By early the next year, a UHF maser was ready to be used in the Millstone radar, resulting in a fivefold increase in sensitivity.

Millstone was the model for the BMEWS AN/FPS-49 tracking radars installed in Greenland and England and the AN/FPS-92 (an improved version of the AN/FPS-49) tracking radar installed in Alaska. It also served as the basis for large tracking and measurements radars at a NASA installation near Wallops Island, Virginia, and for an Air Force downrange tracking station in Trinidad and the Prince Albert Radar Laboratory in Saskatchewan, Canada.

The Millstone radar was rebuilt in 1962 for L-band (1295 MHz) operation. The focus of work at Millstone then changed to basic science, with an extensive study of the physics of the ionosphere, and to space surveillance, which is currently the site's principal task. The original antenna was moved to Turkey, where it replaced the AN/FPS-17, thus evolving from a prototype to an element of the U.S. surveillance network.

The scope of the BMEWS supporting effort expanded in the late 1950s to include overall systems analysis, with special emphasis on the data processing done by the BMEWS Missile Impact Prediction computers. A set of software programs, called the BMEWS Operational Simulation System (BOSS), was written for the Laboratory's IBM 704 computer.

BOSS supported systems studies of deghosting methods, orbit-computation and impact-prediction methods, single-fan discrimination techniques and the use of tracking radars. An improved data-reduction program was designed to simplify the process of getting desired data from BOSS runs.

The Laboratory also designed, developed and vigorously tested a number of components, including the entire organ-pipe feed system that would be required for the BMEWS scanning-beam surveillance radar, the AN/FPS-50. The components and specifications for the organ-pipe feed were turned over to GE, which produced AN/FPS-50 radars for the BMEWS sites at Clear and Thule.

Work continued on advanced radar techniques and components, including pulse-compression methods and phased-array radars. Research on propagation problems gave auroral measurements a high priority.

The BMEWS sites were completed in January 1964, at a cost of more than one billion dollars. The system has been upgraded several times, and it continues in operation today.

Tracking Birds

One result of Lincoln Laboratory's early radar was completely unexpected — an improved understanding of the patterns of bird migration.* The foray into ornithology started during the Cape Cod tests as part of an examination into sea clutter, a term being applied to those overwater targets which were not rejected by the radar moving-target indicator. Sea clutter had been making the South Truro radar beam unusable for the first 50 mi of its range, where the moving-target indicator should have been most useful.

In 1957 Lincoln Laboratory decided to launch an investigation into the cause of sea clutter. Robert Richardson and Joseph Stacey went to Cape Cod and, for several days each month over several months, photographed a PPI display every twelve seconds over a twenty-four-hour period. Playback of the film showed that the sea clutter was concentrated near the shore at dawn, moved out to sea during the day and then returned to the shore at night — behavior that was characteristic of birds.

Richardson modified the radar gain control circuitry to remove the effect of birds from the PPI displays by adjusting the gain to vary with the fourth power of the range so that targets of a specified size would be accepted at all ranges, and echoes from birds would be rejected.

The investigation then shifted from radar clutter to bird behavior. Presentations by Richardson and a cartoon in the *Boston Globe* sparked widespread interest among ornithologists and, at the request of the Massachusetts Audubon Society, Lincoln Laboratory embarked on a year-long study that accumulated a rich store of information on the bird-migration patterns over Cape Cod.

This study changed many long-held views in ornithology. For instance, most ornithologists had believed that birds traveled over land during their migrations, but the radar measurements proved conclusively that overwater travel was common. Bird counts also had to be revised. The study demonstrated that when migrating birds encountered a weather front, they turned, sometimes even reversing direction. This work thus showed that the same birds had often been counted more than once.

The Massachusetts Audubon scientists working in collaboration with Lincoln Laboratory were the first ornithologists to use radar to study the migration of birds. Dozens of subsequent studies drew on the results of their work, and radar has become a standard tool in ornithology.

* This material was contributed by Robert Richardson.

Until supplanted by satellite communications, worldwide communication was possible only through the use of scatter or reflection techniques. Lincoln Laboratory activities in tropospheric-scatter communications permitted contact with remote sites, particularly in Arctic regions. Later, long-range systems were developed to communicate information successfully with submarines in distant locations.

Left: The Round Hill Field Station in South Dartmouth, Massachusetts, with the Round Hills mansion built by Colonel E.H.R. Green.

Each of Lincoln Laboratory's major programs — SAGE, the DEW Line, BMEWS — depended upon reliable long-range communications, because each had radars in remote locations. In the Arctic, on the Texas Towers and for many ships, neither telephone nor line-of-sight communications was possible.

The curvature of the earth sets the limit on direct radio transmissions; a signal can travel long distances only if it is reflected by something above the horizon. This limitation compelled Lincoln Laboratory to begin a complex and extensive program on long-range communications.

Today satellites provide a straightforward solution to the problem of worldwide communication. But before there were satellites, the only way to transmit a signal over the horizon was to use the ionosphere or troposphere to reflect, refract or scatter the signal back to earth. In a sense, ionospheric/tropospheric communications simply used atmospheric layers as natural passive satellites. Natural fluctuations, however, made scatter communications a difficult and complex task. Nonetheless, before satellites, it was the only choice for long-range terrestrial communications.

The programs on long-distance beyond-the-horizon communications technology at Lincoln Laboratory originated at the MIT Research Laboratory of Electronics under the leadership of William Radford. All personnel and equipment of this facility were transferred to Lincoln Laboratory in 1951. These individuals formed the nucleus of the effort that continued the work and started new projects. Through 1958 experiments were conducted over a wide range of frequencies at a variety of sites in the eastern sections of the United States and out to sea.

The ionosphere, located at altitudes of 100 to 250 km, reflects HF (3 to 30 MHz) radio waves over long distances, a phenomenon that amateur radio operators and commercial stations have used since its discovery early in the century. Up to World War II, HF radio was the principal means of long-distance communication for aircraft, ships and fixed stations. During and just after the war long-distance ionospheric- and tropospheric-scatter propagation was discovered; research on these modes became a major undertaking at Lincoln Laboratory. At the same time, however, the Laboratory continued to seek ways to improve conventional HF communications.

High-Frequency Communications

HF has always challenged communications engineers.[1] It can provide worldwide communication with relatively small, low-power transmitting and receiving terminal equipment. However, HF links are subject to strong daily variations and modifications to the ionosphere caused by solar storms. Most problematically for defense applications, HF links are easily jammed because they lack a wide bandwidth for spreading the signal and because it is hard to use antenna directivity to discriminate against jammers.

The central feature of antijam communications is to hide the carrier signal by spreading it over a wide bandwidth. Lincoln Laboratory developed the NOMAC system to conduct jam-resistant HF communications. NOMAC stands for noise modulation and correlation, which aptly describes the system. Transmitted signals were generated with the aid of noise modulation; received signals were decoded by means of a correlation technique.

The carrier signal was hidden by giving it 180° phase shifts with respect to itself according to a pseudonoise pattern, and by supplying the pattern only to the intended receiver. The family of pseudonoise patterns known as direct sequences were used for NOMAC; the binary pattern — to phase-shift or not to phase-shift — was generated by digital circuits.

Notes

3 R. Price and P.E. Green, Jr., "A Communication Technique for Multipath Channels," *Proc. IRE* **46**, 555 (1958).

4 R. Price and P.E. Green, Jr., "Anti-Multipath Receiving System," U.S. Patent No. 2,982,853, May 2, 1961.

5 "1981 Pioneer Award," *IEEE Trans. Aerosp. Electron. Syst.* **AES-18**, 153 (1982); W.B. Davenport, Jr., and P.E. Green, Jr., "The M.I.T. Lincoln Laboratory F9C System," *IEEE Trans. Aerosp. Electron. Syst.* **AES-18**, 157 (1982).

6 The section on scatter communications was written by Burt Nichols, based in part on W.E. Morrow, Jr., and W.T. Burke, "A History of the Effort of MIT Lincoln Laboratory in the UHF/SHF Tropospheric-Scatter Communication Field Utilizing Frequency Modulation," *Lincoln Laboratory Group Report 36-25.* Lexington, Mass.: MIT Lincoln Laboratory, 1 January 1958.

7 W.G. Abel, J.T. deBettencourt, J.F. Roche and J.H. Chisholm, "Investigations of Scattering and Multipath Properties of Ionospheric Propagation at Radio Frequencies Exceeding the MUF," *Lincoln Laboratory Technical Report No. 81,* Lexington, Mass.: MIT Lincoln Laboratory, 3 June 1955.

8 D.G. Brennan and M.L. Phillips, "Phase and Amplitude Variability in Medium-Frequency Ionospheric Transmission," *Lincoln Laboratory Technical Report No. 93,* Lexington, Mass.: MIT Lincoln Laboratory, 16 September 1957.

9 The October 1955 issue of the *Proceedings of the IRE* was entirely dedicated to scatter propagation and is possibly the most detailed and comprehensive report on the topic. Another outstanding overview of scatter communications appeared five years later, entitled "Radio Transmission by Ionospheric and Tropospheric Scatter," *Proc. IRE* **48**, 4 (1960). This article was written by the IRE Joint Technical Advisory Committee Ad Hoc Subcommittee on Forward Scatter Transmission, which was headed by Bill Radford and composed largely of Lincoln Laboratory staff members.

10 (a) Morrow and Burke, "A History of the Effort of MIT Lincoln Laboratory in the UHF/SHF," *Lincoln Laboratory Group Report 36-25,* Lexington, Mass.: MIT Lincoln Laboratory, 1 January 1958; (b) J.H. Chisholm, W.E. Morrow, Jr., B.E. Nichols, J.F. Roche and A.E. Teachman, "Properties of 400 Mcps Long-Distance Tropospheric Circuits," *Proc. IRE* **50**, 2464 (December 1962); (c) B.E. Nichols, "Performance of a 640-Mile 24-Channel UHF-SSB Experimental Communication System," *IRE Trans. Commun. Syst.* **CS-8**, 26 (1960).

The theoretical jamming resistance for NOMAC was 23 dB; the ratio of the spread-signal bandwidth (10 kHz) to the reciprocal of the teletype baud interval (22 msec) provided this processing gain. The time-diversity approach actually enabled the F9C-A to achieve as much as 17 dB of jamming protection. Acquiring the remaining 6 dB required the development of Rake, which detected and summed the received signals from many propagation paths.

The missing 6 dB of jamming protection were lost because the F9C-A processed only the two strongest received signals. What Rake did was to compensate for the effects of all other signal-path delays.

The concept of Rake was to synthesize (and refine) an adaptive matched filter that corresponded to most of the linear propagation paths that produced the received signal.[3] The final output was, to a large extent, exactly what it would have been had there been only one propagation path from transmitter to receiver.

The maximum spread in HF radio was only about 3 msec. Therefore, a delay with thirty taps sufficed to characterize the received signal fully. Each tap output was adjusted in amplitude and shifted in phase by feedback circuits so that the algebraic sum of all thirty taps was a good approximation to the ideal received signal.

The delay line bristling with its taps resembled a garden rake, so the communications system was named Rake. The actual delay line was built in the form of a helix (Figure 4-2).

During the next several years other reports and papers put Rake firmly on record, and the concept was patented.[4] Rake performance approached the bounds of achievable performance. It was tested in 1956 over the same transcontinental link that had been used to evaluate NOMAC, with the same transmissions, and worked very well, achieving nearly the full 23 dB of jamming resistance.

The Army Signal Corps promptly arranged for the National Radio Company of Malden, Massachusetts, to produce twelve Rake modification kits for the F9C-A NOMAC systems that were being built by Sylvania. Production units of NOMAC/Rake equipment saw wide service. Of particular importance was the availability of this spread-spectrum/antijam/antimultipath communications system between Washington and West Berlin during tense times in the early 1960s.

NOMAC/Rake was the first practical implementation of a channel-adaptive communications system. Rake was also the earliest example of what later became the field of adaptive modems.

Beginning with Paul Green's 1953 MIT Sc.D. thesis, NOMAC went through field tests and into production as the F9C-A in less than three years. In 1981 William Davenport, leader of the Communications Techniques Group at Lincoln Laboratory, and Green, the assistant group leader, along with Robert Price, their principal collaborator, each received recognition from the IEEE for their achievements. Davenport and Green received the 1981 Pioneer Award from the IEEE Aerospace and Electronics Systems Society.[5] Price received the 1981 Edwin Howard Armstrong Achievement Award from the IEEE Communications Society.

Long-Range Scatter Communications

Despite the advances of NOMAC/Rake, the HF medium remained difficult and unreliable. Other forms of long-range communications, particularly at the higher frequencies, offered the potential for greater reliability and capacity than HF ionospheric reflection. Therefore, Lincoln Laboratory began a series of programs on three other techniques for long-range communications: HF ionospheric scatter, MF ionospheric scatter and VHF, UHF and SHF tropospheric scatter. These programs began at the start of Lincoln Laboratory in 1951 and continued until 1958.[6]

Figure 4-2
Helical ultrasonic delay line for the Rake receiver.

The work on HF ionospheric scatter showed that, in the frequency range of 20 to 50 MHz, ionospheric-scatter transmissions could be useful for point-to-point narrowband communications of up to 1000 mi. However, because fluctuations in the atmosphere disturbed the quality of HF transmissions, receiving equipment had to be designed to handle a wide dynamic range of received power. At distances of less than 350 mi, differential time delays due to multipath propagation particularly limited the useful bandwidth. High power (10 kW) and high gain (20 dB) antennas were needed. Good antenna directivity was also essential to minimize multipath propagation. During periods of high sunspot activity, the frequency range just above the HF band — close to 50 MHz — gave the best results.

HF ionospheric scatter communications never became widely used except for the DEW Line rearward link. Fading remained a problem, as did the low channel capacity. Lincoln Laboratory concluded the HF scatter study in 1955.[7]

Lincoln Laboratory's study of medium frequency (300 to 3000 kHz) ionospheric-reflection transmissions began at the request of the U.S. State Department. The Voice of America, a radio network affiliated with the State Department, was using a medium-frequency signal to transmit to Eastern Europe. Voice of America was interested in the possibility of improving the strength of its signal by installing an array of high-power transmitters in Western Europe. Because the State Department did not have the technical expertise to assess the value of this scheme, it asked Lincoln Laboratory to determine whether a beam formed by a spaced array on the ground could be sustained by an ionospheric path.

Experiments were carried out at 543 kHz over a 380-mi path between the Round Hill Field Station in South Dartmouth, Massachusetts, and Fort Belvoir, Virginia. This path provided midlatitude ionospheric propagation uncontaminated by a ground wave. In a four-month measurement program, four separate transmitters at Round Hill aimed signals toward the receiving station at Fort Belvoir.

Results were unfavorable. In a technical report issued in September 1957, Donald Brennan and M. Lindeman Phillips wrote that the experiment showed that a broadside array up to about two wavelengths long would perform well on an ionospheric path.[8] When they studied signal propagation from these arrays, however, they measured substantial beam losses. As a result of the study, the Voice of America proposal was not implemented.

Tropospheric Scatter

Most of Lincoln Laboratory's research on long-range terrestrial communications, particularly the most successful research, was on tropospheric scatter, sometimes called forward scatter.[9] Tropospheric-scatter communications utilizes the presence of inhomogeneities in the troposphere to scatter radio signals back to earth. On the basis of the success of the program, numerous military and civilian systems were installed, some of which continue to be used around the world today. Numerous staff members participated in this program, and several reviews of Laboratory work were published.[10]

The tropospheric-scatter mode at the higher frequencies offers reliability, a wide bandwidth and a significant number of communication channels. The Lincoln Laboratory program on tropospheric scatter investigated communications in three frequency bands: VHF, near 50 MHz; UHF, at 385 to 425 MHz, 900 to 950 MHz and 2290 MHz; and SHF, at 3670 to 5050 MHz.

In general, the studies showed that as the communication frequency increased, so did the bandwidth, but that propagation losses decreased the range. In the VHF investigation, for example, it was found that limitations in the available bandwidth made the band useful only for narrowband, low-capacity communications; not many VHF circuits were ever implemented.

Working with experimental results from these test circuits, Lincoln Laboratory staff began to design systems for military applications. In 1953 the Laboratory assisted the Air Force in designing a UHF tropospheric-scatter system along the northeast coast of North America. This system, named POLEVAULT, linked stations along the PINE TREE radar line.

On the basis of the Lincoln Laboratory and Bell Laboratories tests and early results from POLEVAULT, Western Electric developed the WHITE ALICE network of UHF trunk routes for the territory of Alaska. The WHITE ALICE and POLEVAULT systems were subsequently tied into the DEW Line through the use of multichannel, beyond-the-horizon tropospheric-scatter radio relay systems.

New circuits for theoretical studies of tropospheric-scatter propagation continued to be set up. Simultaneous 3670- and 412-MHz propagation tests were added to the Round Hill–to–Crawfords Hill path, and extended to the Rising Sun and Alpha Field Stations in Maryland, at distances of 300 and 350 mi from Round Hill, respectively. A study of short-hop communication was conducted by installing a site at Riverhead, New York, at the midpath of the Maryland-to-Massachusetts circuit. UHF transmissions were recorded at Alpha on a regular basis from May 1955 to July 1957.

A new station at Chillum, near Washington, D.C., 375 mi from Round Hill, extended the path from Round Hill and Coles Signal Laboratory. This circuit became operational in March 1955 and was deactivated a year later.

The underlying reason for Lincoln Laboratory's extensive involvement in long-distance communications was, of course, for SAGE, particularly to support the offshore radars on the Texas Towers. A tropospheric-scatter communications system was designed and built to provide radio communication between the Texas Tower offshore radars and terminals located in North Truro, Massachusetts, and Stewart Air Force Base in Newburgh, New York. An experimental copy of the system was used as the first multichannel communications system for the Texas Tower–to–shore link.

The next step was to extend the range of tropospheric-scatter communications. The transmitter at Round Hill, normally used for the Coles-to-Chillum circuit, was briefly diverted in July 1955 for a study of overwater propagation. A Navy ship was used as a receiver, and signals were propagated via tropospheric scatter out to a distance of 460 mi. The following February, winter overwater propagation was studied at distances exceeding 700 mi, with a new antenna and a higher transmitting power.

Another long-distance propagation study was conducted, this time overland, by setting up a site at Winston-Salem, North Carolina, 619 mi from Round Hill. This site, which began operations in November 1955, was used in conjunction with a new high-power UHF transmitter and a high-gain rotatable parabolic antenna at Round Hill. Operations continued for two years.

By July 1956 the Laboratory was ready for an even more ambitious circuit. A UHF receiving site was installed in Elberton, Georgia, 830 mi from Round Hill. The site, which received transmissions in parallel with Winston-Salem, operated for one year.

Each of these circuits served as a test facility to evaluate the reliability and performance of equipment designed for UHF and SHF communications. These studies led to a steady, rapid series of advances in tropospheric-scatter communications. And the rate of improvement was indeed impressive — the length of the communication paths grew from 161 to 830 mi in only three years.

Major modifications to the design of each system, from the receivers and transmitters to the communication techniques, made these improvements possible. Much of the equipment for the early work on tropospheric scatter was loaned by the military and by other organizations. In early 1953 a program of development and procurement of reliable exciter and multicavity klystron transmitter equipment was started that was designed specifically for UHF or SHF tropospheric-scatter service. The information and experience obtained from developing and testing transmitters led to the fabrication of klystron transmitters that could operate in the 400- and 2000-MHz range with average powers up to 50 kW.

Like the early transmitters, the early receivers were modified commercial units or military equipment. Within a short time, however, Lincoln Laboratory began to produce receivers. Extremely sensitive, low-noise, highly selective FM receivers were designed and placed in use on experimental circuits. The design of the limiter-discriminator section of the receivers included high-speed limiters and wideband, high-linearity discriminators, which were necessary for good performance under multipath conditions.

The first antennas had 28-ft-diameter paraboloidal reflectors. But one of the factors that limited the range of the communication circuits was the gain, determined by the diameters of the transmitting and receiving antennas. Therefore, two 60-ft-diameter paraboloidal antennas were constructed. The usefulness of the antennas for the propagation research program was enhanced by adding two steerable mounts: one capable of rotating a 28-ft-diameter paraboloid 360° in azimuth, the other capable of rotating a 60-ft-diameter paraboloid 360° in azimuth and 105° in elevation (Figure 4-5). Additional work was carried out on reflector configurations other than paraboloidal: helical arrays, corner arrays and dipoles with reflectors.

Other design studies evaluated antenna feed horns. New feed horns were designed, constructed and installed in the 28-ft-diameter paraboloidal reflector at Crawfords Hill, which made the system capable of radiating linearly polarized fields of equal horizontal and vertical amplitudes. A cross-polarized feed horn for reception was also designed, constructed and installed at Round Hill. It permitted simultaneous reception of horizontally and vertically polarized components for a dual-channel receiver. A similar feed horn was subsequently designed for operation at 400 and 2000 MHz.

Each antenna was a large and costly piece of equipment, so diplexed operation (transmitting and receiving simultaneously on two different frequencies) was desirable. Filters had to be added to the systems to prevent the transmitter output power at the transmitter frequency from reaching the receiver input terminals, and to prevent any transmitter output power at the receiver frequency from reaching the receiver input terminals.

By October 1954 a pair of coaxial-line stub filters had been designed, tested and installed on the Truro-Lexington link. These filters (407.45 and 415.15 MHz) provided over 70-dB attenuation in the stop band and less than 1-dB attenuation in the pass band for a bandwidth of 0.7 MHz. A diplexer was also designed and fabricated for use at Round Hill on the Round Hill–to–Coles 400- and 2000-MHz dual-diversity circuit. This diplexer provided more than 100-dB isolation and an insertion loss of less than 0.25 dB. Waveguide diplexer units were designed and fabricated for use with the 10-kW transmitters at Stewart Air Force Base and Truro. The transmitting and receiving frequencies in this case were separated by 50 MHz around a nominal frequency of 900 MHz. The experience in the design, fabrication and operation of various types of branching filters at many frequencies and power levels led to long-stub and cavity-type filters for quadruple-diversity service on a 400-MHz duplex circuit with transmitters of 50-kW peak power capability.

Diversity, a technique that makes use of multiple independent transmission paths to generate a received signal, can help to reduce the effects of fading. Investigations into the use of diversity techniques to improve UHF and SHF tropospheric-scatter communications systems began as early as 1953. At that time two small, horizontally polarized receiving antennas were set up at Round Hill to receive 425-MHz signals transmitted from Alpine. A few months later, five dipoles — with reflectors spaced at 1, 2, 4, 8 and 16 wavelengths — went into dual space-diversity service at Round Hill on that circuit.

In October 1955 Lincoln Laboratory (and, independently, the Federal Telecommunication Laboratories) proposed a new method of diversity that permitted full utilization of the existing path geometry with no increase in either space or spectrum requirements. In this system, the plane of polarization of the transmitting antenna became the characteristic that enabled the receiver to distinguish between sources. With two antennas at a site providing space diversity and by exploiting polarization diversity, any order of diversity up to four could be obtained. After design and fabrication of the necessary dual-polarization, dual-frequency horn feeds, the technique was tested and found satisfactory. The fourth-order diversity technique was used in both the AN/FRC-56 communications system and in the single-sideband (SSB) AN/FRC-47 communications system.

5   **Satellite Communications**

Military satellite systems were designed to address the need for routine, robust communications. Through the development of experimental satellites, terminals and satellite communications payloads, Lincoln Laboratory successfully led the advancement of techniques for reliable communications.

Left: Atlas/Centaur launch of the FLTSAT-7 with an EHF package from Cape Canaveral, Florida, on December 4, 1986.

When the Lincoln Laboratory space communications program began more than thirty-five years ago, the objective was simply to make long-range military communications routinely available for large, fixed terminals. The focus of the program soon shifted to providing satellite-based communications for small, mobile terminals. After that goal was reached, the emphasis changed again, to making the communications systems electromagnetically and physically survivable, capable of functioning despite determined efforts by an adversary to interfere with them by jamming or by physical attack.[1] This work has been conducted within the Communications Division, headed by Thomas Rogers when it was established and under the successive leaderships of Gerald Dinneen, Walter Morrow, Paul Rosen, John Wozencraft, Donald MacLellan, Barney Reiffen and Vincent Vitto.

Project West Ford

The impetus for Lincoln Laboratory's first work in space communications[2] came from the HARDTACK series of high-altitude nuclear tests, which were carried out in the Pacific Ocean near Johnston Island in August 1958. The first of these thermonuclear detonations disturbed the ionosphere over a vast area around the test site, and thus interrupted a great many HF radio communications links.

In 1958 Walter Morrow and Harold Meyer, an employee of Ramo-Wooldridge Corporation, proposed a solution to the problem of HF radio communication failures. They suggested that if the ionosphere became unavailable to serve as a natural reflector, due to thermonuclear detonations or such phenomena as solar storms, an orbiting artificial reflector could replace the ionosphere. Morrow and Meyer proposed the construction of an artificial reflector in space that consisted of a pair of belts (one circumpolar, one equatorial) of resonant scatterers revolving in orbit a few thousand kilometers above the surface of the earth.

The scatterers in each belt would be conducting objects, such as lengths of wire, that would resonate at the system's operating wavelength and therefore reradiate RF signals. The smaller the objects, the shorter the wavelength, and the easier their distribution from an orbiting dispenser. The wavelengths could not be too small, however, or construction of adequate transmitting and receiving terminals would become excessively difficult.

The Lincoln Laboratory group proposed an experiment to demonstrate transcontinental communications by sending full-duplex transmissions between terminals in Camp Parks, California, and Westford, Massachusetts. The orbiting scatterers would act as halfwave dipoles resonating at about 8 GHz, midway between the transmitted frequency limits of 7750 and 8350 MHz. The experiment was planned to release approximately 480 million copper diodes, each with a 0.0007-in diameter and 0.7-in length, into an orbital belt. These dipoles would weigh 40 μg each and have an average separation of 0.3 km (Figure 5-1).

Sixty-ft-diameter paraboloidal antennas would be fed by transmitters on the ground with 20-to-40-kW average power. Maser receivers would provide what was then the lowest attainable system noise temperature at that wavelength, approximately 60K. The waveforms were selected to satisfy the requirements of communication via forward scatter from the orbiting dipoles, and to probe the characteristics of the belt via radar backscatter and forward scatter.

Recognizing that a proposal to place vast numbers of *anything* into orbit would be controversial, Lincoln Laboratory designed the proposed experiment, named Project West Ford,[3] to ensure that the dipole scatterers were in a resonant orbit such that the pressure of incident solar radiation on the orbiting dipoles would cause their orbits to decay. After a few years, the orbits would dip into the upper atmosphere of the earth, where atmospheric drag would rapidly cause them to fall back to earth. Then the experimental dipole belt would disappear.

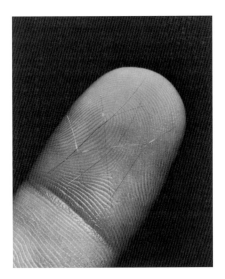

Figure 5-1
The Project West Ford orbiting dipoles were hairlike segments of copper wire.

While Project West Ford had initially been classified secret, the necessity for openness was clear to all involved, and in 1960 Lincoln Laboratory unveiled West Ford in virtually complete detail. Of particular importance was allaying the concerns of optical and radio astronomers who perceived the experimental belt as capable of interference with scientific observations and as a precursor of worse experiments to come.

On October 21, 1961, the first experiment was launched into circular polar orbit. It was unsuccessful; the dipoles did not deploy as planned. On May 8, 1963, a second launch, in the same manner but with improved dipole-dispensing arrangements, achieved a substantial degree of success. The belt formed and closed over a period of about forty days; its density was approximately five dipoles per cubic kilometer.

As expected, the effectiveness of the scatterers proved greatest in the early stages of belt formation, when the dipoles were less widely dispersed. The dipoles' density in the common volume illuminated by the beams of the two terminal antennas allowed communication at data rates of up to 20,000 bps.

Project West Ford demonstrated the feasibility of space communications from orbiting dipole belts. Over the next two years, the belt became progressively less effective for scatter communications, testimony that it was indeed cleaning itself out of orbit. By early 1966 the removal process was almost complete. At the conclusion of the measurements and demonstrations, the Camp Parks and Westford terminals were converted to other uses.

Although Project West Ford was an undeniable success, active satellite communications had already superseded passive scatter communications. The use of passive satellites like the West Ford dipoles required large investments in complex terminals and provided only limited capabilities. Because of their success and burgeoning availability, active communications satellites quickly swept the field.

First Television Transmission via Satellite
The equipment developed for Project West Ford was used to transmit a television picture via satellite for the first time on April 24, 1962. The Echo I satellite, actually a balloon that had been launched almost two years earlier by the National Aeronautics and Space Administration, was in an orbit approximately a thousand miles above the earth. The satellite had been in use for transcontinental voice and facsimile experiments by the California Institute of Technology's Jet Propulsion Laboratory and the Bell Telephone Laboratories. Following the conclusion of these experiments, Lincoln Laboratory began an effort to use Echo I to bounce a television signal across the United States.

The microwave frequency transmission and receiving equipment utilized was developed at the Laboratory. The transmitter was located at the Project West Ford site in Camp Parks, the receiver on Millstone Hill. The Lincoln Laboratory team responsible for the first transmission of a television picture via a communications satellite included Daniel Hamilton, Harold Hoover, Richard Locke, Donald MacLellan, Walter Morrow, Burt Nichols, Thomas Rogers and Philip Waldron.

By the time of this experiment, the balloon had deflated partially, making it difficult to track. In addition, its orbit was unpredictable over more than a short period because of the effects of solar pressure. The effects of solar pressure on Echo I had actually been discovered first by the Millstone radar a few days after the satellite's launch.

For this experiment, Echo I was tracked by optical telescopes to determine its exact orbit and to permit the narrow transmitting and receiving antenna beams to be maintained on the satellite. Both the transmitting and receiving sites were equipped with 60-ft-diameter antennas; the receiver also included a low-noise maser amplifier. Signals were transmitted at a frequency of 8.350 GHz with a power of 20 kW. Although the low received signal level relative to the electrical noise background limited the quality of the transmission, the picture was clear. This simple televised message added yet another first to MIT's accomplishments (Figure 5-2).

Notes

1 This chapter is largely taken from W. W. Ward and F.W. Floyd, "Thirty Years of Research and Development in Space Communications at Lincoln Laboratory," *Linc. Lab. J.* **2**, 5 (1989).

2 An entire issue of the *Proceedings of the IEEE* was devoted to Project West Ford, including an overview, a discussion about the concerns of scientists and detailed descriptions of the program. See *Proc. IEEE* **52**, 449 (1964).

3 This effort was initially called Project Needles, because of the shape of the dipoles. But the name attracted negative publicity, and was soon changed to Project West Ford.

4 The characteristics of Lincoln Laboratory's communication satellites have been extensively reviewed by three sources: (a) H. Sherman, D.C. MacLellan and P. Waldron, "The Lincoln Satellite Technology Program through 1 January 1968: An Annotated Bibliography," *Lincoln Laboratory Technical Report 450*, Lexington, Mass.: MIT Lincoln Laboratory, 12 June 1968, DTIC AD-679-559; (b) M.T. Brown, Jr., *Compendium of Communication and Broadcast Satellites — 1958 to 1980*, New York: IEEE, 1981; (c) D.H. Martin, *Communication Satellites 1958–1988*, El Segundo, Calif.: Aerospace Corp., 1988.

Space Communications at Superhigh Frequency

Lincoln Laboratory's first program in active satellite communications emphasized enhancing satellite downlinks. The downlink signal (from a satellite to a surface terminal) is generally the weak link in satellite communications. The uplink can be improved by increasing the power of a transmitter; the downlink can be strengthened only by maximizing the effective radiated power per unit mass in orbit — a more complex task.

To resolve the downlink problem in satellite communications, the Lincoln Laboratory group set out to develop high-efficiency spacecraft transmitters in the downlink frequency band. These and other spacecraft-related technologies were addressed by a series of Lincoln Experimental Satellites (LES), which were launched between 1965 and 1976.[4]

High-efficiency systems of modulation and demodulation, together with encoding and decoding signals for detection and correction of errors, promised significant advantages for communication terminals. Also needed were interference-resistant, multiple-access signaling techniques that would permit simultaneous use of a satellite by tens or hundreds of users, some of them mobile, without invoking elaborate systems for synchronization and centralized control. These and other terminal-related problems were addressed by a series of Lincoln Experimental Terminals (LET) that went hand in hand with the LESs.

The Lincoln Laboratory satellite-communications program got under way in 1963 with a charter to build and demonstrate satellite-communications systems that addressed military needs. The initial program objective was to build a LES and a LET that would work together as a system and demonstrate practical military satellite communications (MILSATCOM). The availability of Project West Ford's advanced RF technology at superhigh frequency (SHF) — 7 to 8 GHz — contributed to the decision to design LES-1 and LET-1 for that band.

Figure 5-2
First television picture transmission via satellite.

Notes

5 P. Rosen and R.V. Wood, "The Lincoln Experimental Terminal," *IEEE Communications Conv. Rec., Boulder, Colo.,* June 1965, p. 355; P.R. Drouilhet, Jr., "The Lincoln Experimental Terminal Signal Processing System, *IEEE Communications Conv. Rec., Boulder, Colo.,* June 1965, p. 335; I.L. Lebow, "Sequential Decoding for Efficient Channel Utilization," *IEEE Communications Conv. Rec., Boulder, Colo.,* June 1965, p. 47.

6 J.M. Wozencraft and B. Reiffen, *Sequential Decoding.* Cambridge, Mass.: MIT Press, 1961.

7 K.E. Perry and J.M. Wozencraft, "SECO: A Self-Regulating Error Correcting Coder-Decoder," *IRE Trans. Inf. Theory* IT-8, S128 (1962).

8 R.M. Fano, "A Heuristic Discussion of Probabilistic Decoding," *IEEE Trans. Inf. Theory* IT-9, 64 (1963).

9 H. Sherman, D.C. MacLellan, R.M. Lerner and P. Waldron, "Lincoln Experimental Satellite Program (LES-1, -2, -3, -4)," *J. Spacecr. Rockets* 4, 1448 (1967).

1955

Both LES-1 and its twin, LES-2, were built as small polyhedrons with masses of 37 kg, solar powered and spin stabilized. Each satellite's communications transponder acted as a bent pipe in the sky; it translated signals received at the uplink frequency to the downlink frequency after passing the signals through a 20-MHz-wide filter at intermediate frequency and a hard limiter. In response to measurements by visible-light sensors of the earth's position, an autonomous electronic antenna-switching system would connect one of eight SHF horn antennas on the corners of the polyhedron to the transponder. A magnetic attitude-control system (pulsed electromagnets working against the earth's magnetic field synchronously with sensor outputs) kept the satellite's spin axis oriented perpendicular to the line of sight with the sun, and thus avoided thermal problems.

The Titan III-A boosters that carried LES-1 and -2 were capable of carrying satellites to inclined circular orbits at altitudes of about 2800 km. To reach a higher altitude, which would allow tests that would better represent operational MILSATCOM systems, LES-1 and -2 were each equipped with a perigee kick motor, a solid rocket that would place the satellite in an inclined elliptic orbit with 15,000-km apogee.

LES-1, launched from Cape Canaveral on February 11, 1965, accomplished only a few of its goals. Apparently because of ordnance-circuitry miswiring, the satellite never left its circular orbit. LES-2 did much better: on May 6, 1965, it achieved its planned final orbit.

A complete, self-contained, transportable ground terminal, LET-1 was equipped to test and demonstrate evolving satellite-communications techniques in realistic environments.[5] The terminal included a modulation/demodulation system based on 16-ary frequency-shift keying (FSK), frequency hopped over a 20-MHz-wide band at SHF. Sequential decoding[6] had been demonstrated at Lincoln Laboratory with the design and construction of a sequential encoder-decoder (SECO), a convolutional encoder and sequential decoder for a two-way communications system.[7] For the LET-1, a more efficient decoding implementation that used the Fano algorithm reduced the equipment substantially.[8] This set of features, tailored to match the characteristics of LES-1 and -2, provided protection against interference, whether by happenstance or by intention, and was applicable for communication over dispersive channels that used orbiting scatterers such as the moon or the West Ford dipole belt.

LET-2 and -3, each consisting of only a signal processing van (thus not incorporating a transmitter or an antenna), were built at about the same time as LET-1. One of these terminals was used with the SHF West Ford terminal at Westford; the other was transferred to the Army Signal Corps for service with SHF terminals at Camp Roberts, California, and Fort Monmouth, New Jersey. The signal processing features of LET-1, -2 and -3 included advanced vocoders for speech compression and reconstruction, and convolutional encoders and sequential decoders for detecting and correcting errors in the received data stream. The incorporation of cryogenically cooled varactor-diode parametric amplifiers, which provided a system noise temperature of about 55K, improved the sensitivity of LET-1's receiving system.

The next step in Lincoln Laboratory's program in satellite communications was to place a satellite in geosynchronous orbit, and LES-4 was built to fulfill that mission.

T.F. Rogers

G.P. Dinneen

W.E. Morrow, Jr.

The satellite was an outgrowth of LES-1 and -2; the 53-kg satellite had a greater number of solar cells and an enlarged array of sun and earth sensors.[9] The SHF transponder on LES-4 was essentially identical to the ones on LES-1 and -2, although its electronically switched SHF antenna system to despin the antenna beam was more sophisticated. LES-4 carried an instrument for measuring spatial and temporal variations of the energy spectrum, in five energy ranges, of trapped electrons encountered in orbit. This instrument was added to provide information of scientific interest and for use in the design of future spacecraft.

A Titan-IIIC booster was to carry LES-4 and its companion, LES-3, to a near-geosynchronous altitude and deposit them in circular, near-equatorial orbits with eastward drift in subsatellite longitude of about 30° per day. These satellites did not have on-board propulsion systems. The satellites would be visible to any given terminal for about five days, then disappear in the east. Unfortunately, the booster failed to finish its job, leaving these satellites stranded in their transfer ellipses. This disappointment, however, had its bright side: LES-4's repeated trips between perigee (195 km) and apogee (33,700 km) gave it many opportunities to measure the radiation environment over a wide range of altitudes.

LES-4's communications system worked as well as it could under the handicap of being in the wrong orbit. Ultimately, as with the West Ford dipoles, LES-4 descended into the upper atmosphere and burned up.

Lincoln Laboratory's accomplishments in SHF satellite communications opened up a part of the electromagnetic spectrum that remains heavily used today. In fact, SHF satellites now form the space segment of the Defense Satellite Communication System (DSCS).

Space Communications at Ultrahigh Frequency

LES-1, -2 and -4 and the LETs demonstrated the capabilities of SHF for reliable communication between large fixed and mobile ground terminals. These technologies, however, were not useful for small tactical units such as vehicles, ships, aircraft and infantry, all of which needed direct, dependable communication. Only a large command-post airplane or a sizable ship could be equipped with an SHF terminal that could work with the DSCS satellites in orbit and those planned for the immediate future.

Because high levels of RF power at SHF could not be generated in the satellites, the downlink continued to limit system performance. Each terminal needed a large antenna aperture to capture enough of the weak downlink signal, and the price for a large antenna aperture at SHF was a narrow antenna beam that had to be pointed precisely toward the satellite. Small tactical units could not accommodate such complex antenna systems, particularly if the platform carrying the terminal would be in motion.

Communication links at much lower frequencies (in the military UHF band, 225 to 400 MHz) solved the downlink problem. Solid state circuits could generate substantial amounts of RF power at UHF in a satellite. A relatively uncomplicated low-gain terminal antenna could provide a sizable effective receiving area, which permitted closing of the link, and a broad beam, which simplified the task of pointing an antenna in the direction of the satellite. Such antennas were particularly appealing for aircraft installation. UHF terminals promised to be comparatively simple and inexpensive, and they could be readily produced in large numbers.

1960

Project West Ford orbiting dipole belt

Project West Ford terminal, Westford, Mass.

Project West Ford terminal, Camp Parks, Calif.

First photograph transmitted by satellite

Notes

10 D.C. MacLellan,
H.A. MacDonald,
P. Waldron and H.
Sherman, "Lincoln
Experimental Satellites
5 and 6," *Progress
in Astronautics and
Aeronautics, Vol.
26, Communication
Satellites for the 70s:
Systems,* eds. N.E.
Feldman and C.M. Kel-
ly. Cambridge, Mass.:
MIT Press, 1971, p.
375.

11 I.L. Lebow, K.L.
Jordan, Jr., and P.R.
Drouilhet, Jr., "Satellite
Communications to
Mobile Platforms,"
Proc. IEEE **59,** 139
(1971).

12 P.R. Drouilhet, Jr.,
and S.L. Bernstein,
"TATS — A Band-
Spread Modulation-
Demodulation System
for Multiple Access
Tactical Satellite Com-
munications," *EASCON
'69 Conf. Rec.* New
York: IEEE, 1969, p.
126.

13 E.A. Bucher and
D.P. White, "Time
Diversity Modulation
for UHF Satellite Com-
munication during
Scintillation," *National
Communications Conf.,
Vol. 3.* New York: IEEE,
1976, p. 43.4-1.

In 1965 the DoD approved a program to evaluate the potential usefulness of satellite communications in the military UHF band, and it was agreed that Lincoln Laboratory would provide the satellites essential to the test program.

Lincoln Laboratory carried out two programs to measure the characteristics of the UHF environment. In the first, receiving equipment was installed in aircraft and flown over representative cities and varied terrain to measure RF noise. In the second, propagation phenomena between satellites and airborne terminals were examined. For this program, LES-3 was built in haste, with technology from LES-l, -2 and -4, and was launched along with LES-4 on December 21, 1965.

LES-3 was essentially a signal generator in orbit. It radiated a signal near 233 MHz that was biphase modulated by a 15-bit maximal-length shift-register sequence at a clock rate of 100,000 bps. Correlation of the signal received in an aircraft with a replica of the known sequence brought out time-delay structures in the propagation path. Multipath propagation effects were expected, and they were observed: relative to the 1-m free-space wavelength of 300 MHz (the middle of the military UHF band), much of earth's surface is mirrorlike, so electromagnetic waves can be propagated between the satellite and the airborne terminal by a direct path and also by paths involving reflection off the earth's surface. By knowing the likely parameters of the signal delays, the Lincoln Laboratory group was able to design systems of modulation and demodulation for UHF satellite communications that would not be confounded by multipath-propagation effects.

As mentioned, booster problems trapped LES-3 and -4 in elliptical transfer orbits. The orbit of LES-3, however, was quite adequate for gathering multipath-propagation data over a wide variety of terrains. Like LES-4, LES-3 descended, reentered the atmosphere and disintegrated.

LES-5, launched by a Titan-IIIC booster on July 1, 1967, and LES-6, launched in the same way on September 26, 1968, share a strong family resemblance.[10] Each satellite is powered by solar cells and is spin stabilized around an axis nominally perpendicular to the near-equatorial orbit plane. The central feature of each of these satellites is a broadband, hard-limiting, frequency-translating UHF-to-UHF transponder (Figure 5-3).

The Lincoln Laboratory program showed that satellite communications in the military UHF band worked well.[11] The Tri-Service terminals in ships and aircraft and in the field communicated readily through LES-5 in orbit. To enhance satellite communications at UHF to and from mobile platforms, Lincoln Laboratory developed a special antijam/multiple-access system of modulation and demodulation based on frequency hopping and coded multiple-frequency-shift keying (MFSK). The Tactical Transmission System (TATS) that worked with LES-5 was completed at the last minute, after the launch, but before the insertion into final orbit! TATS met its performance goals and was put into production by the DoD.[12]

LES-6 placed substantial communications resources in geostationary orbit (Figure 5-4). Since the LETs for UHF were small, with relatively low-gain antennas, the DoD decided to procure large quantities of UHF terminals.

As will be discussed, it is very difficult to defend a communications satellite with a UHF uplink against a determined jamming attack. Nevertheless, since the simplicity and comparative cheapness of UHF MILSATCOM terminals make this part of the spectrum highly attractive, it is likely to remain in use for a long time.

UHF satellite communications tests soon revealed that electromagnetic signals were sometimes subject to amplitude scintillations due to propagation through the turbulent ionosphere that could disrupt communication links. Because these effects occurred most often near the geomagnetic poles and the geomagnetic equator, the Laboratory studied transmissions from Guam. These observations were used to develop and test a successful time-diversity system for use with the Navy UHF fleet broadcast.[13]

Figure 5-3, left
Earl Hunter (left) and Benjamin Steinberg (right) with an antenna model of LES-6 in an anechoic chamber.

Figure 5-4, above
Andy Howitt (left) and Claude Gillaspie (right) inspect the LES-6 satellite. Launched on September 26, 1968, LES-6 had a long and useful career before it was retired after many years of service. A test conducted in December 1993 showed that the satellite remained functional.

As the number of UHF satellite-communications terminals grew, so did the importance of increasing the utilization efficiency of the UHF satellite transponders. Lincoln Laboratory developed a system that accomplished this goal by improving the ground terminals. A laboratory demonstration of the Terminal Access Control System (TACS) led to the Navy's procurement of the demand assigned multiple access (DAMA) system for its UHF satellite-communications systems.[14]

LESs have often accommodated space-technology experiments. LES-6 carried a solar cell experiment for measurement of degradation effects, a detector for measurement of particle radiation (similar to one on LES-4), a pulsed-plasma-thruster system for orbit control, a system for autonomous attitude control and a system for automatically stationkeeping the satellite in longitude. Lincoln Laboratory also conducted a study of the characteristics of the RF environment near the altitude of geosynchronous orbit.

After LES-6's test program was successfully completed, it began a long period of operational communications support. The satellite was placed on reserve status in March 1976.

A condition check of the LES-6 communications transponder, carried out on December 13 through 15, 1993, showed that it still worked after twenty-five years in space. The satellite's output power and receiving sensitivity were found to be significantly poorer than they were during the years just after launch. However, LES-6 is still available for limited communications support if needed; its stalwart endurance testifies to the extremely long, useful lives of spacecraft systems.

Multiple-Beam Antennas

Although UHF technology had been the main focus for LES-5 and -6 because it would permit affordable operation to mobile platforms, SHF was more desirable for MILSATCOM applications. In particular, the greater bandwidth of SHF permitted the use of antijam communication links and of higher data-transfer rates. Moreover, LES-1, -2 and -4 and the LETs showed that SHF could provide reliable communication with appropriate ground terminals. Therefore, for the design of LES-7, Lincoln Laboratory returned to the SHF band.

The antenna systems on earlier SHF satellites had been small in terms of wavelength, and their beams were much larger than earth coverage (which is about 18° from synchronous altitude). The next level of sophistication in SHF space communications was a satellite antenna system with a mechanically pointable, less-than-earth-coverage beam. Lincoln Laboratory undertook to develop and demonstrate, in orbit, an antenna system that could allow satellite operators to aim the transmit (downlink) power to receivers and simultaneously reduce the receiving (uplink) sensitivity in directions that might include sources of jamming or other interference.

Lincoln Laboratory adopted the multiple-beam-antenna (MBA) approach to shape the downlink beam. In this method, many separate antenna feeds form a dense set of narrow pencil beams covering the earth. The signals from this collection of beams are adjusted in amplitude and phase and then combined to approximate the desired antenna pattern.

Lincoln Laboratory began a program to demonstrate, in orbit, a nineteen-beam MBA for uplink reception at SHF. A single earth-coverage horn was to be used for transmission. The 30-in-diameter aperture of the nineteen receiving antenna beams was designed to yield a nominal 3° resolution throughout the cone subtended by the earth from geosynchronous-satellite altitude. The nineteen beams could be weighted to approximate the desired antenna pattern.

As a design concept, the MBA would be kept facing the earth by the satellite's three-axis stabilized attitude-control system. Solar-cell arrays were to be sun oriented to collect energy as LES-7 revolved during its orbit around the earth. Work got under way to develop the satellite bus — consisting of structure and housekeeping systems, power, propulsion, attitude control, thermal control, telemetry and telecommand — in parallel with the development of the MBA and of the communications system associated with it.

Notes

14 L.E. Taylor and S.L. Bernstein, "TACS — A Demand Assignment System for FLEETSAT," *IEEE Trans. Commun.* COM-27, 1484 (1979).

15 F.W. Sarles, Jr., L.W. Bowles, L.P. Farnsworth and P. Waldron, "The Lincoln Experimental Satellites LES-8 and LES-9," *EASCON-77 Rec., Arlington, Va., 26–28 September 1977,* p. 21-1A. IEEE No. 77CH1255-9 EASCON.

By early in 1970, it became apparent that LES-7 was ahead of its time. Since there was not enough support in the DoD for the mission, the funding required for the satellite's development, launch and evaluation in orbit was not available. Lincoln Laboratory, with considerable regret, put aside the LES-7 flight program. The critical technology of the MBA was carried through final development and was placed on the shelf. Happily, in a few years the MBA concept found application on DSCS-III, the third generation of the Defense Satellite Communications System, for which it was adopted as the primary antenna system almost without change.

Space Communications at Extremely High Frequency

LES-8 and -9 were a pair of experimental communications satellites that Lincoln Laboratory developed and built to demonstrate high-reliability, survivable, strategic communications technologies (Figure 5-5).[15] They were designed to operate in coplanar, inclined, circular, geosynchronous orbits and to communicate with each other via intersatellite links (crosslinks) at EHF, and with terminals operating on or near the surface of the earth at both EHF and UHF. The overall system provided for assured communications between a limited number of strategic terminals at data rates ranging from teletype (75 bps) to vocoded voice (2400 bps) and computer data exchange (19,200 bps). The system design incorporated a number of band-spreading and signal processing techniques for electromagnetic survivability, including encoding/decoding, interleaving, de-interleaving, multiplexing/demultiplexing, frequency hopping/dehopping and demodulation, crossbanding and remodulation on board the satellite.

The EHF portion of the spectrum held out the promise of abundant bandwidth to accommodate many simultaneous users and spread-spectrum systems of modulation and demodulation for electromagnetically survivable (i.e., hard, antijam) communication links. For reasons of convenience, operating frequencies in the K_a-band (36 to 38 GHz) were selected for the LES-8 and -9 experiment.

One of the strengths of Lincoln Laboratory's program in satellite communications is that it encompasses the development of terminals and of satellites in one organization. The LES-8 and -9 experiments were sufficiently complex

that in 1971 the Communications Division established a project office headed by Donald MacLellan to manage the program.

Transmission and reception for satellite links providing substantial antijam capability, such as links through LES-8 and -9, are complex when compared to links that rely on unprotected transponders such as links through LES-1, -2, -4, -5 and -6. It would be very difficult if the space and terrestrial segments of a modern MILSATCOM system were developed separately and if their first operating encounter took place after launch. Lincoln Laboratory conducted extensive end-to-end testing of communication links before launch, including the terminals that Lincoln Laboratory developed and those developed by the Air Force and the Navy. The generally smooth course of the communication-link testing in orbit owed a great deal to the prelaunch testing at Lincoln Laboratory.

The LES-8 and -9 intersatellite links successfully addressed the key technical problems that confronted the implementation of satellite-to-satellite communications. The two satellites were launched together on March 14, 1976. The Titan-IIIC booster placed them in nearly coplanar, circular, geosynchronous orbits with equatorial inclinations of about 25°.

LES-8 and -9 are powered by radioisotope thermoelectric generators and have no solar cells or batteries. These generators have performed superbly. They provide continuous electrical power throughout the seasonal eclipses of the sun by the earth that geostationary satellites experience.

The daily latitude excursions of LES-8 and -9 (now between 17°N and 17°S) are very different from those of most commercial communications satellites, which are stationkept in latitude and longitude to a small fraction of a degree. (Stationkeeping enables commercial satellites to serve customers who have terminals without a satellite-tracking capability.) But what might seem to be a problem is actually an advantage. The motion of LES-8 and -9 relative to ground-based terminals provides a good way to test the motion-compensation circuitry of terminals that operate on moving platforms. Moreover, the daily north/south excursions yield long intervals of visibility from sites in the Arctic and in the Antarctic.

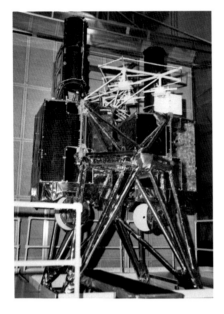

Figure 5-5
LES-8 (left) and LES-9 (right) assembled at Cape Canaveral Air Force Station, Florida. The satellite assembly was integrated with the Titan-IIIC booster.

The resource controller in the orbiting FEP carries out most of its computer-to-computer transactions with users and would-be users without supervisory intervention. Two FEP operations centers have been built: one is installed permanently at Lincoln Laboratory; the other, transportable though by no means mobile, has been installed at a Navy facility near Prospect Harbor, Maine. (The Navy is the operational manager of the FEP communications system.)

During the FEP program, Lincoln Laboratory concentrated on the challenging technologies required for the FEP, taking advantage of the satellite-bus technologies already developed and proven in space by TRW's series of FLTSAT satellites. The success of the FEP program speaks well for Lincoln Laboratory's approach to implementation and its quality assurance in building reliable spacecraft.

Advanced EHF/SHF Terminals
In a Milstar-related activity, Lincoln Laboratory designed and built SCOTT (Single-Channel Objective Tactical Terminal), the advanced-development model of the Army's Milstar EHF/SHF terminal.[17] In 1983 Army personnel successfully tested this terminal, mounted in a tracked military vehicle, against a satellite simulator in the field (Figure 5-7). The Army's production version of SCOTT has many of the features that were first demonstrated in Lincoln Laboratory's advanced-development model.

As an outgrowth of the SCOTT work, Lincoln Laboratory conducted a feasibility study in 1983 that resulted in a conceptual design for a man-portable, Milstar-compatible EHF/SHF terminal. The development of the Single-Channel Advanced Milstar Portable (SCAMP) was completed shortly after the launch of the first FEP, and it operated successfully with the FEP.

The Advanced SCAMP is a complete redesign of the original system (Figure 5-8). Developed in the early 1990s, it provides message or voice communication through a Milstar spot-beam antenna. To achieve the desired size, weight and performance goals, the Advanced SCAMP incorporates miniature solid state RF and transmitter circuitry, displaced-axis petal reflector antennas, application-specific VLSI devices and innovative software codes.

Looking Ahead
In the more than thirty years of Lincoln Laboratory's program, satellite communications has reached a high level of maturity (Figure 5-9). The job, however, is not yet complete. Successes achieved in making communications systems available and survivable must be followed up by breakthroughs in making the technologies affordable, so that both tactical and strategic users can benefit from reliable communications.

1970

Communications Support for Operation Desert Storm

In the fall of 1990, as the U.S. and coalition forces began the buildup of force that led to the liberation of Kuwait, it became clear that additional communications capabilities were needed in the theater of operations. Most U.S. satellites were positioned over the western hemisphere and therefore could not support communications in the Persian Gulf area. Some communications resources were available, but they were inadequate for the demands then being anticipated for Operation Desert Storm.

The command, control and communications support effort of the Joint Staff approached Lincoln Laboratory and asked the Communications Division if it could provide additional communications resources. The answer was affirmative. A Lincoln Laboratory FEP was directed to provide an antijam EHF/SHF communications capability between the United States and the command headquarters in the Gulf area. LES-9 could also be configured to support communications in the Persian Gulf. Although the satellite was approaching its fifteenth year in space, it still worked well. LES-9 was stationed at a longitude of 105°W, but on-board thrusters allowed the satellite to change its position.

On December 20, 1990, LESOC commanded LES-9 to initiate a thrusting operation. The objective was to place the satellite in geostationary orbit at a longitude of 10°W, a position that would provide around-the-clock visibility of the satellite to coalition forces in the theater of operations.

Time was critical. To reach the objective before Operation Desert Storm commenced, LES-9 had to move at a rate of 4.4° per day — about eight times faster than the satellite had ever moved before. To provide enough electrical power for the satellite's heaters, it was necessary to change the UHF transponder transmitter from high- to low-power operation.

LES-9 drifted freely eastward until it was time to commence west-face thrusting to stop the satellite. The stopping operation was complicated by the fact that, as LES-9 approached its new station, it ceased to be visible to LESOC around the clock. Thrusting was carried out only while LES-9 could be seen and controlled from LESOC.

LES-8, meanwhile, was also called to duty. The satellite was shifted from its station at 65°W longitude to a new position at 105°W longitude, where it could replace LES-9 to a significant extent. Thrusting operations for LES-8 began on January 2 and concluded on February 8, 1991.

On January 21, 1991, LES-9 arrived at a longitude of 10°W, and high-power operation of the UHF transmitter was restored. The air war phase of Operation Desert Storm had just begun, and through the rest of the air war, and through the one-hundred-hour ground war in February, the satellite provided an important communications asset for the forces in the Persian Gulf region.

Figure 5-9
Lincoln Laboratory space communications activities.

(Figure 5-9 — timeline chart spanning 50s through 90s)

50s	60s	70s	80s	90s

Project West Ford (SHF)
WF-1 WF-2
Point-to-Point SATCOM (SHF)
LES-1, -2, -4
Mobile SATCOM (UHF)
LES-3, -5, -6   LES-8, -9
Optical Satellite Links   Laser Communications
Multiple-Beam Antennas/Adaptive Nulling
LES-7   UHF   EHF   Lightweight
MBA (SHF) Demo   Demo   MBA (EHF)
Signal Processing Spacecraft
LES-8, -9   FEP-7   FEP-8
Small, Transportable EHF Terminals
Antijam EHF SATCOM
SCOTT   SCAMP   Advanced SCAMP
EHF Higher-Data-Rate Communications
Lighter-Weight Payloads/Terminals

Advanced-development-model SCOTT RF assembly

D.M. Snider with SCAMP

Lincoln Laboratory FEPOC

Transportable FEPOC, Prospect Harbor, Maine

V. Vitto

6   **Ballistic Missile Defense**

Programs in strategic systems have provided an understanding of the phenomenology associated with vehicle reentry into the earth's atmosphere, particularly as it affects target discrimination. Concepts developed in this activity have been applied to the design of missile-defense and defense-penetration systems.

Left: ALTAIR on Roi-Namur Island, Kwajalein Atoll, Marshall Islands.

As ballistic missiles capable of delivering nuclear weapons over intercontinental ranges entered the arsenals of both the United States and the USSR in the late 1950s, the DoD asked Lincoln Laboratory to take on a new challenge — ballistic missile defense (BMD).[1] The skills Lincoln Laboratory had developed in the SAGE air defense effort provided a strong starting point for developing BMD techniques. In particular, the concept of computer-controlled sensors and interceptors developed for SAGE was also essential to the design of BMD systems. The Lincoln Laboratory BMD program grew significantly in the 1960s and again in the 1980s under the leadership of assistant director Jerome Freedman. The Radar Measurements Division assumed primary responsibility for the Laboratory's BMD program under the leadership of Stephen Dodd, Jr., William Lemnios and Wade Kornegay. BMD projects have had significant support across the Laboratory, involving the Engineering, Aerospace, Solid State and Optics Divisions. Under the leadership of V. Alexander Nedzel and Herbert Kottler, the Laboratory's Aerospace Division developed penetration aids that could be utilized in a reentry system to impair or defeat BMD systems.

In earlier work Lincoln Laboratory had joined with the National Advisory Committee for Aeronautics (NACA), which became the National Aeronautics and Space Administration (NASA), in a reentry measurements program.[2] Daniel Dustin and Glen Pippert were instrumental in the establishment of the ARPA-sponsored Reentry Physics Research program, which lasted from 1958 to 1965.

Missile defenses and air defenses are similar in that they both must be able to detect, track, identify, intercept and kill their targets, but they differ in how they carry out these functions. Ballistic missile weapons or warheads are smaller than aircraft, travel much faster and approach from much higher altitudes. Decoys and hardware from the deployment of a missile's weapon or weapons can accompany a warhead on parallel ballistic trajectories. Therefore, target identification for missile defense must include the additional task of discrimination — distinguishing real warheads from accompanying decoys and deployment hardware.

Intercepting and killing an intercontinental ballistic missile (ICBM) is more difficult than it is for an aircraft. In contrast to aircraft, an ICBM has a significant speed advantage over an interceptor. However, ballistic missiles move on predictable trajectories, so it is possible to fly an interceptor to a point within error bounds of a target's ballistic path. Furthermore, an ICBM warhead is extremely rugged. Even if the ballistic missile is hit, substantial portions, including the warhead, may survive and will continue on a ballistic trajectory, rather than crash like an airplane. Until interceptor guidance technology advanced in the 1980s, it was generally assumed that killing a ballistic missile would require an interceptor with a nuclear warhead, because both a large kill radius and a destructive kill mechanism were required.

The Lincoln Laboratory effort in BMD has focused on two key problems: the development of long-range, high-traffic-capability sensors that can discriminate targets and the design of high-speed computers and flexible software to identify targets and control engagements.

While the nation's BMD program has undergone many important changes, Lincoln Laboratory's effort has consistently followed four basic technical threads. The first is the collection of high-quality radar and optical data on targets of interest: foreign and U.S. systems and U.S. test models of potential future threats. The second is the study of the phenomenology of threat-complex objects in different environments and of how the phenomenology relates to measurable differences. The third is the design of defense sensors that can make sophisticated discrimination measurements and of algorithms and processors that can handle realistic threats created by high traffic levels of warheads, decoys and deployment hardware in real time. The fourth is the fitting of the sensors and their measurements into an overall BMD system. Each of these technical threads has been continuous at Lincoln Laboratory, though the major objectives of the DoD BMD program have seen radical changes over the past four decades.

Figure 6-15
Theater countermeasures missile
launch from Wake Island toward the
Kwajalein Atoll.

The shift from hardened silo defense to soft target defense pushed up the minimum intercept altitude in the reentry phase and, consequently, the required discrimination altitude. Lincoln Laboratory concentrated its efforts in this area on studying which discriminants would be available at the start of high-altitude reentry into the thin atmosphere. The discriminants tended to depend on very small levels of target deceleration or heating, and on very precise measurement of these effects.

The Strategic Defense Initiative — The Second Phase
By the late 1980s the threat posed by the Soviet Union had diminished, but concerns had increased about the possibility of accidental or unauthorized launches. Ballistic missiles had spread to more countries, heightening the importance of defense against short-range theater missiles. In response to the changed political picture, the emphasis of SDI shifted away from the near-leakproof defense against a massive attack and toward developing a capability known as Global Protection Against Limited Strikes (GPALS). GPALS work focused on defense systems that could be deployed in a few years, rather than on research for very advanced defenses. Near-term applications emphasized ground-based radars and ground-based interceptors. Research for longer-term GPALS concepts augmented the ground-based system with space-based sensors and interceptors.

Following Operation Desert Storm, theater missile defense (TMD) came to prominence. To reflect the emphasis on TMD as opposed to defense against ICBMs, the Strategic Defense Initiative Organization was renamed the Ballistic Missile Defense Organization. Theater missiles generally employ relatively unsophisticated technologies and have shorter flight times (particularly the exoatmospheric portion), which limits the types of penaids that can be used. Much of the missile trajectory occurs within the view of a ground radar, making discrimination easier. The lower speed of these missiles also makes it easier to hit them with non-nuclear interceptors. Other aspects of TMD, however, are quite difficult. The short time of flight limits the coverage the defense can achieve, particularly in the boost phase. In addition, theater missiles can have a variety of warheads: high explosive, chemical, biological or nuclear. The requirements to

kill each of these are different and a single defense concept is unlikely to be able to handle all possibilities. Finally, although a theater missile may not be designed for the high reliability and extreme accuracy of a strategic missile, it can still be effective against a city.

To obtain a database on potential defense problems for TMD, Lincoln Laboratory has been conducting a series of flight tests of theater missile critical measurements at the Kwajalein Missile Range (Figure 6-15). In these tests, simulated theater missile payloads are flown from Wake Island to Kwajalein, a distance of about a thousand kilometers. The Kwajalein radars, along with other radars and infrared sensors, collect data during the tests; these data are used to develop techniques to handle possible countermeasures. The Laboratory is supporting the design of radars for TMD and the development of discrimination techniques for use by the radars.

The continuing possibility of a limited attack — either an accidental strategic launch or a deliberate strategic or theater attack against the United States and its allies — means national missile defense (NMD) and TMD will continue to be a significant national problem. Moreover, both NMD and TMD are exceedingly difficult problems that stretch the state of the art in many technologies. A key difficulty is that the requirements for BMD systems are, like the missiles themselves, moving targets. Whenever the defense develops a working system, the potential enemies develop countermeasures, forcing the defense to evolve again. The defense can only strive to develop a robust capability, because the specifics of the threat will not remain fixed.

The Lincoln Laboratory BMD program has greatly advanced the potential of the United States to protect itself against the threat of ballistic missiles. Activities in theater missile defense, measurements on missile systems, advanced sensor and component design and the development of highly robust algorithms and discrimination techniques for BMD will continue to serve the needs of U.S. defense forces.

Space Science

A program in radar astronomy led to the mapping of the moon, a refinement in the value of the astronomical unit and verification of the General Theory of Relativity. Haystack's operation as a radar and as a radio telescope contributed to planetary science and radio astronomy.

Left: Haystack's 120-ft-diameter antenna inside the radome.

Radio astronomy is the study of the natural radio-frequency signals emitted by celestial bodies; radar astronomy, by contrast, looks at signals that have been emitted by earthbound transmitters and reflected by objects in the sky. Since manmade transmitters are not nearly as powerful as naturally occurring cosmic transmitters, and since the radio wave intensity falls as the square of the distance (hence as the fourth power for radar), radar astronomy can be used only for the study of objects within the solar system. Radio astronomy, on the other hand, can be used to detect objects in other galaxies and even at the very edge of the universe.[1]

For studies within the solar system, optical and radar astronomy complement each other well. Optical astronomy can determine angular separations between objects with precision, but provides little accuracy in the direct measurement of distance. Thus, although precise determinations of the elements of the orbits of the planets were available in the nineteenth century, the sizes of their orbits were known accurately only in astronomical units of length, not in terrestrial units. Radar astronomy has relatively poor angular resolution; however, it offers extraordinary accuracy in the determination of distances and radial velocities. The goal for radar astronomers in the 1960s, therefore, was to determine the size of the astronomical unit (the mean distance between the earth and the sun) and to explore the radio reflection properties of planetary bodies and the sun.

The idea that radar could lead to new insights in astronomy had been discussed since the end of World War II, when researchers in Hungary and the United States transmitted radio signals toward the moon and detected their echoes. The sensitivity of the equipment at that time was poor, however, so it had not been possible to carry out any real science. Lincoln Laboratory was able to make its mark in the field of radar astronomy because it had developed sensitive radars that were available for science, and it had a staff that was interested and knowledgeable.

In the years between 1958 and 1969, Lincoln Laboratory achieved and maintained a position of international prominence in radar and radio astronomy.[2] Under the successive leaderships of John Harrington, James Meyer and Stephen Dodd, scientists in the Radio Physics Division mapped the moon, measured the orbits of the terrestrial planets, determined the size of the solar system, verified a prediction of the theory of general relativity, studied the sun's corona and identified a molecule in interstellar space for the first time.

Although the Millstone radar at the Millstone Hill field site in Westford, Massachusetts, was built for the BMEWS effort, its first achievement was the detection of radar echoes from Sputnik I, the first artificial satellite, in the fall of 1957. The radar's success in finding nearby objects in space, combined with its great sensitivity, meant that it could also look at objects farther away. Therefore, researchers in the Radio Physics Division decided to use this instrument for the first radar astronomy measurements beyond the earth-moon system.

The Millstone radar operated at a wavelength of 68 cm and employed a fully steerable 84-ft-diameter antenna. It was coupled to a transmitter with a peak output power of 1 MW and an average output power of 60 kW. The radar was later upgraded to operate at 23 cm with greatly improved performance.

Soon after the Millstone radar went into operation, Lincoln Laboratory proposed construction of the Haystack radar in Tyngsboro, Massachusetts (part of the Millstone Hill site) as the next significant step in the development of high-performance microwave systems. Haystack, designed by a team led by Herbert Weiss as an experimental facility for research on space communications and radar, became a true state-of-the-art system. After operations began in 1964, the radar was used in space communications and radio propagation experiments, as a tracking and measurements radar and as a high-resolution radio telescope.[3] Following the conclusion of Project West Ford, the Haystack radar was assigned to basic science, and because its sensitivity was much greater than that of the Millstone radar, it became Lincoln Laboratory's primary planetary astronomy radar for the next decade.

Notes

1 Material for this chapter was contributed by John Evans and Irwin Shapiro.

2 Much of Lincoln Laboratory's work is collected in the book *Radar Astronomy*, eds. J.V. Evans and T. Hagfors. New York: McGraw-Hill, 1968.

3 The main motivation behind the decision to construct the Haystack radar was its intended application as a high-sensitivity ground terminal for the Project West Ford space communications activity. At the time the radar was named, Project West Ford was still known as Project Needles (see chapter 5, "Satellite Communications") — hence the name Haystack.

4 For a review of Lincoln Laboratory's work on the surfaces of the moon and planets, see J.V. Evans, "Radar Studies of Planetary Surfaces," in *Annual Review of Astronomy and Astrophysics, Vol. 7*, eds. L. Goldberg, D. Layzer and J.G. Phillips. Palo Alto, Calif.: Annual Reviews, 1969, p. 201.

5 G.H. Pettengill, "Measurements of Lunar Reflectivity Using the Millstone Radar," *Proc. IRE* 48, 933 (1960).

1960

The Haystack radio telescope operated at a wavelength of 3.8 cm; its central element was a fully steerable paraboloidal Cassegrain antenna, 120 ft in diameter. The antenna was fully enclosed in the world's largest space-frame radome, which improved antenna pointing by protecting the antenna from snow, ice, wind loading and direct radiation from the sun.

Also employed for some experiments were the Camp Parks, California, and Westford systems of the Project West Ford experiment with their radar-mode capability. These systems operated at a wavelength of 3.6 cm and employed 60-ft fully steerable parabolas, together with CW transmitters that could be chopped.

Lunar Studies

Scientists in Britain and the United States began studies of the radio-wave scattering properties of the moon in the mid-1950s.[4] Their investigations found that the largest portions of the reflected signals were returned from a region near the center of the lunar disk with a radius about one-third that of the moon, suggesting that the returns were coming from a largely smooth and undulating surface, termed *quasi-specular.*

Lunar studies began at Millstone Hill in 1958 with a much more powerful radar than had been used up to that time. These measurements showed that there was a second, weaker component of the reflections that came almost uniformly from the entire surface; it was termed *diffuse.* These weaker signals exhibited considerable depolarization, unlike the quasi-specular returns, suggesting that a very different type of scatterer was responsible.

Measurements were subsequently made at wavelengths shorter than the 68 cm first used at the Millstone radar, including 23 cm at Millstone in 1965 and 3.6 cm at Camp Parks in 1962. These observations demonstrated that the quasi-specular returns were wavelength dependent. The scattering appeared to come from a larger region at the center of the disk as the wavelength was shortened. The strength of the diffuse component increased, suggesting that the reflectors responsible for this component were more numerous and/or better scatterers at shorter wavelengths.

Theoretical studies of the scattering from smooth undulating surfaces were carried out by a number of researchers. Theory could best be matched to the observed results when the correlation between the height of two points on the surface was assumed to fall exponentially with the distance separating them.

The radar results were of particular significance when the United States undertook the mission to carry out a landing on the moon. The smallest feature on the lunar surface visible from terrestrial telescopes is about 1/2 km in size. Early in the 1960s, little was known about the roughness on the scale of a landing vehicle; the radar results suggested a smooth surface with an average slope of about one part in eight.

This conclusion was subsequently borne out by close-up television pictures taken by the lunar Ranger probes. The pictures also revealed the presence of boulders lying on the surface, presumably ejected from below during the impact of meteorites. It seemed very likely that these were responsible for the weaker diffuse component. Careful polarization studies made at 23-cm wavelength at the Millstone radar supported this view, because they showed that the diffuse component was partially linearly polarized in a direction radial to the center of the visible disk.

El Campo radar dipoles

S.N. M. N Weinreb, MIT Professor A.H. Barrett and M.L. Meeks

I.I. Shapiro

The radar studies contributed to the lunar landing in other ways. Prior to the landing, there was concern that the lunar surface could be fine dust many feet deep into which any heavy object would sink. From the strength of the radar reflections, however, it was possible to deduce that the average dielectric constant of the surface was about 2.7 — a value very close to that of terrestrial sand, with corresponding weight-bearing properties. Subsequent in situ measurements confirmed the correctness of this result.

The use of radar to map the surface of the moon became possible when the radar beam was made small enough to discriminate between two points on the surface that would contribute echoes at the same range and Doppler shift. The first application of this technique (originally suggested by Paul Green, leader of the Communication Techniques Group) to a solar system target was made at the Millstone radar by Gordon Pettengill, associate leader of the Surveillance Techniques Group, who published a short description of the results in January 1960.[5] Range-Doppler mapping was used extensively over the following decade, first with the new 23-cm Millstone radar system and later with the 3.8-cm Haystack radar. These studies identified regions of anomalous scattering such as (newer) rayed craters, and older craters with rough rims. Increased reflectivity could be accounted for by increased roughness associated with these features, although increased intrinsic reflectivity may also have been a contributor (Figure 7-1).

Another technical innovation at Lincoln Laboratory — the use of interferometry — later enabled altitude data to be added to the two-dimensional radar reflectivity maps, thereby yielding three-dimensional maps of the moon. By using this technique, the Haystack system was able to produce very-high-resolution topographic maps of parts of the moon.

Venus Studies

Although radar echoes from the moon had first been detected in the 1940s, none of the planets had been observed through radar astronomy at the time that Lincoln Laboratory entered the field. The object that came nearest the earth and had the largest radar cross section after the moon was Venus, so the Laboratory initiated an effort to detect its radar echo. The task proved vastly more difficult than was at first expected. In the attempt to observe radar echoes from Venus in February 1958, the group initially believed that Venus had been detected, but subsequent observations proved that their supposed detection had been caused by noise. The next set of measurements was taken about eighteen months later, but because the data were analyzed with the value of the astronomical unit of length in terrestrial units inferred from the 1958 observations of Venus, no acceptable evidence of an echo was obtained.

By 1961 the power of the Millstone transmitter had been increased to 2.5 MW, but by this time the search for radar returns from Venus had become an international race. Four other laboratories were competing to report the first definitive measurement: the Jet Propulsion Laboratory's (JPL) Goldstone facility in California, RCA in Moorestown, New Jersey, Manchester University's Jodrell Bank radar in England and the Institute for Electronics and Radiotechniques' radar system in the Soviet Union (in what is now Ukraine). On March 10, 1961, the JPL radar obtained unmistakable evidence of a return from Venus.

P. B. Sebring

J. Evans

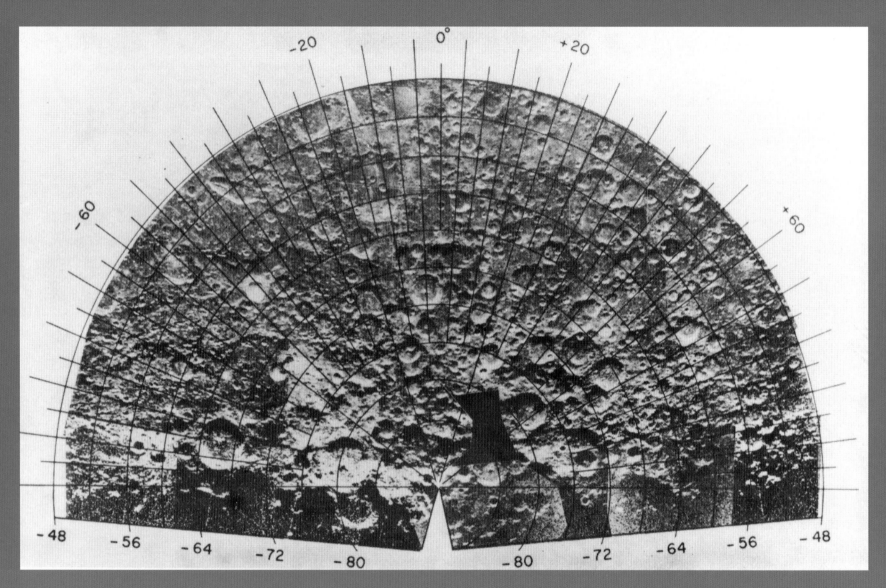

Figure 7-1
Radar map of the surface of the moon
from latitude 48°S to 90°S and
longitude 104°W to 104°E.

Notes

6 M.E. Ash, I.I. Shapiro and W.B. Smith, "Astronomical Constants and Planetary Ephemerides Deduced from Radar and Optical Observations," *Astronom. J.* **72**, 338 (1967).

The principal cause for the difficulty in detecting a radar echo from Venus was the uncertainty in the value of the astronomical unit (the mean distance between the earth and the sun) in terms of a terrestrial unit of length. The astronomical unit was then known only to an accuracy of about one part in 10^3 in terms of terrestrial units of length, and this uncertainty contributed to the difficulty of integrating a sufficient number of echoes (in a computer) to detect the echo. Lincoln Laboratory attempted a ranging experiment by transmitting pulses of radio energy toward Venus. Although the Laboratory found clear echoes in measurements recorded on March 6, 1961, this fact was not known until March 24, by which time enough data had been collected to resolve an inherent ambiguity in the echo delays due to the uncertainty in the value of the astronomical unit. The British and Soviet groups each reported successful detection of echoes from Venus in April.

The error in the astronomical unit could have caused intolerable errors in planetary space-probe missions. The most significant accomplishment of the Venus race, therefore, was the correction to the astronomical unit. Over the next few years, the value was refined further. Lincoln Laboratory eventually determined a value of 499.004786 light sec — nine significant digits.[6]

With the astronomical unit determined, the Lincoln Laboratory researchers then reanalyzed their 1959 data, which had been preserved on magnetic tape. The results showed clear evidence of echoes and provided the first indication that Venus rotated in a retrograde fashion.

Besides contributing to an improved measurement of the size scale of the solar system, continued radar studies of Venus revealed other unexpected aspects of the planet. Not only does Venus rotate in a direction opposite to the earth's, but the period of its rotation is extremely long: about 243 days. These results were dramatic in two respects. With the exception of Uranus, no other planet in the solar system is known to execute retrograde rotation. Moreover, a period of 243.16 days would cause Venus to present exactly the same face to the earth at successive inferior conjunctions, implying capture of Venus's spin by the earth's gravitational field. More recent measurements show the spin period is significantly less, 243.02 days, ruling out capture. Some form of cosmic collision must be responsible for Venus's slow retrograde rotation.

The average scattering properties of Venus were found to exhibit considerable similarity to those of the moon. The returns could be divided into both a quasi-specular component and a diffuse component, with the diffuse component weaker for Venus than the moon. The average surface slope deduced from the quasi-specular component was also less than that for the moon; the average surface slope was found to be about one part in twelve. Venus exhibited considerable surface differentiation, with regions of intense anomalous scattering. These features were studied by using the Haystack radar at 3.8 cm as the illuminator. For reception, the Haystack and Westford antennas were arranged as an interferometer to resolve the ambiguity between points of equal range and Doppler coordinates.

Lincoln Laboratory found that at meter and decimeter wavelengths Venus had a scattering cross section of about 15% of its physical projected area, in contrast with 7% for the moon. This result suggested that the surface of Venus is less porous than the sandy surface of the moon — possibly solid rock with only a thin soil covering.

Initial attempts to observe Venus at the 3.6-cm wavelength were unsuccessful. These experiments were carried out in 1961 at the Camp Parks, California, site by using the Project West Ford equipment. A later attempt in 1964 that used the Westford site yielded weak returns, indicating a radar cross section one-tenth of that observed at decimeter wavelengths. This result was confirmed with the more powerful Haystack radar in 1966. Near-simultaneous range measurements at Millstone (23-cm wavelength) and Haystack (3.8-cm wavelength) demonstrated that the centimeter-wave reflections were from the solid surface, indicating that the difference must be attributed to absorption in the atmosphere of Venus, and that only 30% of the incident 3.8-cm signal reached the surface.

The round-trip times of the radar echoes from Millstone and Haystack also yielded the first reliable value for Venus's radius, showing it to be about 35 km smaller than had been deduced from the Soviet spacecraft Venera 4, which had been thought to have stopped transmitting when it hit Venus's surface. The radar data showed that the transmission had stopped well above the surface and hence that the surface was far hotter and the atmospheric pressure there far higher than had been deduced from the Venera 4 measurements. Radar results obtained at JPL confirmed Lincoln Laboratory's determination of Venus's radius.

These results, along with the surprisingly high temperature of Venus's surface (about 750K) deduced from radio astronomy observations, supported the view that Venus is blanketed by a very thick atmosphere with a surface pressure perhaps a hundred times that of the earth. This atmosphere gives rise to a powerful greenhouse effect, trapping thermal radiation.

Mercury Studies

Radar reflections from Mercury were first reported by the Soviet team in 1962. These were followed by observations reported by the JPL group in 1963 and Millstone and Arecibo in 1965.

The scattering properties of Mercury were studied by the Arecibo team and later by the Lincoln Laboratory team using the Haystack radar. The total radar cross section of Mercury (about 6%) and the distribution of the returns proved extraordinarily close to those observed for the moon. This result implied that Mercury has a similarly eroded and cratered surface; high-resolution photographs taken in 1974 by the Mariner 10 spacecraft provided confirmation. The limited sensitivity of the radar systems then available and the short interval that Mercury spent close enough to earth to be studied made it impossible to discern regions of anomalous scattering.

Mars Studies

Mars never approaches the earth as closely as Venus, which, combined with its smaller size, makes detection difficult even at favorable oppositions. Moreover, the high rotation rate of Mars (24.6 hr) increases the frequency dispersion of the reflections. Therefore, the apparatus necessary to detect Mars must be a hundred times more sensitive than that to detect Venus.

The first detections of Mars were made in 1963 by the JPL and the Soviet groups. At subsequent oppositions, measurements were also made by the Arecibo group and Lincoln Laboratory, initially using the Millstone radar (23-cm wavelength) and later the Haystack radar (3.8-cm wavelength). Measurements of Martian topography at Haystack revealed surprisingly large variations, up to 12 km from the mean.

Studies of the radar echo intensities showed the average radar cross section of Mars to be about 10%, suggesting that the dielectric constant was slightly larger than the value found for the moon. This fact indicated that the surface of Mars was more compact, though still somewhat unconsolidated.

On the basis of the average distribution of echo power over the disk observed at Haystack, the Lincoln Laboratory team concluded that Mars had the smoothest of the planetary surfaces so far investigated, with average slopes of about one part in twenty. These were average properties, however, and the JPL and Arecibo teams both reported large variations in the reflectivity of the subradar point with Martian longitude, with values in the range of 3 to 15% of the physical area of the disk.

There seemed to be a definite association of increased radar reflectivity with the dark-appearing regions on the surface, for example, Trivium Charontis and Syrtis Major. It was not clear whether these variations were caused by changes in the composition of the surface material, its compactness or its roughness, or a combination of properties.

Notes

7 J.H. Chisholm and J.C. James, "Radar Evidence of Solar Wind and Coronal Mass Motions," *Astrophys. J.* **140,** 377 (1964).

Asteroid, Comet and Satellite Studies

The improved Haystack radar system was also able to detect small objects that came near the earth. On June 14, 1968, the asteroid Icarus passed the earth at a distance of 6.5 million km and was successfully detected with the Haystack radar. This measurement marked the first such detection of an asteroid. An attempt to detect Comet Kohoutek, however, failed; the radar system had insufficient sensitivity. Only later, in the 1970s and 1980s, when radar systems with greater sensitivities were developed, were echoes from comets detected.

Even in 1968 greater sensitivity was possible by combining the Haystack and Goldstone antennas in a bistatic configuration. The extra performance of this system permitted the detection of Callisto, one of the major satellites of Jupiter.

Solar Studies

Other than the moon and the terrestrial planets, the only other body that presented a large enough cross section to be detected by radar in the early 1960s was the sun. However, the frequency range over which radar systems could be built to detect echoes from the sun was very limited. For the best signal-to-noise ratio, calculations had predicted the wavelength had to be greater than 6 m. This conclusion was based on the expectation that higher frequencies would penetrate farther into the solar corona, and that the physical conditions prevailing there would cause greater absorption losses. The Millstone radar then operated at a wavelength of 68 cm, so its use was ruled out.

Radar reflections from the sun were first reported in 1960 by a group from Stanford University that employed a radar operating at a wavelength of 11.7 m. No systematic scientific studies were carried out, however.

Lincoln Laboratory had built a powerful VHF transmitter in 1955 near El Campo, Texas, to study signal propagation on a path from El Campo to Oakhurst, New Jersey. Four years later, the Laboratory began to build an array of dipoles to use with the El Campo antenna to permit the use of the system for radar astronomy of the sun. This effort was completed in 1960, and in 1961 the first systematic radar studies of the sun were begun. Over the next three years, the El Campo radar made roughly six hundred separate radar observations of the solar corona (Figure 7-2).

Echoes from the sun showed considerable variability from day to day, indicating equivalent solar cross sections between zero and three times the projected area of the solar disk. The bulk of the energy appeared to be returned from solar plasma residing between 0.5 and 1.5 solar radii above the photosphere. Moreover, there was a wide spread in the energy with Doppler frequency, corresponding to returns from reflection points with speeds between 60 and 150 km/sec along the line from the earth to the sun. Also, the shortest delayed echoes tended to exhibit the largest positive Doppler shift.

The reflections seemed to be caused by irregularities in the solar wind — an ionized plasma that flows radially away from the sun as a consequence of being heated to a temperature of about one million degrees centigrade, sufficient for plasma to escape the sun's gravitational field. However, the spread of the velocities observed appeared to be larger than the simple expansion velocity predicted by the theory of the solar wind, suggesting that perhaps some of the reflections arose from shock waves traveling through the plasma. These measurements provided one of the first confirmations of the existence of the solar wind.[7]

Lincoln Laboratory's study of the solar corona ended in 1964 when the El Campo radar was transferred to the MIT Center for Space Research. Measurements continued for a short time and were then concluded.

The General Relativity Experiment

The possibility of detecting radar echoes from Mercury prompted thoughts about measuring precisely the relativistic advance of Mercury's perihelion; this effect is one of the predictions of Einstein's theory of general relativity. This measurement and two others had been the only known methods for testing Einstein's theory experimentally. The theory also predicted, however, that the speed of a light wave depended on the strength of the gravitational potential along its path, so that a radar pulse passing near the sun would be delayed.

In 1964 Irwin Shapiro published an article suggesting that general relativity could be tested by measuring the round-trip time of radar pulses transmitted toward Mercury or Venus when either was close to superior conjunction, that is, on the opposite side of the sun from the earth. These measurements would provide a fourth test of the theory of general relativity, one that had not been previously considered.

An intensive program was undertaken in 1965 to build a new transmitter and receiver system to provide Haystack with the capability to measure these round-trip delays to an accuracy of about ten microseconds. The improved radar was put into operation in 1966 and tests were carried out over the next year.

The results showed that the sun's gravity did indeed slow the speed of propagation of light. The predicted increase in round-trip delays was confirmed to within about 10%.* The predicted general relativistic advance of Mercury's perihelion was also confirmed, to within about 1%. Lincoln Laboratory had successfully carried out the fourth test of the theory of general relativity.

* I.I. Shapiro, G.H. Pettengill, M.E. Ash, M.L. Stone, W.B. Smith, R.P. Ingalls and R.A. Brockelman, "Fourth Test of General Relativity: Preliminary Results," *Phys. Rev. Lett.* 20, 1265 (1968).

Space Surveillance

The Soviet launch of Sputnik I on October 4, 1957, transformed the military application of space from abstract concept to reality. The threat posed by foreign satellites called for detailed monitoring and evaluation, and thus space surveillance became a vital component of national security.[1]

Space surveillance encompasses detecting, tracking, identifying and cataloging all artificial objects in earth orbit, including payloads, rocket bodies and debris from launches and fragmentation. Keeping a catalog of satellites enables the United States to assess, and respond to, the military potential of satellites launched by other countries, whether overtly or surreptitiously.

Lincoln Laboratory became involved in space surveillance essentially because of lucky timing. The Millstone radar on Millstone Hill in Westford, Massachusetts, had been designed to explore problems relating to early warning of intercontinental ballistic missile launches, but it would prove to be well suited for satellite tracking. The Laboratory was just bringing the radar on line in the fall of 1957, so it was available, although only at low power and with manual tracking, to take data at the time of the Sputnik launch. Through an intense effort on the part of the staff, the skin return from Sputnik was observed within a few days of the satellite's injection into orbit (Figure 8-1). The Soviet Union launched three more satellites over the next year, and Lincoln Laboratory staff members Gordon Pettengill and Leon Kraft, Jr., were able to report that the Millstone radar had successfully detected each of the four satellites.[2]

Responsibility for space surveillance was assigned to the Aerospace Defense Command (ADCOM), the Air Force component of the North American Air Defense Command (NORAD). Over the next decade the Millstone radar occasionally tracked satellites for ADCOM; space surveillance, however, did not become a major program effort at Lincoln Laboratory until deep-space satellites were developed.

In 1963, the original Millstone antenna was shipped to the Pirinclik early-warning site near Diyarbakir, Turkey, and an 84-ft-diameter parabolic reflector with a monopulse feed was installed in Westford (Figure 8-2). The radar wavelength was converted from UHF (450 MHz) to L-band (1295 MHz). The shorter wavelength increased the antenna gain by a factor of 10, although at the cost of a narrower beamwidth (about 0.5° instead of 2°). The average power was increased to 150 kW from a nominal 20 kW. Because of the increased power and antenna gain, as well as a somewhat lower receiver noise figure, the sensitivity increased by a factor of about 60, or about 18 dB, with a corresponding single-pulse detection range on a 1-m² target of approximately 6400 km. The corresponding detection range for the UHF system had been 1800 km.

With the new sensitivity, Millstone was able to track SYNCOM II, the first of a series of experimental geostationary satellites. The existing sensors in the SPACE-TRACK system had been capable of performing space-surveillance operations on objects in near-earth orbit. However, they could not see objects in *deep space,* that is, with circular orbits having a period greater than 240 min and an altitude in excess of 5000 km.

Since the mission of the U.S. Air Force SPACETRACK system was to maintain surveillance of all earth-orbiting satellites and to detect newly launched foreign satellites, the Millstone radar became a key component in the system. For many years the Millstone radar was the only SPACETRACK radar that could acquire and routinely track satellites in deep space.

The first operational geostationary satellite, the Applications Technology Satellite (ATS-1), was launched in September 1967. After ATS-1 reached a geostationary altitude, a rocket burn established a more or less circular orbit above the equator, where the ATS-1 moved in synchronism with the earth's rotation. Millstone tracked the booster stage as it injected ATS-1 into geosynchronous orbit.

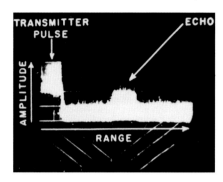

Figure 8-1

The Millstone Hill UHF radar detected the first Soviet satellite, Sputnik I, in 1957.

Notes

1 Material for this chapter was provided by Robert Bergemann.

2 G.H. Pettengill and L.G. Kraft, Jr., "Earth Satellite Observations Made with the Millstone Hill Radar," in *Avionics Research: Satellites and Problems of Long Range Detection and Tracking*. New York: Pergamon Press, 1960, p. 125.

A year later, Lincoln Laboratory deployed LES-6 into a geostationary orbit. Baker-Nunn cameras, which employ a modified Schmidt tracking telescope for satellite tracking, were used to detect LES-6 optically, but the reflected sunlight was fainter than could be detected on film.

In the summer of 1971, Robert Bergemann and Gordon Guernsey, while investigating the Soviet capability to detect U.S. geostationary satellites, persuaded the Haystack planetary-radar team to attempt acquisition of the LES-6 satellite. On the third attempt, the narrow radar beam — only 0.06° — encountered LES-6. Moreover, the team was able to measure the satellite's spin rate and wobble.

The measurement showed that spin-stabilized payloads, which were the principal class of synchronous payloads, yielded coherent radar returns, and that paved the way for exchanging integration time for radar beam power. Not surprisingly, this achievement spurred interest in measuring the radar characteristics of all deep-space satellites.

Two major classes of deep-space communications satellites needed investigation. The most important orbit class was the geostationary, the 24-hr orbit first proposed for global communications in 1944 by the science fiction writer, Arthur C. Clarke. Three geostationary satellites equally spaced in longitude over the equator, revolving in synchronism with the earth's rotation, can provide communication between any two points on earth between the latitudes of 80°N and 80°S with no more than two relays. Geosynchronous satellites must be located at an altitude of 22,000 mi above the earth.

The other important class of deep-space satellites are those in the Soviet *Molniya* ("lightning") orbit. A minimum-energy Hohman transfer from a circular low-earth orbit raises the apogee of the Molniya orbit to approximately 40,000 km. This clever high-eccentricity orbit, with a plane inclined to the equatorial around 50°, requires neither a rocket burn for circularization at apogee nor a burn for changing the inclination of the plane from the latitude of the launch site. Substantially greater payloads can be deployed in Molniya orbits (with a given booster capacity) than in geostationary orbit. At the high-latitude cities and military bases of the Soviet Union,

Molniya satellites loiter, nearly stationary, nearly overhead, for about nine hours, minimizing the tracking antenna requirements at the communication ground sites. Near perigee, the Molniya scoots over the southern hemisphere and rises to apogee over the United States, where it loiters for another nine hours. A constellation of four to eight Molniyas in the plane ensures that an operating satellite is always nearly overhead.

The Soviet Union began launching Molniya satellites for military and civilian interrepublic communication in 1965. More than twenty were in orbit by 1972.

ADCOM had no deep-space sensors at this time, with the exception of a few Baker-Nunn cameras that did not provide real-time observations to ADCOM. The SPACETRACK system was, however, able to maintain surveillance of the Molniya satellites because the high eccentricity of their orbit meant that about a third of the orbit was inside the near-earth sensor coverage.

Late in 1972, the desirability of deep-space coverage was dramatically demonstrated when what was thought to be a routine Molniya launch was not acquired. The lost payload, Cosmos 520, was the first in a series of Soviet launches having high-apogee, high-eccentricity 12-hr orbits in which the apogee occurred over 25°N, approximately, instead of near 60°N, as in the Molniya class. The possibility that the payload was an antisatellite interceptor caused considerable consternation within the space-surveillance community. However, the Cosmos 520 payload was acquired several months later, and soon identified as the Soviet Union's first ballistic-missile launch-detection satellite.

Lincoln Laboratory's space-surveillance group was asked to stand by for the launch of the second launch-detection satellite the following year. With precious little lead time from the announcement of the launch, Antonio Pensa was able to use the Millstone radar to acquire the new satellite, Cosmos 606, before the first revolution was completed. An initial orbit was determined from the metric data that confirmed Cosmos 606 was indeed the same class as Cosmos 520.

Figure 8-2
Millstone radar with 84-ft antenna.

Tracking a Satellite

Within a few days of the launch of Sputnik I on October 4, 1957, several radars at Lincoln Laboratory and elsewhere in the Western world successfully detected echoes from the satellite. These radars could not, however, track Sputnik; they could observe the satellite only briefly during each orbit.

The sight of a Soviet satellite passing over North American skies every 95 min prompted serious concern within the DoD about U.S. strategic defenses. Optical instruments could track the satellite under clear conditions at night, but only radar could track under all weather and light conditions. Therefore, a high priority was assigned to the task of developing a radar that was able to track space objects.

Although the original plans for the Millstone radar had called for a tracking capability, it had not been implemented up to that point. Within a few days of the Sputnik launch, however, the DoD instructed Lincoln Laboratory to build an automatic tracker as soon as possible.

Two Communications Division staff members, Victor Guethlen and Leo Sullivan, were assigned to lead the project. In a sense it was an engineer's dream — no expense was to be spared — but it was also a nightmare. The work schedule was relentless and the calls from the Director's Office were frequent. But within six months, the team had completely designed and constructed a conical-scan automatic angle-tracking system that permitted the Millstone radar to lock onto and follow a satellite as it traveled across the sky.

Installation of the automatic angle-tracking system was completed on April 11, 1958. During that afternoon the radar successfully tracked the sun. By sunset the team was ready to initiate the first automatic track of a satellite. The radar was not yet able to acquire a satellite automatically. The Air Force, however, had supplied the coordinates of Sputnik II (Sputnik I had reentered the earth's atmosphere and disintegrated by that time), so they knew the target could be found easily. There was just one problem. The automatic angle-tracking system used the moon as a reference, and the night was cloudy.

The tracking team could not find the moon. The radar was able to see through clouds, but they had to know where to point it. Not wanting to be forced to explain another delay in the project, the members of the team pulled out their slide rules and an ephemeris table for the moon. And at that point, they began a very brief study in the use of an ephemeris table.

No one there had ever calculated the position of an astronomical object from an ephemeris table before, but by about 9:00 pm the group had converged on one set of coordinates. They pointed the radar and, to their astonishment, the moon indeed was there.

With the last crisis behind them, they pointed the radar to the spot on the horizon where they expected the satellite to appear on its next orbit. When Sputnik II rose over the horizon, the Millstone radar locked onto the signal and tracked the satellite from horizon to horizon.

The value of a radar that could track a new foreign launch (NFL) in deep space had already been demonstrated to the surveillance community. By 1975 ADCOM had initiated the Satellite Tracking (SATTRK) program with the Lincoln Laboratory Aerospace Division, and Millstone, which was the only available deep-space radar, had become a contributing sensor in the SPACETRACK system.

SATTRK was initiated by Alexander Nedzel, the first head of the Aerospace Division, and subsequently managed by Jack Slade. The program is currently supervised by Antonio Pensa and Herbert Kottler, respectively the associate head and head of the Aerospace Division. Assistant director Daniel Dustin, followed by assistant director Donald MacLellan, provided guidance and support for the space-surveillance program.

The Lincoln Laboratory missile defense program had been reoriented as a result of the signing of the Antiballistic Missile Defense Treaty in 1972, and a substantial fraction of Millstone's support was then cut off. However, ADCOM increased SATTRK funding to make up the difference and Millstone became dedicated to space surveillance.[3]

The space-surveillance group began to develop the techniques required for Millstone to achieve a high probability of detection, precise tracking, high-accuracy metric measurement and rapid initial-orbit determination for deep-space satellites. Millstone's 0.6° beamwidth gave the radar a limited but useful search capability, along orbit and transverse to orbit, to aid target acquisition. Nevertheless, unannounced foreign launches as well as U.S. non-nominal rocket burns deployed objects that required considerable searching before detection was achieved.

One important addition was the capability for real-time data communication to ADCOM. Initial-orbit observation data determined on a new foreign payload were still being driven by courier from Westford to the Electronic Systems Division (ESD) Communications Center in Lexington so that data on punch cards could be transmitted to ADCOM. Millstone's request for an on-site AUTODIN terminal was approved by the NORAD commander-in-chief on his first visit to Millstone.[4]

Notes

3 When Jack Slade
requested that ADCOM
replace the Millstone
shortfall, the Air Force
colonel directing
ADCOM's SATTRK
program, a chronic
gesticulator, acciden-
tally knocked over
his coffee cup and
drenched Slade. Morti-
fied by his loss of
control, the colonel
apologized and found
a million dollars for
Millstone before Slade's
clothes had dried. Lin-
coln Laboratory scien-
tists are used to having
cold water thrown on
their proposals, but not
hot coffee!

4 Just after he had
been listening to a
series of complaints
about inefficient data
communications, the
commander of NORAD
spotted a horse
tethered near the Mill-
stone entrance with a
sack thrown over the
saddle. The sack
strongly resembled the
courier's data pouch.

The primary goal of the space-surveillance group, there-fore, was to transform Millstone into a stand-alone, semi-automatic, interactive, real-time deep-space sensor by developing powerful integrated software programs and databases to run efficiently on the site computers. The CG-24 that had initiated computer tracking in the UHF epoch had been replaced by a Scientific Data Systems SDS-9300 shortly after Millstone came up on L-band, and that computer was then superseded in 1978 by two Harris 24-bit S220/7 machines.

The Millstone radar was able to achieve a detection signal-to-noise ratio of about 13 dB on a 1-m^2 target at 6000 km. However, the signal-to-noise ratio at geosta-tionary distance, reduced by the fourth power of the range ratio, was only −21 dB, requiring a thousandfold gain. This improvement and more was achieved with SATCIT (Satellite Acquisition and Tracking using Co-herent Integration Techniques) software, and the break-through allowed Millstone to detect and close-loop-track most geostationary satellites within several seconds of real-time processing.

Real-time coherent integration was achieved by running a fast Fourier transform (FFT) on the site computer to process 256 pulses at a pulse-repetition frequency of 60 Hz. The integration gain of a factor of 256 allowed real-time detection of geostationary satellites as small as 5 m^2!

Even more impressive was the coherent integration of 60,000 pulses. This task required not only that the satellite be stable (which spin-stabilized cylinders are), but that the coherent radar signal phase be corrected for the mismatch between the true acceleration and the predicted target line-of-sight acceleration (from the element set driving the radar). This error was determined by observing the successive drift in the peak Doppler frequency of sequen-tial FFTs. When the small mismatch of only 3×10^{-5} m/sec^2 was corrected, the gain achieved was 47.3 dB, only 0.5 dB from the theoretical limit. Without accelera-tion mismatch correction, the same integration yielded 35.8 dB. Thus the smallest payloads of a few-square-meters radar cross section could be detected in or near the geostationary belt with only a few seconds of coherent integration.

Millstone satellite observations using SATCIT provide positional data that are transmitted to the NORAD Space Surveillance Center in Cheyenne Mountain, near Colo-rado Springs. On site, the observations are stored in the Master Object File and inputted to ANODE (Analytic Orbit Determination), the powerful program that com-putes an initial orbit for uncataloged objects or differen-tially corrects an existing orbit.

The Millstone dynamic scheduler (MIDYS) is a major part of the overall satellite tracking system. MIDYS optimizes satellite tracking operations by automatically sequencing objects to be tracked. The program uses task-ing category, age-of-element sets, radar cross section and coherence or noncoherence of objects to prioritize tasks. By contrast with manual session scheduling, MIDYS tolerates such interruptions as real-time requests for high-interest tracks, equipment outages and missed detections. After MIDYS was installed on the Harris computer in mid-1979, the number of tracks increased from about 250 to 450 per week.

The New-Foreign-Launch Processor program (NFLP) bears some similarity to MIDYS in that a number of orbits are automatically examined sequentially. However, only the high-priority components of an NFL are sought. From a set of several dozen historical foreign-launch pat-terns, a few are selected for sequential search on the basis of the launch-detection sensor report of launch site, launch direction, if available, and other possible informa-tion from intelligence sources. NFLP controls Millstone's search near a satellite's probable orbit, centered on the position computed from the selected historical launch patterns and reported launch time. A detected target ini-tiates tracking; a missed detection during a programmed pattern search initiates a search around the next pro-grammed orbit.

The current surveillance tasks, in approximate order of priority, include NFL acquisition, deep-space catalog maintenance, initial-orbit determination, and object identification for orbit and for signature correlation and uncorrelated target resolution.

station *Freedom*. The only available source for such data was the Haystack LRIR, which could detect orbiting objects as small as one centimeter. Lincoln Laboratory proposed that if NASA would fund HAX construction, it would get Haystack and HAX debris data in return. The proposal was accepted by NASA and the U.S. Space Command, and an agreement to exchange funding for debris data went into effect in 1989. Since then Haystack has provided NASA with more than 2300 hr of space-debris measurements.

The HAX was completed in the fall of 1993 (Figure 8-4). HAX wideband data produced finer and sharper images than even the Haystack radar. The detailed information derived from these images has already refined several satellite models. In 1993, the HAX became a contributing sensor, like Haystack and ALCOR, and also began collecting space debris data for NASA.

Electro-Optics for Space Surveillance

In 1971 Robert Bergemann proposed that the emerging electro-optical technology could support the search and detection of small, distant satellites by their reflected sunlight. An electro-optic low-light-level television (LLTV) camera at the focal plane of a modest 1-m²-aperture telescope promised a clear advantage over the Air Force's Baker-Nunn cameras; because the LLTV camera had no film to be developed, it could provide real-time output. Electronic cameras also promised high sensitivity to point-source objects (unresolved stars and unresolved satellites), principally because of the quantum efficiency of the photoemissive detector chemistry. The telescope field of view could be as large as several square degrees, and because of the short exposures required (1/30-sec television rate), that feature promised a high search rate, as much as 1000 square degrees per hour.

Electro-optical detection of distant satellites capitalizes on sun illumination of deep-space satellites with a visible-band flux on the order of 1000 W/m², which is about 10^9 times greater than the Millstone radar flux at geostationary distance. Since, unlike Millstone, solar illumination is not phase coherent, the net power gain from solar illumination is actually the square root of 10^9. The flux is considerable nevertheless. More importantly, all satellites except those eclipsed by the earth are illuminated simultaneously, greatly aiding object searches.

Figure 8-4

Haystack radar site. The LRIR Haystack antenna is in the large radome on the left; the HAX radome and equipment building are on the right. HAX was completed in 1993 to collect satellite-imaging and space-debris data.

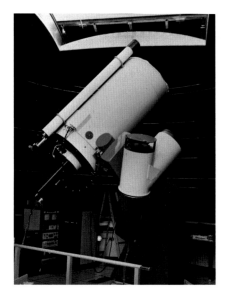

Figure 8-5
The 31-in main telescope of the ETS with an intensified Ebsicon camera at Cassegrain focus. The 14-in wide-field auxiliary telescope is on the declination axis, helping to counterbalance the main telescope.

Notes

7 The magnitude scale is a quantification of stellar brightness. The scale is logarithmic and also reversed: the fainter the star, the larger the magnitude number. The brightest stars are about 0 Mv; the Sun is –26.8 Mv.

A system of two telescopes with electro-optical cameras, separated by several kilometers and searching synchronously, was proposed as a means of star subtraction and satellite range detection from the parallax. A goal was set to detect the smallest geostationary payloads having a projected area A of 1 m^2. The reflectivity coefficient ρ was expected to be about 10%, resulting in an estimated brightness for $\rho A = 0.1$ m^2 at geostationary distance of about 16 stellar magnitudes (Mv).[7]

A search of the geostationary belt viewable from a site in one night seemed a minimum goal: about $120° \times 20°$ (to allow $\pm 10°$ inclination spread). Since satellites at geosynchronous distance move relative to the stars at about 15° per hour, the required search rate was $120° \times 15°$ per hour, or 1800 square degrees per hour.

The sine qua non of the system was the camera tube. Laboratory experiments indicated that the best LLTV tube for this purpose was the Westinghouse Ebsicon. This camera tube was chosen and, for even greater sensitivity, an external image intensifier was mounted between the focal plane and the Ebsicon tube. With this enhancement the camera noise, referred to the first photocathode, was only a few electrons. The sky background, not the camera noise, limited the detection performance. The external intensifier soon became available with an 80-mm fiber-optic faceplate to couple to a 32-mm Ebsicon, easing the design of a wide-field telescope.

In less than a year a portable intensified Ebsicon camera was assembled and tested at the focal plane of the 31-in telescope at Lowell Observatory, in Flagstaff, Arizona. Three field trips, culminating in October 1973, produced videotapes of some two dozen satellites in the geosynchronous belt and one about four times farther out.

The television playbacks were spectacular. A satellite appearing as an unresolved star slowly drifted across the screen from west to east, taking two minutes to transit. Some satellites brightened and faded regularly, the result of wobble in their spin stabilization.

Observations of calibrated star fields showed that on dark nights satellites and stars as faint as 16.5 Mv were detectable on the video monitor without an automatic processor. Robert Weber, who constructed the camera and conducted the field tests, quantified the solar flux as hav-

ing a value of 5×10^{10} photons/sec/m^2 and the quantum efficiency of the photocathode as 7.2% in the visible-wavelength region.

The results of the camera field tests warranted the construction of the Experimental Test System (ETS) to be located where the nights were predominantly clear. A short study produced the ETS design, which was accepted by the ESD in 1974. The Space Surveillance Group, led by Robert Bergemann, was then established to construct the ETS and develop technology to support the acquisition of an operational Air Force System. A field site on the White Sands Missile Test Range near Socorro, New Mexico, was selected by the Air Force, and construction of the telescope building and dome began. The real-time site software and detailed system design were managed by Donald Batman, the first site manager.

The telescope chosen as the largest affordable aperture was a Boller-Chivens 31-in Ritchey-Cretien with a focal ratio of $f/5$ (155-in focal length) at the Cassegrain focus (Figure 8-5). With the 80-mm faceplate of the intensified Ebsicon camera, the field of view was 1.2° diagonal, 0.93° horizontal in the television format and 0.6° with the intensifier zoom. The angular-resolution element with 400 television horizontal half-amplitude picture elements (pixels) was approximately 9 arc sec. On zoom, the 4-arc-sec-resolution elements were about twice the site's average seeing disk. Subsequent implementation of a prime focus approximately doubled the field of view. A comounted 14-in $f/1.7$ folded-Schmidt telescope provided a 7° field of view for rapid search of bright satellites. ETS became operational in the fall of 1975, eighteen months after ESD approval. LES-6 was easily detected electro-optically, without the 4-hr search that the Haystack radar had performed four years earlier.

During the time that a database on the brightness of existing satellites was being established, site investigators discovered that old spin-stabilized solar-panel-covered satellite cylinders, a major class of inactive payloads, were fainter than expected by about two stellar magnitudes.

Two remedies were found to this problem. In the first approach, thirty television frames were summed with an electronic scan converter (the kind used to hold X-ray images at airport boarding gates). With noncoherent inte-

Figure 8-6
The 31-in telescope camera and cold-shield assembly adapted for medium-wavelength infrared (1 to 5 μm) satellite-tracking experiments.

gration, the gain was the square root of 30, about equal to the lost brightness. In the second approach, a later version of the electro-optical camera allowed integration on the silicon target while the read beam was gated off. Either integration technique provided a sensitivity of about 18.5 Mv.

The desire to have a second tracking telescope led to making the ETS a duplex site; it had two main telescopes, including a second console and a second site computer. Lincoln Laboratory continued to develop electro-optical sensors and techniques, and a second site was established, so that a military crew from ADCOM could conduct operational tasks and communicate nightly position measurements to the NORAD Space Surveillance Center. ADCOM used this site for deep-space surveillance for five years, until a permanent site went into operation.

The ETS was used to test a variety of surveillance concepts. One of the most interesting was daylight satellite tracking, called DAYSAT. It had become apparent that a silicon target vidicon, without intensification, could detect and track near-earth satellites in broad daylight. When extended-red-sensitivity vidicons, filters to reduce the bright blue sky and a Quantex digital-image-storage processor to add the two camera signals were used, a Soviet *Salyut* spacecraft was detected at a distance of about 300 km, with 4-in lenses, by looking out through a basement laboratory window! Daylight electro-optical observations were carried out on about two dozen satellites; the maximum range was about 2000 km. Experiments on the 31-in telescopes reached 9.3 Mv in a daylight sky brightness of 4 Mv.

The panoramic sky camera, PANSKY, was developed at Lincoln Laboratory and tested at ETS. An electro-optical camera on a 35-mm fish-eye lens with 160° field of view provided detection of bright stars to compare with those in computer storage. Atmospheric extinction could be estimated, and the ability to report regions of clouds obviated fruitless observations.

Daniel Kostishack and Michael Cantella used Schottky-barrier detectors to initiate an entirely new approach to medium-wavelength infrared satellite surveillance. One ETS 31-in telescope was modified to investigate a camera intended for space-based surveillance of near-earth satel-

lites (Figure 8-6). Thermoelectrically cooled megapixel medium-wavelength infrared (1 to 5 μm) detector arrays, operated in a stare mode, were shown to provide more effective surveillance of objects in earth shadow than scanning long-wavelength infrared detector arrays. The atmospheric window near 4 μm permitted successful ground-based detection of several large satellites, including the Soviet space station *Mir*.

Perhaps the most important experiment was the first search of the geostationary belt by Larry Taff and John Sorvari during the spring specular season of 1978. (The specular seasons are the periods two weeks before the spring equinox and two weeks after the fall equinox, when geostationary satellites exhibit mirrorlike specular reflections, one hundred times brighter than usual.) Both main telescopes were operating, one to provide a leak-proof fence, the other to record photometric light-curve signatures. After a few observation nights, thirty UCTs had been detected and tracked by dead reckoning and had their initial orbits determined. About one-third of the signatures had measurable periods, one-third had distinctive features and one-third had constant but distinct brightness levels; this collection of signatures proved adequate to reacquire the ensemble of UCTs even after the specular season ended.

The ETS also participated in astronomical measurements, particularly observations of comets (Figure 8-7). Larry Taff and David Beatty also conducted the first electro-optical search for asteroids, resulting in the discovery of eight new asteroids. The Smithsonian Astrophysical Observatory assigned the name MIT Lincoln Laboratory to Asteroid No. 2460; the name Tammy (Beatty's wife) was assigned to Asteroid No. 3404. Other names are pending reacquisition. The most important function of ETS was that it proved the concept of using electro-optical technology for deep-space surveillance. As a result, ESD used technical specifications developed by Lincoln Laboratory, and initiated the procurement of five globally deployed operational sites.

Operational GEODDS
On May 15, 1978, ESD awarded TRW and their partner for camera production, Itek, a contract to produce five ground-based electro-optical deep-space surveillance (GEODSS) sites (Figure 8-8). General Robert Marsh, commander of ESD, expressed his thanks to Walter

Figure 8-7
Intensity contours of Halley's comet measured by the ETS during 1986 apparition.

Figure 8-8
The electro-optical space-surveillance site near Socorro, New Mexico. The ETS with its three telescope domes is in the foreground; the operational GEODSS CONUS site is the large building farther back. The operational GEODSS site has one auxiliary and two main telescope domes attached to the building.

Morrow, director of Lincoln Laboratory, for the technical accomplishments of ETS that made the production contract possible. The concept of electro-optical space surveillance was so well proven that the request for quotation was for a fixed price. The operational system was designated AN/FSQ-114. The Laboratory provided technical support to ESD throughout the procurement and in the selection of operational sites.

Rather than operate at television rates with post-read integration, as had been done at ETS, TRW chose to use an 80-mm faceplate tube without an external intensifier and integrate on the camera tube. Lincoln Laboratory was concerned that this technology posed technical risk. When it was learned that TRW had selected the RCA electro-optical silicon intensified-target (SIT) tube for the operational systems, the tube was quickly ordered and tested.

The worst fears were realized when Lincoln Laboratory bench measurements indicated the sensitivity would suffer a shortfall of more than a factor of two. ESD directed TRW and Itek to design the camera to accept both the RCA SIT tube and the Westinghouse Ebsicon, and asked the Laboratory to manage a manufacturing techniques program at Westinghouse.

Lincoln Laboratory continued to support the GEODSS procurement by guiding TRW's tests at Newbury Park, California. It soon became apparent that the sensitivity shortfall of the RCA electro-optic tube was at least as great as had been predicted by bench measurements, and greater when skies were bright. The Laboratory initiated a GEODSS upgrade program in anticipation of replacing the Ebsicon camera tubes with solid state charge-coupled device (CCD) cameras offering far greater quantum efficiency and long operational life. The Microelectronics Group at Lincoln Laboratory developed visible-band CCDs, and various camera configurations were tested at the ETS during the 1980s. These tests demonstrated the performance advantages that would be gained from CCD camera technology.

Finding locations for the first three of the five GEODSS sites went quickly. The continental U.S. (CONUS) GEODSS site was built adjacent to ETS. The mid-Pacific site was collocated with the DARPA Maui Optical Site (now called the Air Force Maui Optical Station) in Hawaii; the western Pacific site was established near Tague, South Korea.

Siting the remaining two GEODSS installations brought international negotiations into the effort. The U.S. State Department was unable to obtain host country agreements for the eastern Atlantic and Mideast sites. The island of Diego Garcia, located in the Indian Ocean at 7°20′S, 72°25′E, was finally selected to serve as the site for Mideast coverage. Rewriting the telescope-mount software was avoided by aligning the polar axis with the north celestial pole, 7°20′ below the northern horizon, rather than following the astronomical convention of south polar alignment for the southern hemisphere. This solution was workable, but limited the zenith distance (elevation) coverage to the south.

The Diego Garcia site became operational in 1984. Baker-Nunn cameras in San Vito, Italy, and Saint Margarets, New Brunswick, Canada, helped to fill the eastern Atlantic gap. The GEODDS equipment slated for the eastern Atlantic site was installed instead in Socorro as the GEODSS Test Site (GTS) to aid in the development of GEODSS upgrades.

Late in 1989 the Air Force asked Lincoln Laboratory to construct a transportable optical system (TOS) to fill in gaps in space-surveillance coverage. An available 22-in Ritchey-Cretien $f/2.3$ telescope was provided with a commercially available silicon target vidicon having two stages of image intensification to achieve background-noise-limited sensitivity. The fiber optic 18-mm faceplate gave a field of view of about 0.3 square degrees.

Under the direction of Robert Weber, the TOS was completed and installed in the Baker-Nunn site in San Vito in nine months. With a signal-to-noise ratio of 6, a sensitivity of 16.7 Mv at the telescope on calibration stars — against a 21-Mv/(arc sec^2) sky background — was achieved with 2-sec integration in the image processor.

The San Vito site nearly closed the coverage gap on geo-stationary satellites between the CONUS and the Diego Garcia GEODSS sites. The coverage gap overlapped if both sites operated very close to the horizon, but the astronomical seeing then spoiled the detection sensitivity and the metric accuracy.

In 1991 the Space Surveillance Group at Lincoln Laboratory conducted a survey of the state of the art in imaging technology to seek a replacement for the large Ebsicon vacuum-tube cameras used in GEODSS, which would soon become obsolete. Although CCD imaging technology had advanced and vendors were producing imagers that would meet some of the requirements of GEODSS, none were making fully suitable devices. However, the Laboratory Microelectronics Group was fabricating CCD imagers that would meet all the requirements except focal-plane size. In late 1992 the Air Force funded Laboratory development of the CCD imager for the GEODSS Upgrade Prototype System (GUPS) program. This imager would have the required large (80 mm diagonal) gap-free focal plane with 2560 × 1960 imaging pixels and frame-transfer readout for real-time applications. The successful fabrication of this imager was accomplished in 1994 and supplied to Photometrics to build the prototype CCD camera under a Laboratory contract.

Deep-Space Sensor Networks and Controls
The GEODSS sites, despite their wide-field search capability and rapid position update capacity, had their limitations. Electro-optical surveillance of a satellite was possible only when a site was in darkness, the sun was illuminating the satellite and clouds did not obscure the line of sight. By contrast, a radar could detect an NFL injection into geostationary orbit under all weather conditions.

In 1977 the Millstone space-surveillance group participated in ADCOM's study of a leakproof multiradar fence: a Pacific barrier that could detect all prograde launches from Asia. An experiment using the dual-wavelength (VHF and UHF) ARPA Long-Range Tracking and Instrumentation Radar (ALTAIR) at Kwajalein demonstrated the efficacy of the fence, and the radar was upgraded to provide an operational low-altitude surveillance capability.

At the same time, ADCOM decided to augment Millstone's all-weather radar coverage of about half of the geostationary satellite belt by upgrading both ALTAIR and Pirinclik to a deep-space capability. (The three radars are more or less equidistantly spaced.) Millstone's software provided the technology transfer basis for both ALTAIR and Pirinclik. Since both radars operated in the deep-space mode at UHF, rather than L-band, the upgraded

sensitivities achieved were not quite as good as that of Millstone.

Some five years later Lincoln Laboratory played a major role in upgrading the AN/FPS-85 phased-array surveillance radar at Eglin Air Force Base, Florida, to provide a limited deep-space-surveillance fence. In addition to hardware upgrades, the SATCIT integration/tracking program was added to the system.

By 1985 the large number of Air Force Space Command (the organization that succeeded ADCOM) sensors deployed around the world — at Millstone, Pirinclik, ALTAIR, the AN/FPS-85 radar at Eglin, the GEODSS sites — gave the Millstone space-surveillance group the opportunity to form an integrated deep-space-surveillance system: the Deep-Space Network Control Processor (DSNCP). In simplified terms, DSNCP takes the Air Force Space Command deep-space tasking priority list, computes a satellite's pass geometry from each site for several days and optimally tasks the sites for observations. Equipment availability status and weather conditions at optical sensor sites are considered during the scheduling process. DSNCP algorithms scheduled support of catalog maintenance, coordinated search and acquisition of the components of NFLs and processed data to provide signature data.

From time to time, the value of sensor network coordination was demonstrated by the reacquisition of a missing inactive payload. The element set of LES-5, launched in 1967, was not maintained after the communications transmitter expired in 1970. Because the telemetry transmitter continued to operate, the location of LES-5 was known in a rough sense, but the lack of an element set precluded tracking by the Millstone radar's narrow beam.

On February 6, 1987, during the optical specular season, ETS detected a UCT with an inclination of about 7.2°, drifting eastward at a rate of 29° per day. Millstone acquired the UCT from ETS's rough initial-orbit determination, and the satellite was identified with high confidence as LES-5 by the spin period and low radar cross section.

A notable achievement related to radar networks was the use of Lincoln Calibration Spheres (LCS) to calibrate sensitivity and metric position simultaneously. Each LCS

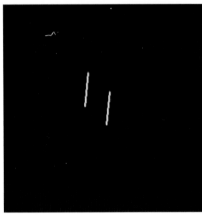

Figure 8-10
Streak-detection processing by the visible-band sensor system allowed star-background-clutter removal with high throughput and high sensitivity. Top: Output display before streak-detection processing. Bottom: Output display after processing.

was a polished, hollow, rigid aluminum sphere with a diameter of 1.129 m, an optical cross section of 1 m^2 and a radar cross section at 1300 MHz of 1 m^2 (Figure 8-9). These passive satellites were designed to be calibration objects for ballistic-missile and satellite-tracking radars and for optical telescopes.

LCS-1 was placed in a circular orbit of 2800 km on May 6, 1965 — too high to be used by any but the most powerful radars (but where the booster had been scheduled to dispense its prime payload). LCS-2 and -3 were lost to booster failures. LCS-4 was placed in a circular near-polar orbit at an altitude of 850 km on August 7, 1971, and continues to be a useful calibration object.

Mike Gaposchkin refined the orbital drag and solar-pressure models for LCS-1 and -4 and, with frequent observations, enabled them to be used as metric standards, secondary to the primary standard, LAGEOS. Because both LCS satellites have an area of exactly 1 m^2 compared to LAGEOS's 0.3 m^2, the radar signal-to-noise ratio is typically 35 dB greater for LCS-1 and 15 dB greater for LCS-4 than for LAGEOS in a 6000-km orbit.

The Space-Based Visible-Band Sensor
Both ESD and Lincoln Laboratory always regarded GEODSS as an interim system; the long-term goal was *space-based* surveillance. A space-based system would always be above the clouds. Perhaps more importantly, it would be above the geopolitics that plagued the siting of the eastern Atlantic and Mideast GEODSS sites. In addition, a sensor in space always sees a dark sky when looking away from the sun, the moon, the zodiacal light and the earth limb.

A spaced-based sensor always has a clear line of sight to all satellites except when they are in the earth's shadow. Such eclipses occur for a maximum of about one-third of the orbit period for a near-earth satellite; for geostationary satellites, earth eclipse occurs only near the equinoxes, a maximum of 70 min in a 24-hr period, and then only for about a week.

The Air Force SDIO supported the development of a space-based space-surveillance system, the Midcourse Space Experiment (MSX). This spacecraft, managed by

Johns Hopkins University, is planned to include long-wavelength infrared, ultraviolet and visible-band sensors. Lincoln Laboratory's contribution to this effort is in the visible band: the Space-Based Visible (SBV) sensor.

The MSX infrared sensor requires cooling to cryogenic temperatures, but because the SBV sensor can take on the tasks of near-earth surveillance when targets are sun illuminated, and deep-space surveillance at all times, the visible-band sensor should reduce cryogen consumption in an operational space-surveillance system.

The weight and power allocations to the Lincoln Laboratory SBV package are 172 lb and 98 W. With these restrictions, the space-based telescope is limited to a 6-in aperture, small compared to GEODDS and TOS. But the CCD imaging devices at the focal plane, with a quantum efficiency of about 20% and a read noise smaller than 10 electrons, should achieve about 14.5 Mv with a 1-sec exposure against a nominal 20-Mv sky background (Figure 8-10).

A critical problem is the nonrejected earth reflectance when the sensor is pointed close to the bright sun-illuminated earth limb. However, high rejection of light from sources outside the field of view has been achieved by developing a three-mirror off-axis-reimaging telescope design with an intermediate field stop and a diffraction stop. Because mirrors for this design must be exceptionally clean, fabrication and laboratory measurements have been conducted in a clean room. The performance has met Lincoln Laboratory's specifications.

MSX does not have real-time communication with the ground. Therefore, Lincoln Laboratory has set up the SBV processing operations control center, which converts experiments from concept to spacecraft instructions: pointing, sensor settings and formats, taking into account the constraints of spacecraft power, the position of the sun, moon, earth limb and zodiacal light and the geometry between MSX and the target.

About twenty experiments have been designed for MSX. Plans include metric measurements to bound the limiting accuracy of angular position measurements from an orbiting spacecraft. Other high-priority experiments include

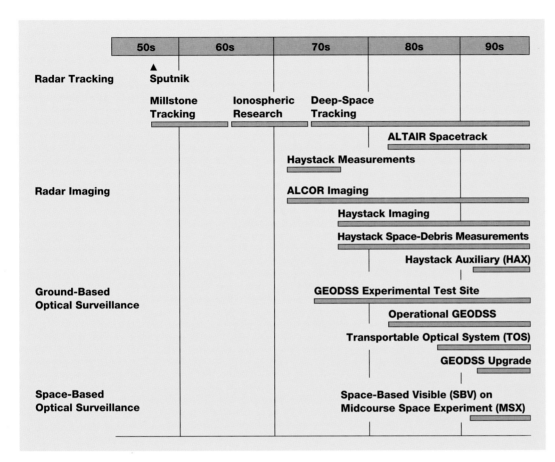

	50s	60s	70s	80s	90s

Radar Tracking

▲ Sputnik

Millstone Tracking

Ionospheric Research

Deep-Space Tracking

ALTAIR Spacetrack

Haystack Measurements

Radar Imaging

ALCOR Imaging

Haystack Imaging

Haystack Space-Debris Measurements

Haystack Auxiliary (HAX)

Ground-Based Optical Surveillance

GEODSS Experimental Test Site

Operational GEODSS

Transportable Optical System (TOS)

GEODSS Upgrade

Space-Based Optical Surveillance

Space-Based Visible (SBV) on Midcourse Space Experiment (MSX)

Figure 8-11
Lincoln Laboratory space-surveillance activities.

geosynchronous belt search, NFL search acquisition, space-shuttle satellite deployment to deep space, debris search after satellite fragmentation and tasking observations for catalog maintenance.

Summary
Until 1975 the Millstone radar was the only deep-space radar available to the SPACETRACK system. Four radars and five GEODDS sites subsequently became operational within a very short time, with the help of Lincoln Laboratory technology and the close cooperation of the Air Force Space Command (Figure 8-11).

The cataloged space population has grown to about ten thousand, of which about one thousand are in deep-space orbits. Lincoln Laboratory has played a significant role in space surveillance, from the detection of the Sputnik, cataloged as 1957 alpha, through the development and technology transfer of deep-space sensor innovation, at radar and electro-optical wavelengths.

Despite the decrease in Russian military launches and the absence of antisatellite tests that deliberately create debris, the deep-space catalog is continuing to grow. Pollution of space has become an international concern. Furthermore, increased sensor sensitivity and improved wide-area search techniques are detecting a greater number of debris pieces as time goes on. As space-object identification techniques improve, smaller resident space objects and long-lost large ones are being added to the catalog. The annual Space Surveillance Workshop, initiated by Ramaswamy Sridharan thirteen years ago, continues to provide an efficient means for Lincoln Laboratory to transfer space-surveillance technology.

National and international interest in space surveillance is extending to solar system debris — asteroids and comets smaller than those currently detectable by the astronomical community. Of particular concern is interplanetary debris that could collide with the earth.

International agreements already provide for graveyard orbits, where dying payloads are to be relegated, outside the geostationary belt. Nevertheless, the drive to catalog all debris that threatens high-value satellites, space shuttles and the proposed space station *Freedom* will continue.

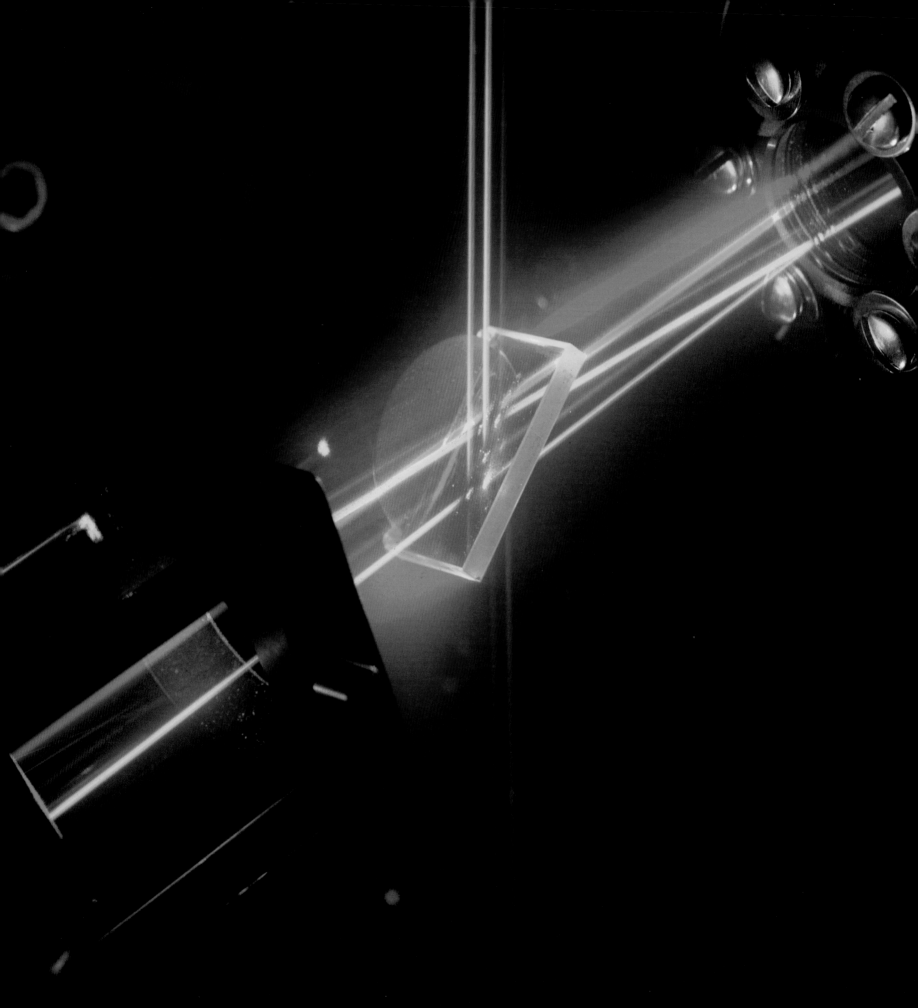

Optics and Laser Systems

The continuing development of lasers prompted Lincoln Laboratory director Milton Clauser to form the Optics Division in 1969, under the leadership initially of Alan McWhorter and then of Robert Kingston. Laser activities brought together in the Optics Division included the gas laser work that was to lead to the development of a wideband high-power laser radar and the optical propagation studies that were to lead to the development of adaptive optics. These two central themes — high-energy laser beam propagation and laser radar — persisted throughout the existence of the Optics Division, with binary optics subsequently joining the activity as an outgrowth of work on tactical lasers.

Optical research on incoherent pulse-to-pulse radar systems is described in chapter 6, "Ballistic Missile Defense." Additional material on both passive-IR-sensor research and tactical lasers is presented in chapter 11, "Tactical Battlefield Surveillance."

As the development of high-power lasers progressed, ARPA identified the potential of these devices for application in ground-based laser weapons and asked Lincoln Laboratory to participate in the effort. The Laboratory initiated an activity to increase the understanding of propagation phenomenology and to plan critical field measurements. Industry was tasked to develop the high-energy lasers. The Laboratory's ballistic range was converted to a laser measurement facility by Seymour Edelberg. Louis Marquet then continued the research and performed beam measurements with a high-power CO_2 gas dynamic laser at a Pratt and Whitney facility in West Palm Beach, Florida.

Lincoln Laboratory was the first to arrive at a theoretical understanding of the nonlinear atmospheric propagation of high-energy laser beams, a phenomenon now referred to as thermal blooming. A Lincoln Laboratory–built 500-J single-pulse CO_2 laser was used to validate the theory of thermal blooming in fog-hole-boring experiments and in experiments in laser beam material coupling and atmospheric breakdown. Concepts to use flexible mirrors for thermal-blooming correction were initiated.

The Firepond Optical Research Facility in Westford, Massachusetts, was built to perform laser radar measurements, and the facility began operations in 1968. Measurements were made with a 1000-W narrowband carbon-dioxide laser. Although the laser radar demonstrated the capability to acquire, track and collect targets, difficulties in the development of the high-power laser amplifier prevented the system from meeting its objectives. The failure to produce range-Doppler images and achieve the average power goal led to termination of the high-power laser radar program.

The Strategic Defense Initiative Organization (SDIO) decision to concentrate on the use of optical sensors and weapons greatly changed the character of the Optics Division in 1985. In that year the Optics Division undertook the Optical Discrimination Technology program for DARPA, a major activity that led the division to grow substantially. The proposed use of an orbiting laser radar sensor for discrimination led to the reestablishment of the Firepond facility for laser radar measurements, and the first high-power, wideband, range-Doppler imaging laser radar was successfully constructed and tested. SDIO also proposed the development of a ground-based laser system in which a beam would be sent to a relay mirror in space; efforts to implement this concept increased the work in adaptive optics for atmospheric compensation. Changes in the direction of SDI that began in late 1991 shifted the emphasis toward theater missile defense, and the optical discrimination and adaptive optics work was rapidly reduced. In 1993 the remaining efforts were transferred to other divisions.

Laser Radar

In May 1962, less than two years after the invention of the laser, a team of researchers from the MIT campus and Lincoln Laboratory used a liquid-nitrogen-cooled, photon-counting, direct-detection laser receiver to perform the first laser radar range measurements on the moon. These experiments, titled Project Luna See, were performed with a visible 50-J/pulse ruby laser radar located in the Laboratory's Annex 4. This demonstration was a historical first, but laser radar research at Lincoln Laboratory did not take on major significance until after the invention of the carbon-dioxide laser in 1964.[1]

The carbon-dioxide laser was at once a temporally coherent signal source and a high-power source of infrared radiation. Earlier collaborations among Professors Ali Javan and Hermann Haus of MIT and Charles Freed at Lincoln Laboratory had led to fundamental measurements on the photon-counting statistics of frequency-stable helium–neon lasers. In 1966, at the suggestion of Robert Kingston, Javan's laser construction techniques were applied to carbon-dioxide lasers to produce the first frequency-stable CO_2 laser at Lincoln Laboratory; its stability was at least a hundred times greater than that previously reported.

In 1967 the first coherent CO_2 laser radar was demonstrated at the Laboratory. This CW Doppler laser radar employed the stable laser and used a conical scan system for angle-tracking targets. Additional radar components had to be developed to take full advantage of the new signal source. The first InSb 10.6-μm optical isolator, a device necessary to maintain master-oscillator and laser-transmitter stability, was also built in 1966. Experiments with laser amplifiers during 1968 led to master-oscillator/power-amplifier (MOPA) combinations that produced 100 W. High-speed photomixers were developed to accommodate the large Doppler frequency shift produced by satellites. By 1968, researchers in the Solid State Division had developed a high speed (1.25 GHz) copper-doped germanium photoconductor that could operate as a photomixer in an optical heterodyne circuit.

In parallel with the laser radar developments at Lincoln Laboratory, ARPA and the Office for Naval Research were funding the development of a 1000-W CW carbon-dioxide laser oscillator at the Raytheon Corporation. After Raytheon had evaluated the oscillator, it was given to the Laboratory for laser radar experiments.

In late 1968 the Laboratory completed the Firepond Optical Research Facility, located near the Millstone Radar in Westford, Massachusetts, to provide a facility for performing laser radar measurements on aircraft and satellites (Figure 9-1). Within a few months members of

the newly formed Optics Division had modified the Raytheon laser oscillator, turning it into a 1000-W CW laser amplifier with an optical gain of 33. Initial laser radar measurements were made at a power of 200 W on a corner cube retroreflector placed on the Groton Fire Tower, located on a hill 5.4 km from Firepond. Additional measurements were made on buildings, trees and calibration spheres and on an aircraft at a range of 10 km.

The first laser radar images of several different stationary objects were collected with a flying-spot scanning system in 1971. The year closed with the installation of a 1.2-m telescope at the Firepond site (Figure 9-2).

Coherent wideband radar offers an approach to imaging that circumvents the conventional *angular* resolution limits associated with diffraction and atmospheric turbulence. A range-Doppler radar can use the aspect changes of a target, such as a satellite, as it moves along its orbit, to form an image that has resolution in *range* and in *Doppler frequency*. Moreover, the resolution of the range-Doppler image is independent of range to the target.

In 1972 a Lincoln Laboratory study under the direction of Robert Cooper examined the feasibility and role of a wideband, very-high-power range-Doppler laser radar for space object surveillance and identification. The study group concluded that development of a laser radar was feasible and that Lincoln Laboratory should undertake the task.

Accordingly, in 1973 the Laboratory developed specifications for a high-power CO_2 laser radar capable of imaging unenhanced satellite targets in low earth orbit at slant ranges out to approximately 1000 km, with downrange and cross-range resolutions of less than 30 cm. To obtain the necessary Doppler resolution, the waveform had to have a duration of 4 msec in a wideband mode. The specification for long range meant that the output power amplifier had to generate a high-energy pulse with a wide bandwidth, which led to the requirement that the carbon-dioxide laser amplifier operate at close to atmospheric pressure.

Notes

1 Material for this section was provided by Leo Sullivan and William Keicher.

Figure 9-1
Firepond infrared radar complex.

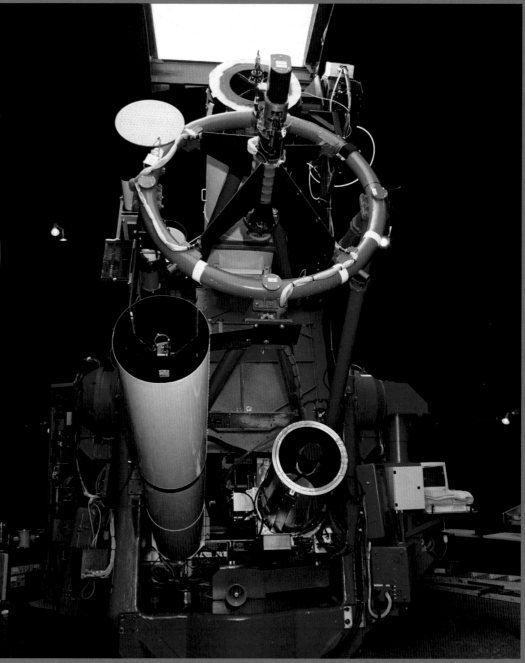

Figure 9-2
Front view of the Firepond 1.2-m
Cassegrain telescope. The three
auxiliary telescopes collect radiant
energy for a variety of other sensors.

The First SDI Experiment in Space

In the early days of SDIO, the basic concepts behind the Strategic Defense Initiative were provoking passionate debate over their feasibility. Therefore, when the SDIO revealed that it was about to conduct its first experiment in space, the announcement became front-page news. Whether fortunately or not, that experiment was Lincoln Laboratory's test of the use of adaptive optics for atmospheric compensation.

The plan was to propagate a 4-W, 488-nm argon-ion laser beam from the Air Force Maui Optical Site, retroreflect it from the space shuttle and correct it on the ground. NASA installed an 8.5-in-diameter laser retroreflector on the left mid-deck side-hatch window of the space shuttle orbiter *Discovery,* and described the test at a press briefing. By the time of the shuttle's launch on June 17, 1985, intense media coverage was focused on the atmospheric-compensation experiment.

The test began on June 19. With reporters present, NASA transmitted the altitude of the ground station to the orbiter computer in units of feet, rather than in the nautical miles the computer was expecting. The shuttle flipped around, searching for a 10,023-nmi-high mountain.

About seven minutes before reaching Maui, as the orbiter passed over Guam, Mission Commander Daniel Brandenstein informed mission control in Houston that the orbiter was oriented with its left side — the one with the retroreflector — pointing toward space. Because it was impossible to reorient the orbiter within the time left before reaching Maui, the atmospheric-compensation test could not be conducted. The Lincoln Laboratory team did illuminate the shuttle with the laser, and the shuttle crew reported seeing a blue light. But with the shuttle facing the wrong way, none of the test objectives could be achieved.

The mistake was immediately reported worldwide by network television and numerous newspapers. Opponents of SDI used the opportunity to advance their arguments against the program, and the Lincoln Laboratory staff on Maui received a message relayed from high levels within the DoD that the next test had to succeed.

NASA juggled the shuttle schedule to permit a test opportunity on June 21. As tensions mounted, the day of the test arrived with gale-force winds. Gusts reached 55 mph; winds were steady at 40 mph. Normally, astronomical domes are kept shut under such conditions. For this experiment, the high winds also meant increased difficulty in compensating for atmospheric turbulence.

The NASA mission director asked Charles Primmerman, who was heading the Lincoln Laboratory effort, if he wanted to conduct the experiment on the next pass. In an agonizing decision, Primmerman declined. NASA, however, made the decision to turn the shuttle around anyway, just to test that part of the experiment. Deciding it was a no-lose proposition, the Lincoln Laboratory team opened the domes and illuminated the space shuttle. If they failed, they could report that it was only an engineering test. But if it succeeded. . . .

It was night when the space shuttle passed over Maui, so the crew ignited a one-million-candlepower docking light in the left flight deck window for optical acquisition. The orbiter was also acquired by radar, with the laser beam director slaved to the radar.

The experiment worked precisely as planned. The argon-ion laser beam bounced from the retroreflector, was measured by detectors at the observatory and then was corrected by the deformable mirror of the adaptive optics system. The active tracking sequence lasted two minutes, thirty seconds.*

The news flashed around the world, from the front page of the *New York Times* to the evening news. The SDIO had conducted its first successful experiment in space.

---

* E.H. Kolcum, "Discovery Crew Tests Laser Tracker, Surpasses Mission Goals," *Aviat. Week Space Technol.* 123, 19 (1 July 1985).

deformable mirror that was manually adjusted according to the computer predictions to maximize the intensity of the laser beam on the target. In a subsequent experiment, named Closed Loop Adaptive Single Parameter (CLASP), the shape of the deformable-mirror correction was fixed but the amplitude was adjusted automatically to maximize the far-field intensity.

In the mid–1970s Lincoln laboratory carried out a long series of field experiments with the Pratt and Whitney XLD — a 10.6-μm CO_2 gas-dynamic laser that was, at the time, the most powerful laser in the nation — at the Pratt and Whitney high-energy laser-beam-propagation range in West Palm Beach, Florida. This propagation range is fondly remembered by the researchers for its location in the middle of Florida swampland and for its resident alligators (Figure 9-4). The experiments were conducted with a cooled 52-channel deformable mirror, the first deformable mirror to be used with a high-power laser. The XLD laser beam was expanded to 1.2 m and propagated over a 2-km horizontal path to an instrumented vehicle (affectionately known at the Everglaser) that ran on a short stretch of railroad track. This arrangement enabled the Lincoln Laboratory team to produce the first thermal-blooming compensation with a high-energy laser. CLASP tests were also completed successfully — the first closed-loop thermal-blooming compensation of a high-energy laser beam.

The 52-channel deformable mirror was used in several experiments to correct for aberrations on the XLD laser beam itself. The most successful of these experiments was the Optical Compensation of Uniphase Laser Radiation (OCULAR), which used a multidither technique that had been pioneered several years earlier by Hughes researchers. OCULAR demonstrated the first-ever compensation for device aberrations in a high-power laser. A second atmospheric-compensation experiment performed with the XLD was the Target Return Adaptive Pointing and Focus (TRAPAF). To explore the efficacy of simple, low-order adaptive optics systems, TRAPAF used a mirror that could correct only for tilt and focus instead of the 52-channel deformable mirror. Successful high-power and low-power tests were conducted along the 2-km path, although the lack of a fully deformable mirror limited the correction achieved.

Figure 9-4
Pratt and Whitney high-energy-laser propagation range in West Palm Beach, Florida, site of thermal-blooming tests. An alligator is just visible at the bottom center of the photograph.

Figure 9-5
Air Force Maui Optical Site on top of Mount Haleakala on the island of Maui, Hawaii.

Figure 9-6
ACE using the space shuttle *Discovery*. The ACE system illuminated a retroreflector mounted on a side-hatch window of the shuttle and used the return signal as a beacon to perform atmospheric compensation.

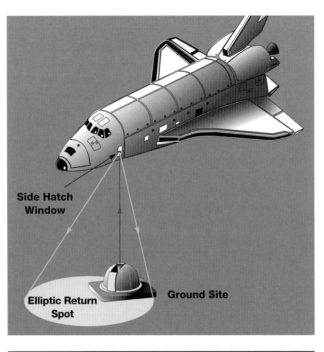

Side Hatch
Window

Elliptic Return
Spot

Ground Site

Figure 9-7
Sodium-beacon experiment at White Sands Missile Range, New Mexico. A 589-nm-wavelength laser beam is sent skyward to generate a synthetic beacon in the sodium layer at an altitude of 90 km.

Atmospheric-Compensation Experiment

In the late 1970s the DoD emphasis on lasers shifted from tactical to strategic applications that involved ground-to-space propagation. As a result, Lincoln Laboratory began to develop the Atmospheric-Compensation Experiment (ACE) system to explore ground-to-space compensation.

ACE was a complete 69-channel adaptive optics system; it used a deformable mirror and a shearing interferometer built by Itek. The sensor had photomultipliers for low-light operation and the system had a correction bandwidth of 600 Hz. The ACE system was built on the technology of the pioneering 21-channel real-time atmospheric-compensation system developed by Itek in the mid-1970s, and used technology similar to that of the 168-channel compensated-imaging system Itek researchers used to perform the first star-imaging-compensation experiments in 1982.

Tests of the ACE system began in 1981 with turbulence simulated by rotating phase screens. During the following year the system was shipped and installed on the 60-cm laser beam director at the Air Force Maui Optical Site on the top of Mount Haleakala on the island of Maui in Hawaii (Figure 9-5). Thus began a decade of adaptive optics experiments at the Maui field site. Most people think of Maui as a warm-weather paradise, but Lincoln Laboratory researchers mostly remember the arduous three-hour round-trip commute to the top of the 10,023-ft Mount Haleakala. The mountaintop is always cold and occasionally snowy.

From 1982 through 1985 Lincoln Laboratory conducted an extensive three-phase field test of ACE under the overall direction of Darryl Greenwood. In Phase I, completed in 1982, atmospheric compensation was demonstrated for a beam propagating along a 150-m horizontal path (with integrated turbulence equal to that for vertical propagation through the entire atmosphere). In Phase II, conducted from 1983 to 1984, atmospheric compensation was demonstrated for a laser beam propagating to a small aircraft flying above the site. The aircraft tests demonstrated compensation to a dynamic target.

The third and culminating phase of the ACE tests was a demonstration of compensation from ground to space. In the first experiment of this phase, a laser beam was bounced off a retroreflector carried by the space shuttle *Discovery* and the return signal was used as a beacon to perform atmospheric compensation (Figure 9-6). This was the first SDIO space experiment and, as such, received considerable publicity.

The experiment with the space shuttle did not involve compensating an outgoing beam; that was subsequently demonstrated in experiments with four instrumented sounding rockets. These rockets, developed for Lincoln Laboratory by Sandia National Laboratory, were launched from Barking Sands on the island of Kauai in Hawaii and reached altitudes of about 600 km as they went by Maui. Each rocket carried a retroreflector, which was illuminated to serve as a beacon, and a linear array of detectors to detect the outgoing beam. The beam detected at the rocket clearly showed a dramatic increase in irradiance when atmospheric compensation was applied. The ACE sounding rocket tests were the first to demonstrate atmospheric compensation of a beam propagating from the ground to space.

Short-Wavelength Adaptive Techniques

In the principal high-energy-laser scenario of interest to SDIO, the laser beam was to be sent from the ground to a relay mirror in space. The relay mirror may be regarded as a cooperative target; that is, it can provide a beacon source suitable for the adaptive optics system. Many targets, however, are uncooperative in that they do not come equipped with a beacon suitable for the adaptive optics system. For short-range tactical targets, optical energy either emitted by or reflected from the target can be used as a beacon. For long-range targets like satellites, such a beacon is usually too dim and, more importantly, will not lead the aimpoint by the correct angle.

A solution to the uncooperative target problem is to generate a synthetic beacon (also called an artificial beacon and sometimes a laser guide star) by atmospheric backscatter from a ground-based illuminator laser. In this concept, the ground-based laser beam is sent skyward in the proper direction (Figure 9-7). The beam generates a synthetic beacon either by backscatter from atmospheric oxygen and nitrogen or by backscatter from atomic sodium in the mesosphere at approximately 90-km altitude. Once the synthetic beacon is generated, the atmospheric compensation is performed in much the same manner as in the cooperative-beacon scenario.

At the same time that Lincoln Laboratory was conducting the ACE cooperative-compensation program, a new program — called Short-Wavelength Adaptive Techniques (SWAT) — was initiated to explore uncooperative atmospheric compensation. This program, under the overall direction of Charles Primmerman, comprised a variety of experiments and hardware-development efforts.

Ronald Humphreys conducted the first SWAT experiment at the White Sands Missile Range in New Mexico in 1984 and 1985. This was a phase-measurement, not a phase-compensation, experiment: a synthetic beacon was generated in the mesospheric sodium layer and the phase measured from the beacon was compared to the phase measured from a star in the same direction. The experiment was the first to demonstrate that atmospheric phase distortions could be measured with a synthetic beacon in the mesospheric sodium layer.

Following completion of the initial tests, the main SWAT system — a 241-channel adaptive optics system — was constructed. The system mirror, built by Itek, used discrete lead-magnesium-niobate actuators. The phase sensor was a Hartmann design developed by the Laboratory; it included advanced CCD focal planes developed by the Laboratory. The wavefront reconstructor, which was also developed by the Laboratory, was based on an all-digital matrix-multiplication technique.

10 Seismic Discrimination

Project VELA UNIFORM, a program in seismic monitoring under ARPA sponsorship, aided the United States in monitoring underground nuclear tests and in verifying international compliance with the Limited Test Ban Treaty. Lincoln Laboratory had a major role in the deployment of the Large Aperture Seismic Array.

Left: LASA seismometer subarray showing open trenches for cable installation near Miles City, Montana.

Public concern about nuclear testing in the atmosphere reached a peak in the late 1950s and compelled the nuclear powers — the United States, the Soviet Union and the United Kingdom — to continue their nuclear testing programs underground. The problem with underground testing, however, was that it made test-ban verification difficult. In December 1958 the U.S. government appointed a panel to study seismic monitoring of nuclear testing. In its report, published six months later, the panel argued that seismic methods were capable of detecting only explosions with yields over 20 kton, and recommended the initiation of an aggressive program in seismic detection and discrimination. In response to this recommendation, the VELA UNIFORM program was established, and responsibility for the program was assigned to ARPA.[1]

Primarily because of its substantial expertise in antenna and wave propagation theory, Lincoln Laboratory became involved with the VELA UNIFORM program in 1962. At the suggestion of director Carl Overhage, a small group was asked to explore possible Laboratory participation. Their report, presented in September 1962, advocated a serious commitment. Overhage accepted the recommendation and started a small effort in December 1962.

Lincoln Laboratory's involvement in VELA UNIFORM began with its participation in the addition of mobile digital-recording equipment to the Tonto National Forest array in Arizona. As a result, Lincoln Laboratory was one of the first groups to record seismic data in digital form. Using these data, as well as data from other networks, the group began to develop and apply a variety of propagation-theory, statistical and data processing methods to seismic discrimination.

The Lincoln Laboratory team formulated a plan to construct a large seismic array that could be used to study the feasibility of monitoring underground nuclear explosions. The plan was accepted and the ARPA-supported VELA UNIFORM program at the Laboratory was initiated in October 1963.

The Limited Test Ban Treaty was signed by the United States, the United Kingdom. and the USSR in August 1963; it eliminated all future atmospheric testing. The treaty led to a substantial increase in the importance of VELA UNIFORM, and the program became the focus of much activity and new funding. As a result, in late summer 1964 the Lincoln Laboratory effort was enlarged and aimed specifically at the immediate development and deployment of a Large Aperture Seismic Array (LASA).

Seismologists were hired and assigned to the problem, and by December 1964 the array design was complete and construction had begun on LASA. The array consisted of 525 seismometers arranged in 21 subarrays, configured with a 200-km aperture and installed near Miles City, Montana (Figure 10-1). The Air Force Tactical Applications Center was assigned responsibility for installation of the seismometers and for communications from the sensors to the subarray vault. Lincoln Laboratory was assigned responsibility for signal transmission beyond that point, for the construction of an array data analysis center and for all processing functions at that center.[2]

A site for the data center was selected in Billings, Montana, and by the summer of 1965 the seismometers and communication links had been installed, computer equipment was operating at the data center and testing had begun (Figure 10-2). LASA began operations in October and its technical performance exceeded expectations (Figure 10-3). Within six months the experimental period ended and routine operations began.

Lincoln Laboratory was then assigned overall system responsibility for control and maintenance of LASA. Operations and maintenance were handled by subcontract to Philco Corporation. The program became heavily involved in processing the LASA data and applying it to the basic problems of detection and discrimination; the processing of array data dominated the program for the next seven years.

Notes

1 This section is based on a report by M.A. Chinnery, *Seismic Discrimination, Final Report to the Defense Advanced Research Projects Agency.* Lexington, Mass.: MIT Lincoln Laboratory, 1982. Report No. ESD-TR-82-099.

2 R.V. Wood, Jr., R.G. Enticknap, C.S. Lin and R.M. Martinson, "Large Aperture Seismic Array Signal Handling System." *Proc. IEEE* **52**, 1844 (1965).

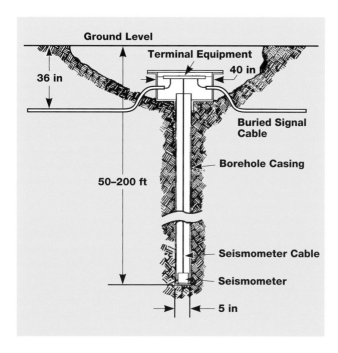

Ground Level

Terminal Equipment

36 in

40 in

Buried Signal Cable

Borehole Casing

50–200 ft

Seismometer Cable

Seismometer

5 in

Figure 10-1
LASA seismometer installation.

The Seismic Discrimination Group during this period was at the forefront of the development and exploitation of modern high-resolution array processing and spectral analysis techniques. Major accomplishments included significant developments in digital time-series analysis, the formulation of a frequency-wave number approach to array analysis, the invention of velocity-spectral analysis, the application of sonograms and considerable work in array calibration both for travel times and for amplitudes. The group developed time and spectral-domain versions of the maximum-likelihood method of array processing and was among the first to apply and popularize the Burg maximum-entropy method.

A notable accomplishment in this period was the introduction of interactive computer graphics for the analysis of array waveforms. Using two PDP-7 computers, Lincoln Laboratory constructed a display system called CONSOLE, which advanced the state of the art for the analysis and display of seismic waveforms.

CONSOLE was easy to use. With little preparation, a user could select a tape containing a given event, play it into the computer and view the waveforms. Facilities were provided for such standard analysis operations as filtering and spectral analysis. The system attracted visitors from all over the world, and many Ph.D. theses were based on LASA data and CONSOLE.

In 1967 an experimental subarray was installed in Norway. Lincoln Laboratory played an active part in the site evaluation.

However, the array program, while successful technically, was not successful in seismic detection and discrimination because the earth has a complex seismic environment. Signals arriving at subarrays were more incoherent than

1960

C.F.J. Overhage

P.E. Green, Jr.

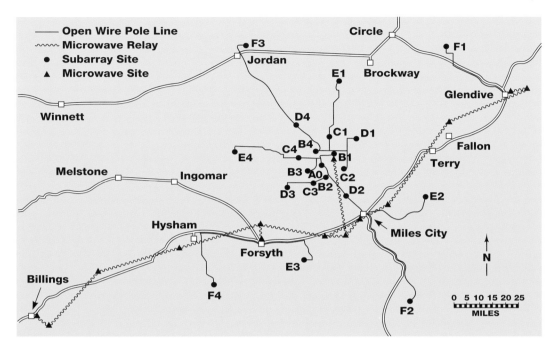

Figure 10-2
LASA communication network for transmission of seismometer data from subarrays to the LASA data center in Billings, Montana.

had been expected, and this incoherence placed a fundamental limitation on the usefulness of the large aperture of the array. The inferred degree of inhomogeneity in the crustal section beneath LASA became a new standard for the way geophysicists think about the continental crust. As the Norwegian array began to produce data, these effects were observed to an even larger degree.

Clearly, the analysis of seismometer array problems needed the services of geophysicists as well as data processors. The emphasis of the program shifted toward seismological research.

By 1969, LASA had become an operational entity, and the routine operations passed to IBM, leaving Lincoln Laboratory free to focus on the data-analysis and seismic issues. Realizing that the LASA data were raising questions at the forefront of academic seismology, the Lincoln Laboratory group moved into new quarters on the MIT campus, where it could interact closely with academia.

About this time, Paul Green, who had directed the seismology effort from its start, left the Laboratory. Because of the new emphasis, David Davies, who had been reviewing seismic monitoring methods for the Stockholm International Peace Research Institute, joined the Laboratory to lead the research. Richard Lacoss took over responsibility for the computer systems and signal processing aspects.

The end of the array era was approaching, however, as it became clear that scattering in the earth provided a natural limitation to the usefulness of seismic arrays. By 1970, interest in array data had diminished considerably, and although LASA was not finally closed until the mid-1970s, it received little attention.

1965

Seismometer

LASA maintenance console

Figure 10-3
Laurice Fleck and a Philco employee in the LASA data center in Billings, Montana.

Interest in the overall VELA UNIFORM program was revitalized in 1971, largely as a result of a series of Senate hearings by the Foreign Relations Subcommittee on Disarmament. Several influential senators spoke strongly for an expansion of the U.S. seismic discrimination program.

Since the large-array program had not proven as successful as had been hoped, the program returned to an earlier idea — a global distribution of single stations. Such a network, especially if equipped with low-noise-sensitivity instruments, would lead to a substantial improvement in detection capability and, by providing wide azimuthal coverage, would allow more sophisticated studies of the source mechanism of seismic events.

The VELA UNIFORM program at Lincoln Laboratory became increasingly oriented toward geophysical problems. By the 1970s, most of the staff in the program were professional seismologists, and research was focused on understanding earthquake source mechanisms and path effects.

The emphasis on global networks led the Laboratory to organize an international project to clarify the detection capability of the existing seismic stations. With cooperation from many countries, the seismic records for one month (February 20 to March 19, 1972) were analyzed and the results sent to Lincoln Laboratory, where they were checked and assembled into a list of events. The results of the International Seismic Month project were surprising. Existing organizations that produced global lists of earthquakes were able to identify about three hundred events per month; the International Seismic Month event list, however, contained one thousand events. The study thus showed clearly the need for care in reading and analyzing seismic records.

During 1973 David Davies left the Laboratory to become the editor of the scientific journal *Nature,* and Professor Michael Chinnery of Brown University joined the Laboratory, taking over the leadership of the program.

The new federal administration in 1977 changed the test-ban treaty situation completely. President Jimmy Carter initiated new negotiations with the objective of formulating a comprehensive test ban treaty. Early in these negotiations it became clear that a key element in any potential treaty would be the deployment of sensitive seismic stations that were within the national boundaries of both the United States and the USSR. This plan raised a new issue that changed the Lincoln Laboratory program.

The possibility that internal stations might send continuous densely sampled seismic data raised concerns about data management. The only existing system for handling digital data in an operational way was at the Seismic Data Analysis Center in Alexandria, Virginia. That facility, however, did not have the capacity to handle the new data flow. Lincoln Laboratory had already been considering ways to update the Seismic Data Analysis Center. The Defense Advanced Research Projects Agency (DARPA), as ARPA had been renamed in 1975, asked the Laboratory to design an entirely new system that would be capable of fulfilling whatever requirements might be specified by the test-ban treaty.

DARPA's request altered the Lincoln Laboratory program substantially. Research in seismology was reduced, computer scientists were brought into the program and the program focus changed to computer hardware, software and database management.

The design for the new Seismic Data Analysis Center was submitted in September 1979, and Lincoln Laboratory completed construction of the system two years later. DARPA moved the hardware and software to the Center for Seismic Studies in Rosslyn, Virginia.

The completion of the new Seismic Data Analysis Center signaled the end of the Lincoln Laboratory VELA UNIFORM program. During its twenty years, the Lincoln Laboratory effort made major contributions to the fields of seismic discrimination and seismic data management and analysis, and it counted some of the foremost seismologists in the country on its staff.

Seismic Events

Soon after LASA became operational in 1965, it recorded data on both natural and manmade seismic events.* Two events of particular note were an earthquake in the Rat Islands, a group of islands in the Aleutian chain, and a presumed explosion detected in Kazakhstan, a republic within the USSR. By combining all subarray outputs in a central signal processing computer, LASA scientists were able to detect and analyze these events successfully.

The recorded data for these events shows the amplitude of the detected signal and smoothed envelope of the signal on the vertical axis with time progressing to the right on the horizontal axis.

* H.W. Briscoe, J. Capon, P.L. Fleck, Jr., P.E. Green, Jr., R.J. Greenfield and E.J. Kelly, Jr., "Interim Report on Capabilities of the Experimental Large Aperture Seismic Array," *Lincoln Laboratory Technical Note No. 1966-16.* Lexington, Mass.: MIT Lincoln Laboratory, 24 February 1966, DTIC AD-631285.

Earthquake near the Aleutian Rat Islands, November 11, 1965

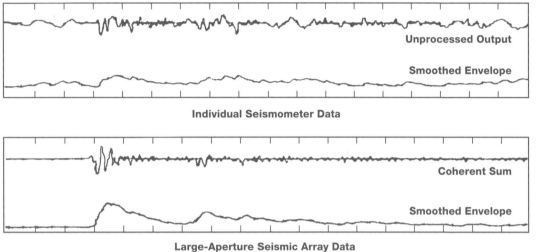

Individual Seismometer Data

Large-Aperture Seismic Array Data

Presumed Explosion in Kazakhstan, USSR

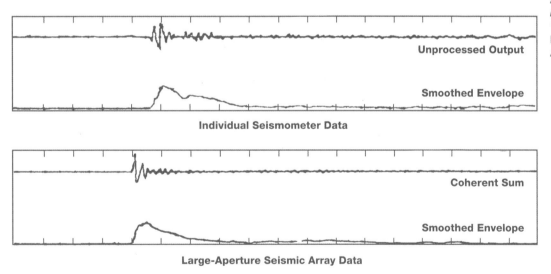

Individual Seismometer Data

Large-Aperture Seismic Array Data

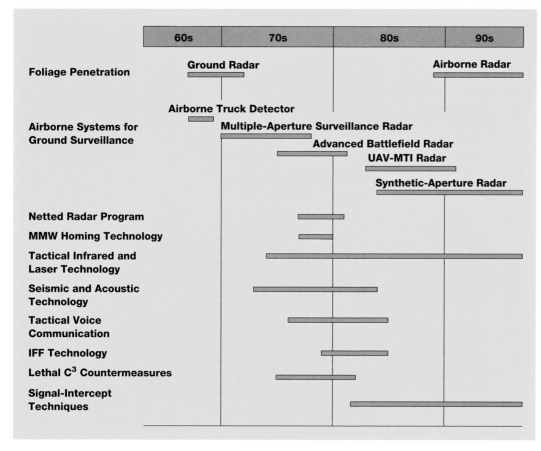

	60s	70s	80s	90s

Foliage Penetration — Ground Radar / Airborne Radar

Airborne Systems for Ground Surveillance — Airborne Truck Detector / Multiple-Aperture Surveillance Radar / Advanced Battlefield Radar / UAV-MTI Radar / Synthetic-Aperture Radar

Netted Radar Program

MMW Homing Technology

Tactical Infrared and Laser Technology

Seismic and Acoustic Technology

Tactical Voice Communication

IFF Technology

Lethal C³ Countermeasures

Signal-Intercept Techniques

Figure 11-1
Time line of major efforts in the surface-surveillance program area.

Notes

1 The tactical battle-field-surveillance program has also been known as the surface-surveillance program. Organization and editing of this chapter were directed by William Delaney. Contributors included John Beusch, Thomas Bryant, Thomas Goblick, Robert Hull, Herbert Kleiman, Melvin Labitt, Richard Lacoss, Edward Muehe, Edward Schwartz, Jay Sklar, Irvin Stiglitz, Melvin Stone and Donald Temme.

2 A summary of the Florida measurements program appears in a 1971 report: M. Labitt, J.H. Teele and R.D. Yates, "The Lincoln Laboratory Foliage Penetration Radar Measurements Program," *17th Ann. Tri-Service Radar Symp. Record, Vol. 1, 25–27 May 1971,* Fort Monmouth, New Jersey: U.S. Army Electronics Command, AMSEL-CT-DT.

Three critical questions about the propagation of radar signals within foliage had to be answered: (1) How much does the foliage spread the frequency spectrum of a signal reflected from a target? (2) What is the frequency spectrum of clutter signals reflected from windblown foliage? (3) What is the effect of multipath propagation on range and azimuth resolution and on subclutter visibility?

The Laboratory built two radar systems to answer these questions. The initial system, the Camp Sentinel Radar-I, took measurements locally. It worked well, and it was used in demonstrations to military observers in the fall of 1967. A second version was mounted in a van and sent to Bisley, Puerto Rico, where foliage closely simulated the conditions in Vietnam. By January 1968, enough measurement data had been accumulated to go ahead with a more advanced radar, the Camp Sentinel Radar-II.

The design of the Camp Sentinel Radar-II incorporated unique and innovative concepts. The antenna was mounted high above the ground on a rapidly deployable tower so the electromagnetic waves could reach a target by propagating over the tops of the trees and then be diffracted to the ground, rather than by propagating directly through the foliage. An electronically scanned cylindrical array sequentially stepped the antenna beam through thirty-two positions of azimuth to cover 360°. Methods to cancel out moving clutter due to wind were successfully demonstrated.

The radar control was designed to allow an operator to construct two intrusion fences. These fences could be made irregular in shape, matching them to the desired defense perimeter. The operator did not need to monitor the radar unless an alarm sounded. If a detection occurred, the operator simply checked the display to see which range/azimuth sector contained the intruder and to see if the target was incoming or outgoing.

After a short local testing period, the first Laboratory-built Camp Sentinel Radar-II was shipped to Vietnam in August 1968. Leonard Bowles and David Rogers spent two months in Vietnam, introducing the radar to the Third Brigade, 1st Infantry Division, and instructing Army personnel in its operation and maintenance. The radar received immediate acceptance and the Army used it until the end of the war (Figure 11-2).

Additional development work was carried out by the Army's Harry Diamond Laboratory. The improved version, the Camp Sentinel Radar-III, included a more powerful transmitter to increase the detection range and additional display options. Six of these radars were manufactured and sent to Vietnam, where they remained until U.S. combat troops were withdrawn.

The Long Range Demonstration Radar

The success of the Camp Sentinel radar encouraged the DoD to support a program to investigate the feasibility of developing a much longer-range foliage-penetration radar. This effort began early in 1969 with the design of equipment that could measure electromagnetic propagation and clutter spectra in foliated areas. Measurements were then carried out in the Florida Everglades between June 1969 and December 1970.[2]

The Florida program collected detailed and precise data on the effect of foliage on radar, including measurements of the spectra and amplitude statistics of signals from windblown clutter, the spectra of signals from moving men in the clear and in clutter, and the variation of the signal strength and polarization of the electromagnetic field as a function of height above ground. These measurements at 435 and 1305 MHz verified the lossy dielectric slab model of propagation in foliage, as well as a randomly moving tree model that explained the observed spectra.

The design and construction of the Long Range Demonstration Radar, an electronically scanned radar featuring an 80-ft semicircular antenna, proceeded in parallel with the Florida measurements. The radar was operational from the fall of 1971 through June 1972. Its antenna was mounted on a 100-ft tower on Katahdin Hill near the Laboratory. Most of the signal processing — the Doppler filter bank and thresholding in each range-azimuth cell — was performed in real time by the Fast Digital Processor (FDP), which had been developed by the Laboratory's computer division as a general-purpose signal processor.

The Long Range Demonstration Radar reliably detected a single walking man at distances greater than 7 km. Subclutter visibility varied from 45 to 60 dB, depending on whether the clutter was distributed or from a single large scatterer. Military observers attended demonstrations

In Vietnam

Certainly no Lincoln Laboratory assignment has called for greater physical courage than the one given in 1968 to Leonard Bowles and David Rogers. Their task — to install the Camp Sentinel Radar in Vietnam, operate it in the field and train Army personnel in its use.

When Bowles and Rogers arrived in Saigon on August 11, the city was under attack. Five rockets hit nearby parts of the city, one only about a hundred feet away. Ironically, Saigon was considered safe.

They flew to Lai Khe, about fifty miles northwest of Saigon, where the 3rd Brigade, 1st Infantry Division, had established a large base. The Vietcong had established a route through the village of Lai Khe and were slipping onto the base at night. They had already blown up the officers' club, three helicopters and four barracks; the commanding officer, Colonel William Patch, was eager to bring the Lincoln Laboratory team on board.

The Camp Sentinel Radar had been shipped to South Vietnam in three boxes, all of which were left out on the runway in the tropical weather. When Bowles and Rogers opened the boxes, they found the radar equipment sitting in several inches of water. Working with military personnel in weather that alternated between 100°F and torrential rain, they replaced corroded parts, cleaned circuit boards, dragged equipment through deep mud and set up the radar.

The radar proved its value immediately, detecting targets during each of the first three days. Mortars and M-79 grenades were fired each time moving targets were detected, and each time the targets were then observed moving away. Patrols during the following days found items dropped by the enemy along the trail in hasty retreats.

After a month of operations at Lai Khe, Bowles and Rogers moved the radar by helicopter to an even more hazardous site: Bandit Hill, a night defensive position near the village of Tam Binh. Located deep in Vietcong country, Bandit Hill was suffering frequent attacks by mortar, rocket and ground intrusion. A first sergeant came out to greet the Lincoln Laboratory team; all of the commissioned officers were wounded.*

Setting up the radar called for extraordinary courage; while working on the tower, Bowles and Rogers were completely exposed. But once the Camp Sentinel Radar became operational, it was immediately successful in detecting targets under foliage. And when the Vietcong realized that their movements were being detected, attacks declined markedly.

Over the next month, Bowles and Rogers trained military radar mechanics and operators to detect moving targets. Averaging about five hours of sleep each night throughout their tour, both men were more than glad to leave Vietnam on October 10. But the real proof of the importance the Vietcong assigned to the Camp Sentinel Radar came just two days later.

On October 12 Army radar mechanics took the Camp Sentinel Radar antenna down from its tower for routine maintenance. The radar position immediately came under heavy ground and mortar attack, and the radar was damaged and unable to function. The maintenance battalion personnel and enlisted men Bowles and Rogers had trained were able to replace or repair the damaged parts. Three days later they brought the set back into operation. The radar had proved its importance, and the Vietcong stayed away from Bandit Hill.

* Letter from Leonard Bowles to John Allen, September 23, 1968.

seeker to the missile guidance system as the range to target decreased. These results were initially developed by using the seeker/target/missile simulation with signature data derived from scaled target models, and then testing the helicopter-mounted MMW seeker radar in realistic field conditions.

By the end of the program in 1980, significant improvements in guided-missile seeker performance had been achieved, and several defense contractors subsequently adopted these improvements in the design of MMW seeker systems.

Tactical Infrared and Laser Technology

Lincoln Laboratory's first involvement with optical systems for battlefield applications began in 1974 as part of the DARPA-sponsored Hostile Weapons Location Systems (HOWLS) effort. The work continues to this day, and a wide variety of techniques, processes, sensor systems and related experiments have been developed.

Early Infrared Work

Two major issues needed to be addressed to assess the utility of optical and IR sensors on the battlefield: the statistical effects of the environment (weather, clouds, obscurants) and the detection of targets, particularly stationary targets, in background clutter. Worldwide databases of IR transmission were translated into statistics of operational utility to resolve the issue of environmental effects. Cloud statistics were combined with weather statistics, yielding complete statistical descriptions of the probable operational utility of a sensor. This effort was one of the first systematic examinations of sensor utility, and the IR community still routinely uses these databases and computer techniques to predict sensor performance.

Two IR sensors were developed under the HOWLS program. The first was a mortar location system made up of several linear arrays of passive IR staring sensors low on the horizon. As mortar or artillery shells passed through the coverage of the arrays, the arrays would report several angular position points for the projectile trajectory. The uppermost staring array was also coupled to a Nd:YAG laser radar programmed to make a single range measurement. This combination of sensors could measure shell trajectories and backtrack to launch points with high

accuracy. The system successfully demonstrated its predicted performance in 1978 at the China Lake Naval Weapons Center, California. After the field tests, responsibility was transferred to the Army Night Vision Laboratory, but the techniques were never carried forward into advanced system development.

The second IR sensor developed during this early effort had a longer-lasting impact. It was a multispectral IR sensor for developing techniques to allow precision guided munitions to detect IR targets in clutter. A number of clutter suppression techniques were explored, particularly those based on spectral and spatial differences between targets and backgrounds. Algorithms for clutter suppression yielded results that were dependent on the (highly variable) statistics of the instantaneous background clutter. A notable achievement was the development of optimized digital filters for both point targets and targets that could be resolved by the IR sensor. These filters were essentially two-dimensional equivalents of the matched filters in radar signal processing.

IR sensors mounted in a truck and on a fixed-wing aircraft were used to gather a large, well-calibrated database on background IR clutter. This database became the basis for testing clutter-rejection algorithms, and a generation of heuristic spatial filters with improved performance against various types of backgrounds was developed.

The difficult problem of IR detection of a stationary land target in a cluttered IR background is not yet fully solved. Many of the techniques first developed for the HOWLS program have been carried forward to systems currently under development requiring automatic detection — for example, IR search and track arrays for detecting low observable targets and automatic target recognition for IR imagers.

Infrared Airborne Radar

Lincoln Laboratory initiated a program under Air Force sponsorship in 1975 to explore the utility of imaging IR laser radars for tactical applications. The primary impetus for this development was the need for high spatial resolution in an airborne sensor aboard low-altitude air vehicles like the A-10, the F-16 or a cruise missile. The sensor

had to provide high-quality images in any of several domains (intensity, range, Doppler or thermal) for either automated or man-in-the-loop target detection and identification, when applications included navigation with terrain following and obstacle avoidance, fire control or damage assessment. A combination of active and passive IR sensors was chosen because it provided day and night operation, high-resolution images with modest-size apertures and some measure of penetration in bad weather and of many obscurants found on the battlefield (smoke, dust, haze).

A 10.6-μm CO_2 laser radar was built to serve as a test-bed imaging laser radar. The objective was to provide about 30-cm spatial resolution on a target at a range of 3 km. The laser radar used heterodyne detection and operated in a pulsed mode for ranging applications and in a CW mode for Doppler measurements. A 1-W laser transmitter gave a sufficient margin for operation in most weather conditions. The laser radar was completed in 1977 and, from its station in one of the Laboratory's penthouses overlooking Hanscom Air Force Base, was able to image a variety of buildings and other structures. Military tanks (U.S. and foreign) were brought onto the base to establish their signatures; images were collected in fog and rain and even through limited amounts of military obscuring smoke.

A truck-transportable version of the laser radar was designed and its fabrication completed in 1980. The sensor was taken to Camp Edwards on Cape Cod for extensive data collection exercises, during which a tank, an armored personnel carrier and a 105-mm howitzer were imaged at ranges between 700 and 2500 m and at various aspect angles. Targets were imaged both dry and soaked by streams of water. In addition, IR-absorbing smokes were used to mask targets while being imaged. The measurements showed that 10.6-μm radiation was only minimally attenuated by common visual obscurants, and that the range data, displayed as an image, provided reliable identification.

Several DoD programs used the transportable laser radar to support their research. In 1981 the Air Force Armaments Laboratory at Eglin Air Force Base funded the laser radar to collect data on Pershing missiles at Fort Sill. The laser radar also collected transmission measurements on a variety of obscurants during Smoke Week exercises at Redstone Arsenal, Alabama. Measurements were made of the signatures of ships passing through the Cape Cod Canal to establish their signatures at 10.6 μm. Then in 1982 a series of modifications to the transportable system were undertaken to support a chemical-agent detection program managed by the Air Force Engineering and Services Center at Tyndall Air Force Base, Florida. Demonstration of the detection of a gaseous chemical released into the atmosphere was carried out in 1985.

An airborne laser-radar and passive IR system called the Infrared Airborne Radar (IRAR) was designed and built in 1983 under Air Force sponsorship. The system was patterned after the transportable version, but required a twelve-element detector array for the radar to be useful at typical aircraft speeds. Its platform was a Gulfstream G-1 twin turboprop aircraft (Figure 11-7). The laser radar sensor and the passive IR sensor looked forward from a housing mounted on the bottom of the aircraft just behind the wings. First images were collected in 1984, and the wide field-of-view line-scan mode became operational in December 1984.

During the latter half of the 1980s the IRAR was employed extensively to collect data, demonstrate technology and test system concepts in support of such DoD programs as the Air Force Avionics Laboratory's Cruise Missile Advanced Guidance Program, DARPA's Smart Weapons Program, DARPA's Strategic Relocatable Targets Program and the Navy Space and Naval Warfare Systems Command's Radiant Outlaw Program. Various upgrades of and additions to the IRAR sensor on the G-1 aircraft were made during that period. These upgrades included an improvement in the range precision of the basic IRAR CO_2 laser radar from 6 to 1 m, the addition of a passive IR mode in the 8-to-12-μm spectral band, the addition of a real-aperture MMW radar operating at 85 GHz with a range resolution of 0.5 m, the addition of a very high resolution (15 cm in each of the three spatial dimensions) down-looking near-IR laser radar integrated with the forward-looking infrared (FLIR) sensors, and a similar high-resolution down-looking CO_2 laser radar.

Lincoln Laboratory's pioneering effort in IR laser technology broke new ground for many subsequent DoD and industry efforts. Underscoring the impact of this early work most vividly is the widely reproduced image of the Bourne Bridge over the Cape Cod Canal in Massachusetts, taken with the IRAR laser radar in 1984 (Figure 11-8).

Seismic and Acoustic Technology

In 1973, as part of its effort to address the problem of locating hostile indirect-fire weapons, the Laboratory began investigating seismic and acoustic techniques for weapon location, with an emphasis on understanding the basic phenomenology and the use of sensor arrays. This effort continued through 1982.

The hostile-weapons work benefited substantially from the earlier Laboratory involvement in the DARPA VELA UNIFORM program, described in chapter 10, "Seismic Discrimination," which had developed a system for the detection of seismic waves from underground nuclear tests at intercontinental ranges. The array technology and the propagation physics from that program carried over directly to the weapon location problem, although the time and space scales were very different and the hostile-weapons problem included the element of air acoustic propagation.

The DARPA Distributed Sensor effort at the Laboratory, which started in 1977, provided additional acoustic phenomenology and array processing technology inputs to the hostile-weapons work. This project involved the use of geographically distributed sensor sites for aircraft surveillance and emphasized the use of small acoustic arrays. The project culminated in 1986 with the successful demonstration of real-time aircraft tracking by using fused data from multiple acoustic arrays and imaging sensors.

Experimental work on the use of acoustic and seismic signals for hostile-weapons location began in earnest in 1975. Sources included firing weapons, ground vehicles and a weapon surrogate in the form of a modified 4.2-in mortar. The mortar fired a projectile that consisted of a mass of water equivalent to a real mortar projectile; realistic seismic and acoustic signals could be safely generated where real weapons could not be used. Data were obtained at multiple field sites: Fort Devens, Massachusetts; Eglin Air Force Base, Florida; and Twenty-Nine Palms USMC Base, California.

Experiments with microphone arrays indicated that multilateration and time-difference-of-arrival source location methods would allow arrays to be effective for weapon location, and that the arrays would be effective out to operationally useful ranges.

Seismic experiments provided interesting results. As expected, the seismic signals contained many seismic phases in addition to signals generated by the passage of the air acoustic wave. It was concluded that, for a well-calibrated site, the seismic signals could be used for weapon location and probably for distinguishing between weapon firings and shell impacts. However, seismic signal details were geology sensitive and seismic detection ranges were much shorter than typical acoustic detection ranges.

The VELA, Distributed Sensor and weapon location work all involved arrays of ground-based mechanical-wave sensors. The VELA program left a legacy of a network of seismic monitoring arrays around the world. Although the Distributed Sensor and the weapon location efforts have not yet led to such tangible results, ongoing programs in other organizations are building on the work in the use of small arrays for tactical applications.

Between 1983 and 1984 the Laboratory briefly investigated the use of an airborne dual-mode RF and acoustic homing weapon for tactical applications. The idea was to develop a system that would allow an airborne platform to home in on RF emissions or acoustic signals from motors on vehicles, electric generators and other equipment. Acoustic homing was judged to be feasible based on preliminary measurements and analysis, but the program did not proceed to an experimental phase. The present-day Army BAT antitank weapon, which utilizes acoustic-target acquisition methods, is similar in general concept.

Figure 11-8
Laser radar image of the Bourne
Bridge over the Cape Cod Canal in
Massachusetts.

Figure 11-9
Extensive use of digital electronics made it possible to fit this jam-resistant tactical voice-communication equipment into a fighter aircraft.

Tactical Voice Communication

The objective of the Tactical Voice Communication program was to develop a system design and technology to produce highly jam-resistant voice radios for tactical fighter aircraft and related platforms. The challenge was to develop a design that provided secure (encrypted) communications with high jam resistance and a multiple voice and interrupt (conferencing) capability, yet still satisfied the constraints on electromagnetic compatibility to coexist with other users of the UHF voice frequency band. Additional technology development was also needed to implement radios based on this system design in the small volume available in fighter aircraft.

The program, sponsored by the Air Force and the National Security Agency, began in 1976. The brassboard demonstration model was bench tested in 1980 and flight tested in 1981 (Figure 11-9). The program was completed in 1984; in the last few years the focus was on the development of technology to miniaturize the radio for form-fit replacement of existing AM radios and to transfer the technology to an industrial contractor chosen by the Air Force.

The signal waveform employed pseudorandomly phase-modulated pulses that were further spread over the UHF band by frequency hopping. In the bench tests a level of jam resistance very close to the theoretical value was demonstrated against broadband jamming, and the performance was shown to be robust; that is, any strategy of partial-time (pulsed) or partial-band jamming did not give an advantage to the jammer. The flight tests demonstrated successful operation in an aircraft environment.

Equipment miniaturization to permit form-fit replacements for the existing radios using existing antennas in fighter aircraft was an important requirement. By the mid-1980s rapid advances in digital circuitry had solved the problem of digital miniaturization, but significant challenges remained in the RF and analog circuitry, the CCD matched filters and the transmitter. Miniaturization of key circuits was demonstrated with volume reductions ranging from factors of ten to thirty. The CCD matched

filters for the brassboard model were fabricated in a joint effort between Lincoln Laboratory and industry, and a next-generation device with the proper characteristics was defined. A family of transmitters of various sizes and output powers was designed to provide a pragmatic approach to tailoring the transmitter size (and output power) to the space available in a given aircraft type. Transmitters with efficiencies in excess of 40% were demonstrated. Industry development continued for a time after completion of the Lincoln Laboratory program but no production resulted from this effort.

IFF Technology

Identification, friend or foe (IFF) describes an electronic password system that identifies friendly units on a battlefield. In the classic question/answer system, potential targets are interrogated, or "challenged," by an encrypted radio signal before they are fired on. All friendly units carry a transponder that can detect and decrypt the interrogation and can send an encrypted response. The encryption prevents enemies from eliciting responses to their interrogations and prevents interrogated enemies from sending the proper responses. Thus a cooperative IFF system reduces fratricide, an important consideration when targets can be engaged beyond visual identification range.

In the late 1970s the NATO Alliance recognized the need for a common IFF system among the member nations. The United States had the largest amount of IFF equipment in operational use at that time, but the U.S. system design, the Mark XII, was based on 1950s technology, and NATO wanted to develop a new IFF system design that could overcome the shortcomings in the Mark XII.

In 1978 a team of three NATO members (the United States, the United Kingdom and the Federal Republic of Germany) formed a working group to define a NATO Standardization Agreement (called a STANAG) for an IFF system for NATO-wide use. The new system was referred to as NIS (for NATO IFF System). France and Italy subsequently joined the endeavor.

The NIS team became interested in the use of very wideband pseudonoise-modulated waveforms to provide jamming resistance, low probability of intercept and security. The U.S. DoD representative on the NIS team, Michael Keller, from the Office of the Secretary of Defense–Command, Control, Communications and Intelligence (OSD–C^3I), was familiar with the surface acoustic wave (SAW) devices that had been developed by the Lincoln Laboratory Solid State Division for use as programmable matched filters for wideband pulses. These devices, called convolvers, could be used to perform matched filtering of pulses modulated at up to 100 MHz or more within a restricted time window. Keller therefore approached Lincoln Laboratory and requested assistance in designing the NIS around SAW technology.

The Laboratory began its involvement with the NATO IFF project in 1979, and the program lasted until 1985. It began with funding from OSD–C^3I, and later from the Mark XV IFF program, a joint-service development effort with the Air Force as the lead organization. Throughout this program, the Laboratory provided direct technical support to the DoD team involved in the NATO effort and worked with laboratories of all three U.S. military services and with foreign laboratories as well. Lincoln Laboratory personnel were also active participants in the many tense and sensitive negotiations among the NATO working group members.

Because the Mark XII system operated at L-band, it was unable to match the narrow beamwidths of higher frequency (X-band and K_u-band) radars. The mismatch in resolution between the radar sensor and the IFF could lead to ambiguous identification of closely spaced targets. Thus the initial NIS concept was to have multiple interrogation frequency bands that could accommodate target sensors with differing resolutions. Three interrogation modes were proposed: (1) a microwave interrogation and response with wideband direct-sequence pseudonoise (DSPN) modulated waveforms and an S-band operating frequency, distinct from the air traffic control radar beacon system (ATCRBS) band to relax electromagnetic compatibility constraints (by contrast, ATCRBS and Mark XII operated in the same band); (2) an X-band radar interrogation mode with simple waveforms chosen to provide narrow interrogation beamwidths with a better match to the radar resolution; and (3) an optical interrogation mode for ground combat vehicles, to match the resolution of optical sights and FLIR devices.

Lincoln Laboratory's initial work addressed the feasibility of using wideband DSPN modulation for IFF waveform formats in the S-band microwave interrogation and reply modes. The Laboratory played a major role in defining the S-band signals, and designed and built a matched-filter signal processor with SAW convolvers to detect, synchronize and demodulate messages that consisted of wideband (100 MHz) DSPN-modulated pulses. This processor was demonstrated at the Laboratory in 1981. The wideband approach was shown to be technically feasible, but also complex and costly.

Lincoln Laboratory played an instrumental role in persuading the NATO team to reassess the decision to avoid the Mark XII and ATCRBS L-band frequency. The Laboratory conducted detailed electromagnetic compatibility analyses and carried out airborne measurements of the L-band interrogation environment in Europe during NATO exercises to bolster the case for switching the proposed S-band mode back to L-band. After these analyses, measurements and simulations had convinced the NATO working group that electromagnetic compatibility with the air traffic control system could be achieved, the S-band interrogation was dropped in favor of a new L-band interrogation with a smaller bandwidth that would produce a much more affordable IFF system. In 1985 NATO agreed to a STANAG for NIS that included L-band and X-band interrogations and essentially adopted Lincoln Laboratory's Mark XV signals design for the L-band interrogation and reply modes.

Because of serious concerns about fratricide in a major tank battle in an environment that might include fog, haze, smoke, dust and night fighting, Germany expressed a strong interest in developing a battlefield IFF (BIFF) mode for NIS. On the basis of the technology then available at Siemens, the German delegation proposed the use of lasers operating at 1-μm wavelength. However, Lincoln Laboratory's work in IR radar technology indicated that the 1-μm wavelength would not penetrate fog, smoke or dust on the battlefield as effectively as the 10-μm wavelength. A debate ensued within the NATO NIS team; the technical issues were finally addressed by a Lincoln Laboratory program to analyze and verify the performance of 1-μm, 10-μm and millimeter-wavelength interrogations under the conditions of interest. This work, carried out at Cape Cod, Massachusetts, indicated that the 10-μm wavelength was superior to 1 μm, but that the millimeter wavelength was the best.

Although the Air Force dropped the Mark XV program in 1990 for lack of funds, the Navy continues to pursue the design of IFF equipment based on the Lincoln Laboratory waveforms. The Army has become increasingly concerned about fratricide on the battlefield, particularly since the war with Iraq, and has reopened the study of BIFF modes.

Lethal C³ Countermeasures

The DoD recognized in the mid-1970s that there was considerable leverage for tactical antiradiation weapons employed against command, control and communications (C³). The notion was to employ low-cost weapons to target both C³ transmitters and jammers threatening friendly communications. Solutions to two major technical challenges were needed: (1) direction-finding seeker antennas with small apertures (less than 1 ft) capable of effective operation at the frequencies of principal interest (UHF and VHF) and (2) signal processing algorithms capable of homing on a target in an environment consisting of multiple cochannel emitters operating with continuous signals.

The technology base that had been developed for attacking radars under a variety of antiradiation missile programs was unfortunately deficient for this application because of the substantially smaller seeker aperture available (typically between 0.1 and 0.5 wavelength) and because the leading-edge-gating direction-finding technique could not be employed against pulsed emitters. The principal focus of Lincoln Laboratory's program, therefore, was the development of the necessary critical technologies and their validation through flight testing.

An effort was begun in 1975 to conduct an initial concept-feasibility assessment. The early work focused on algorithm development, simulation evaluation and bench testing. The major advance during the first two years was the development of the enhanced interferometer to avoid the centroid homing problem traditionally associated with multiple CW cochannel emitters in the homing sensor's beam. These activities were followed by the design and evaluation of a compact broadband dual-polarized direction-finding antenna, which then led to flight-test validation with an airborne seeker test bed against multiple cochannel emitters.

1980

Transportable laser radar image (bicyclist)

Cylindrical-aperture AGSR

W.P. Delaney

The flight-test program, conducted at Eglin Air Force Base in the summer of 1982, used a miniature UAV platform (XBQM-106). Of the three identical flight-test vehicles built, two were allowed to complete a terminal impact against a low-frequency emitter. The test scenarios represented stressed environments that consisted of three nominally equipowered emitters in the VHF/UHF bands. Of the two impact tests, the first was a near miss, but within the lethal radius of a small warhead, and the second was a direct impact on the radiating antenna of a simulated tactical target (Figure 11-10).

The final phase of the program focused on technology transfer to industry. This activity included formal reporting, inputs to specifications, evaluation of proposed efforts, construction of critical subsystems and direct interactions with cognizant government agencies and industrial contractors.

Signal-Intercept Techniques

In 1982 the Laboratory began an analysis and data collection program to assess the applicability of adaptive-antenna-array techniques to signal intercept. Signal receivers generally must be able to handle various forms of interference, including that from other signals in the same frequency band and multipath signals due to propagation effects. Such interference is difficult enough when the transmissions are cooperatively generated. In the case of signal intercept, however, the transmitter is noncooperative; as a result, the receiver may be poorly sited and the transmitted signals may incorporate features that make reception difficult. Signal intercept can thus be an extremely challenging problem. But, through adaptive antenna techniques that use spatial processing to suppress undesired signals, interference can be mitigated.

The Laboratory's work has focused on four areas: (1) mathematical assessments and simulations to develop and analyze appropriate adaptive-array algorithms; (2) evaluation of such algorithms with data collected in controlled experiments; (3) development of real-time, preprototype demonstration systems based on adaptive-array signal processing; and (4) analysis of operational signal intercept problems to determine the suitability of adaptive-array processing techniques.

The greatest challenge to achieving effective spatially based interference suppression comes when the spatial separation between the signal of interest and the interfering sources is small. When the separation is more than an antenna beamwidth, the undesired interfering signal can be largely attenuated by using well-established sidelobe cancellation techniques. In many situations, however, the available antenna aperture is too few wavelengths in diameter for a narrow beam to be formed, and the desired and interfering sources will fall within the same beam. Super-resolution techniques are then necessary to suppress the interference.

Super-resolution — the ability to place multiple deep nulls closer in angle than the diffraction limit — has been the common thread in most of the Laboratory's work in the signal-intercept area. The techniques were first developed by the geophysics community for spectral-frequency estimation processes, but in recent years they have been applied to spatial resolution processing. Theoretical analysis and simulation had shown that super-resolution techniques should provide sub-beamwidth resolution, but it was unclear whether super-resolution could be made to work with real antennas and their associated pattern mismatches and errors. Furthermore, it was unclear whether such propagation effects as multipath would preclude effective interference nulling.

Vehicular-traffic display

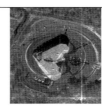
Aerial SAR image of office building

Figure 11-10
Direct impact of an antiradiation
drone on the radiating antenna of
a simulated tactical target.

Figure 11-11
Beech 1900 test aircraft with both a
top- and a bottom-fuselage-mounted
conformal broadband compact-multi-
element array.

Notes

7 R.S. Bucy and L.L. Horowitz, "Maximum Likelihood Direction Estimation for Multiple Emitters with Array Response Vector Distortion and Noisy Observations," *Lincoln Laboratory Technical Memorandum No. 44L-0655*. Lexington, Mass.: MIT Lincoln Laboratory, 1991.

A multiphase program was initiated to cast light on these questions. It was necessary to understand the effects of antenna errors on the performance of high-resolution algorithms, and to learn how array and signal characteristics (number of antenna elements, aperture, signal/interferer spacing) affected performance. For these techniques to be practical, moreover, algorithms had to be developed that would be robust despite array errors. A major breakthrough occurred when Lincoln Laboratory developed unique calibration techniques to compensate for array errors, and it became clear that superior interference suppression capabilities were achievable.[7] But this goal had to be verified with field measurements.

In the first set of measurements, three emitters and a line array of antenna elements were deployed at the Antenna Test Range; data collected there confirmed expectations. Next, an airborne flight-test program was begun with a Beech 1900 aircraft as the test platform to prove that super-resolution was achievable in practice and to provide an extensive source of data from representative scenarios.

The Beech 1900 was initially fitted with arrays of eleven dipole elements on the top and bottom of the fuselage (Figure 11-11). Later, elements were added on each wing and on the tail. Over 150 flights were carried out with a controlled set of emitters operating in the low VHF band as targets. A network of distance-measuring equipment (DME) transmitters located the aircraft position accurately. The data were processed with a number of algorithms and detailed comparisons were made.

Representative data sets were also distributed to industry so that algorithms and results could be compared. The aircraft was decommissioned in 1991, but the large database is still being used for algorithm development and assessment.

This program was the initial effort in super-resolution technology. It spawned several other small programs, however, that continue today: (1) extensions of the technology to the HF band, where sky wave signals propagate via ionospheric refraction; (2) assessment of how the techniques apply to spread-spectrum signals; (3) development of real-time interference cancellation receiver systems for use at VHF/UHF and HF frequencies; and (4) application of these techniques to low-frequency radar imaging in foliage-penetration situations.

Through the combination of theoretical analyses, simulations and realistic field experiments, the Laboratory's efforts since 1982 have validated the use of super-resolution techniques for difficult signal-intercept situations. Several new and effective algorithms have been developed; these algorithms increase performance and are suitable for real-time implementation.

Retrospective

Battlefield technology is of great national importance; our ability to stay ahead of potential adversaries protects the lives of our military forces and our allies. Lincoln Laboratory's accomplishments in MTI radar, laser radar, secure communications and signal processing have made important contributions to the nation's present-day battlefield systems. Current work in stationary-target detection, foliage penetration and super-resolution is forming the basis of future systems. Continuation of the careful attention to scientific analysis and experimentation, and to the development and demonstration of advanced sensor and processing hardware, that has characterized the twenty-seven years of Lincoln Laboratory activities in this area, will provide superior technology for the U.S. forces of the future.

Air Vehicle Survivability and Air Defense

In 1977 the Cruise Missile Detection Technology Program was initiated at Lincoln Laboratory to evaluate the survivability of U.S. cruise missiles penetrating enemy air defenses. An advanced air defense effort that complemented the air vehicle survivability investigations was undertaken in the mid-1980s. These programs returned the Laboratory to an important national role in air defense and now rank among the Laboratory's principal activities.

Left: The Mountaintop Radar complex at North Oscura Peak on the White Sands Missile Range, New Mexico.

Air defense has played a prominent role in Lincoln Laboratory's history. The Laboratory was founded in the early 1950s to address the problem of national air defense, but that work diminished significantly with the completion of the SAGE activity in 1958. By the 1970s little air defense work remained at the Laboratory.[1] In 1977, however, the U.S. development of the modern cruise missile[2] created a new role for the Laboratory in air defense.

The new assignment was initially not the development of an air defense system, but the corollary task of developing insights, techniques, models and experiments that would help to ensure that U.S. cruise missiles could penetrate enemy air defenses. The principal enemy was the Soviet Union, which had built a formidable national air defense system, consisting of thousands of ground radars to guide thousands of aircraft interceptors and about a thousand surface-to-air missile (SAM) batteries around industrial complexes and military bases. The Soviets' modern navy was also equipped with heavy air defenses — mostly of the SAM variety. U.S. cruise missiles were being developed as a long-range weapon that allowed U.S. Air Force and Navy aircraft to avoid these intense defenses.

The Laboratory's initial role in 1977 was to characterize these enemy air defenses. In the mid-1980s the Laboratory took on the additional role of developing air defense technologies against enemy cruise missiles. These two activities, air vehicle survivability and air defense, grew in size so that by 1995 they represented about 25% of the Laboratory's total effort.

Although Soviet weapons and air defenses were the focus of work carried out through 1991, the demise of the Soviet Union has not affected U.S. interest in air vehicle survivability and air defense. As was vividly demonstrated during Operation Desert Storm, cruise missiles have great applicability in regional and theater conflicts, and they continue to be prominent weapons of interest to the U.S. government.

Early Controversy over Cruise Missile Survivability

The introduction of the modern cruise missile caused some controversy, both political and technical. Politically, they were worrisome and complicating devices to the arms control community. Another group, the manned-bomber advocates, also saw them as a threat, and for good reason: in 1977 President Jimmy Carter canceled the production plan for the original B-1 bomber partially on the grounds that cruise missiles launched from outside the Soviet Union from the older B-52 bombers would allow weapon delivery into the heavily defended Soviet Union.

There were also technical controversies that surrounded the cruise missile — mainly in the area of their survivability against air defenses. Proponents of cruise missiles thought of them as nearly invisible to surveillance systems, capable of defeating (in a variety of ways) air defense systems designed to handle much larger signature aircraft. The small size and simple shape of cruise missiles made them difficult to detect by radar, electro-optical and infrared defense sensors. Modern navigation techniques allowed them to fly a low-altitude, terrain-hugging flight path. Thus the air defender faced the challenge of finding and killing low-observable targets that could not only fly close to the ground but could also arrive in large numbers from multiple directions with precise timing.

One Navy proponent of the Tomahawk cruise missile argued:

"Even if you are lucky enough to find it and fire a missile at it and the interceptor missile guides successfully to an intercept, the radar fuze on the interceptor missile won't work because of the low observability of my cruise missile."

Advocates of SAM systems were far less impressed with cruise missile technology. A proponent of the Improved Hawk SAM system, for example, saw cruise missiles in a very different light:

"This cruise missile looks a lot like the target drones I practice on. It can't maneuver aggressively, it doesn't carry electronic countermeasures. It will present my SAM battery with a low altitude target on a straight and level flight. I will kill it easily — probably a direct hit as in many of my tests."

The 1977 Strategic Penetration Technology Summer Study

By the spring of 1977, the controversy over the relative survivability of cruise missiles and penetrating bombers led William Perry, at that time Director of Defense Research and Engineering (DDR&E) and more recently Secretary of Defense, to commission a summer study on two topics: cruise missile survivability and B-1 electronics countermeasures. The study was cochaired by E.C. "Pete" Aldridge of the System Planning Corporation, who later became Undersecretary and then Secretary of the Air Force, and William Delaney of Lincoln Laboratory. A national team of talent was assembled in Washington for the study. Also participating from the Laboratory were Victor Reis, who later became the Director of DARPA and then the DDR&E, and David Briggs, who subsequently led the Air Defense Technology Division of Lincoln Laboratory prior to becoming an assistant director of the Laboratory in January 1994.

The cruise missile part of the 1977 summer study concluded that there was substantial justification for controversy over cruise missile survivability. Air defenders and cruise missile designers alike were ill prepared with experience, analytic models or experimental data to predict the outcome of an engagement involving a low-flying, low-observable cruise missile. And accurate prediction was important: the early cruise missiles had a strategic nuclear deterrent role and the ability to predict survivability with confidence was paramount.

The list of uncertainties was long and included some basic phenomenological effects, such as the magnitude and statistics of radar ground clutter, the complications of very-low-elevation-angle radar propagation and the effects of terrain masking. Practical hardware issues of radar sensitivity and clutter rejection, fuze performance and interceptor-missile-seeker sensitivity and clutter rejection also frustrated predictions for surface or airborne defenses. Electro-optical and IR systems had similarly long lists of uncertainties in predictions.

This study convinced the Lincoln Laboratory management that cruise missiles were an important part of future DoD weapons capabilities and that Lincoln Laboratory had a role to play in their development.

The Air Vehicle Survivability and Air Defense Programs

Late in 1977, with encouragement from the office of the DDR&E, the Laboratory proposed that DARPA take the lead in establishing a sound scientific underpinning to cruise missile survivability and air defense against cruise missiles. The Laboratory proposal outlined a basic scientific, phenomenological effort toward those goals. In 1978, DARPA established the Cruise Missile Detection Technology program at Lincoln Laboratory. Notwithstanding a variety of sponsorship changes and broadening of the charter, that effort has remained a major Laboratory program.

The Laboratory's program began in the Radar Measurements Division in 1977 under Delaney's leadership; the program and the people supporting it joined the Surveillance and Control Division in 1979. The program grew and expanded in that division over the next thirteen years, led first by Delaney and later by Carl Nielsen. In 1992 the Air Defense Technology Division was established under the leadership of Briggs and later Lee Upton to continue the expanding program in air vehicle survivability and air defense.

Notes

1 Material for this chapter was provided by William Delaney.

2 Cruise missiles were not new in 1977; the Germans had launched over 20,000 V-1 "buzz bombs" against England and Allied forces in Belgium during World War II. However, the modern cruise missile was much more sophisticated: smaller, longer range, more accurate and, with its nuclear warhead option, vastly more lethal.

The program was jointly sponsored by DARPA and the office of the Assistant Secretary of the Air Force for Acquisition from 1982 to 1985 and became an Air Force–sponsored program in 1986. It has been called Air Vehicle Survivability Evaluation since 1983.

At the outset the sponsors' goal for this program was ambitious — establishment of a national community of technical understanding and a scientific prediction capability in cruise missile survivability. This goal required Lincoln Laboratory to ensure that its work would be important to and supportive of industry and government efforts throughout the nation. A variety of approaches have been used to make the Laboratory's work widely available and to capture the interest and support of the defense community. Chief among them are the annual Cruise Missile Workshops and the Cruise Missile Technology report series.

A process was developed early in the program to provide confident predictions of cruise missile survivability (Figure 12-1). The intelligence community supplied the enemy air defense models; cruise missile models were provided by U.S. industrial developers via their government sponsors. Lincoln Laboratory's role was to build phenomenological models and predictive models, as needed, and to participate in field tests. Predictions were developed in advance of cruise missile tests; experimental results were subsequently compared with predictions and corrective feedback was given to the modeling process.

Lincoln Laboratory hoped to and did become heavily involved in the field-test part of the process, which the Laboratory's Kwajalein Missile Range experience in the ballistic missile defense area had demonstrated to be critical. The process did work, although it was not always defined as clearly as in Figure 12-1. As an example, the Laboratory found it necessary to commit very substantial efforts to working with the intelligence community to describe and model Soviet air defense systems.

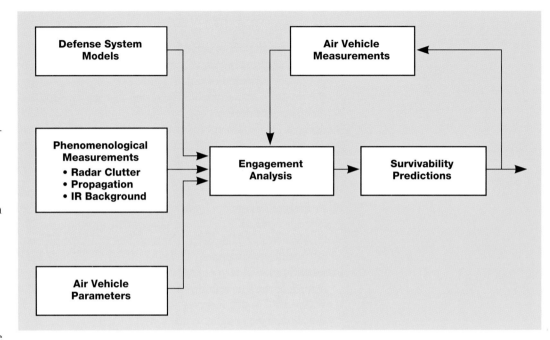

Figure 12-1
Air vehicle survivability prediction process.

Notes

3 J.B. Billingsley, "Ground Clutter Measurements for Surface-Sited Radar," *Lincoln Laboratory Technical Report 786 (Revision 1)*. Lexington, Mass.: MIT Lincoln Laboratory, 1 February 1993, DTIC AD-A262472.

4 S. Ayasli, "SEKE: A Computer Model for Low Altitude Radar Propagation over Irregular Terrain," *IEEE Trans. Antennas Propag.* **AP-34**, 1013 (1986).

5 The DoD never promoted the idea of invisibility, but the press did, and considerable controversy resulted.

6 The U-2 aircraft operated by Gary Powers that was lost in 1960 was shot down by an early Soviet SAM, the SA-2.

Low-Angle Propagation Measurements

A variety of radar propagation experiments were conducted between 1979 and 1990. Initial measurements were performed in Massachusetts, and in 1980 and 1981 measurements were also made at Grand Forks, North Dakota, and at Port Austin, Michigan, the site of the last U.S. VHF air defense radar.

In 1982, the Laboratory built a propagation measurements package that could be conveniently carried on a helicopter. In a typical experiment, the helicopter instruments would record the signal strength as a function of height from the radar of interest. These signal-versus-height profiles would be collected at various ranges and azimuths around the radar, thereby providing a variety of terrain for the signal propagation. Measured terrain profiles would then be used in conjunction with reflection and diffraction theory to deduce the relative importance of each effect.

Clutter and Propagation Models

The previously mentioned data collection enterprise produced a formidable amount of data. (The Phase Zero, Phase One clutter-data tape library contains 4000 high-density computer tapes with a total of about 500 Gbytes of clutter data.) A great deal of effort by many investigators was needed to reduce these data to usable models.[3]

A variety of models of radar clutter have been published. These models offer the user varying degrees of sophistication to suit individual modeling needs. The principal insights of the propagation work have been embodied in the well-known Lincoln Laboratory Spherical Earth with Knife Edges (SEKE) model,[4] which predicts low-angle radar propagation over specified terrain profiles, taking into account multiple combinations of reflection, diffraction and refraction.

Air Defense System Analysis and Modeling

The Lincoln Laboratory approach in a major program area is to conduct broad system studies to guide the phenomenological, technological and experimental work. These studies and concept analyses played an especially prominent role in the air vehicle survivability and air defense program. First, the studies were necessary to guide the design and development of U.S. cruise missiles and aircraft. Second, the concept of low observability was new and much air defense analysis work was needed to assess the impact of low observability on traditional types of air defense and on the design of new defenses. Finally, the prospect of an invisible cruise missile or aircraft piqued the imagination and creative impulses of engineers and scientists throughout the nation.[5] A plethora of ideas to defeat this invisibility flowed forth. Some ideas were conventional, others quite novel. The novel or unconventional air defense approaches also required substantial analysis by the Laboratory.

Conventional Air Defense Analyses

The 1977 Strategic Penetration Technology Study described earlier focused on surface-to-air defenses. These air defense approaches have continued to receive major attention through the ensuing seventeen years of the Lincoln Laboratory program, reflecting the fact that the Soviet Union was the world's most prolific builder and user of such systems.[6] The Laboratory's SAM analyses have looked particularly closely at the SA-10 system, because it is probably the most capable Soviet air defense unit. The Laboratory has issued a substantial number of classified reports on this system.

The second conventional air defense approach involved manned interceptors directed by either ground or airborne radar. Airborne defenses have the very important attribute of being potentially capable of providing broad-area defense against low-altitude targets. In the 1980s, the Soviets had significant defenses of this type, with some three thousand manned interceptors supported by several thousand ground radars.

In 1981 the Laboratory completed a major study of these Soviet defenses. A variety of studies continued over subsequent years on Soviet airborne defenses, with a major focus on characterizing the capability of Soviet look-down, shoot-down interceptors against U.S. cruise missiles.

Unconventional Air Defense Analyses

The Laboratory has also studied a wide variety of novel or unconventional defense schemes. Many of these schemes were applicable to the detection of a low-observable air vehicle at short range, although a robust air defense capability often requires much more than that. An air vehicle should be detected at relatively long range, it should be tracked essentially continuously, some kill mechanism should be guided into close proximity with the air vehicle and the interceptor should kill the vehicle. A weakness in any one of these factors can limit the air defense capability.

Many unconventional defense schemes envision solving the detection problem by proliferating a great number of very simple sensors on the landscape. As pointed out in the section on phenomenology, essentially all sensor systems are limited by background effects. One role of the Lincoln Laboratory investigations has been to characterize these background limitations, which have often been the fatal flaw in unconventional approaches against low-observable vehicles.

The Laboratory has analyzed more than fifty unconventional defense schemes. A partial list gives some idea of the wide range of analyses: acoustic detection and tracking; IR sensor detection and tracking; bistatic radar schemes; occultation of natural cosmic rays by the air vehicle; high-frequency surface-wave radar; detection of chemical emissions from aircraft engines; detection of the aerodynamic wake of an aircraft; radiometric detection approaches; space-based radar and space-based infrared sensors; and ultrawideband or impulse radar approaches.

In many cases, a relatively simple analysis demonstrated that a scheme was unworkable and the investigation stopped there. Other defense schemes required a more substantial investigation, often involving the analysis of existing phenomenological data. A few unconventional defense approaches required a substantial amount of dedicated field testing to be characterized with adequate confidence.

Models and Modeling Tools for Air Defense Analysis

The basic process of Lincoln Laboratory's air vehicle survivability and air defense effort, as diagrammed in Figure 12-1, revolves around the development of a scientific understanding of modern air defense and the embodiment of this understanding in computer models that can predict the outcome of air defense engagements. This process is a substantial challenge, with a wide variety of complicated effects that must be captured in a computer code that must also be easy to use, easy to change, efficient in run time and transparent to the analyst.

The complexities of the low-altitude air defense engagement precluded the possibility of simple generic, or "cookie-cutter," models. The earth's complicated surface, or (in the case of IR systems) complex atmosphere, was heavily enmeshed in the problem. Defense situations had to be analyzed on a site-by-site basis — accumulating statistics from many sites and then finding a way to capture the statistical insight in fast-running computer codes. This process was named site-specific analysis. Lincoln Laboratory became its champion and bore the heavy burden of making it work.

The TRAJ software program, which calculates a radar's signal-to-interference ratio and can separate the effects of terrain masking, clutter, propagation and target radar cross section, became an important radar computer code. TRAJ was used most often to evaluate cruise missile encounters with Soviet surveillance radars. The model was also important for analyses that supported flight testing of U.S. cruise missiles on test ranges.

Soviet SAM systems are often characterized by their footprint, the area on the ground surrounding the SAM battery that is defended by that SAM against a specified model of attacking cruise missile. Lincoln Laboratory developed the premier site-specific predictive air defense, or footprint generator model, the Advanced Surface-to-Air Missile Model (ASAMM).

ASAMM provides the analyst with a tool to examine in detail the performance of each SAM subsystem, and gives an overall system coverage footprint. Multiple computer modules with various degrees of complexity are available for each subsystem of the specified SAM. This flexibility allows the analyst to tune the code to the scenario under study, modeling the key subsystems with the highest fidelity. For example, ASAMM has been used to establish the importance of defensive-missile-seeker clutter rejection in SAM performance against low-altitude cruise missiles. ASAMM is also used for high-altitude intercept modeling, which does not call for seeker clutter calculations. Attention in the high-altitude intercept case can be focused on other issues, such as the endgame, where missile miss distance, fuzing, warhead lethality and endgame countermeasures are important.

In addition to the extensive deployment of SAM batteries, a main line of Soviet air defense comprised numerous manned interceptor aircraft guided by ground radar or airborne AWACS-type systems. Recent Soviet interceptors have sophisticated look-down, shoot-down radar fire-control systems. The Laboratory took on the complex problem of characterizing the limits of such radars against low-observable targets.

A computer model of a look-down fire-control radar was developed through a number of evolutions, finally leading to RADAIR, the current software program. This code was constructed with sufficient modularity so that the user could model many different look-down fire control radars fairly easily. RADAIR allows the user to predict snapshots of the clutter return seen by the radar in any look-down geometry, and also to "fly" a target through a clutter background and emulate the radar's detection process. RADAIR has enabled the Laboratory to understand and to model accurately the inherent limitations in the detection of small, low-altitude targets with an airborne look-down fire control radar. Experimental efforts in this area are described later in this chapter.

Lessons Learned

The Lincoln Laboratory philosophy is that people must analyze problems, aided, but never supplanted, by computer models. No air defense model will ever be broad and flexible enough to capture fully the next tough air defense problem. Therefore, accurate modeling and analysis efforts must continue to rely on talented people whose judgments are based on scientific principles, experimental results and computer models.

Field Instrumentation and Experimentation

Field experimentation has played a critical role throughout the seventeen-year history of the air vehicle survivability and air defense programs. It is the element of the prediction process that ensures the development of confidence in predictions of air vehicle survivability or air defense performance.

The Laboratory's philosophy on field experimentation was enunciated early in the program by William Delaney, the first program manager of the Laboratory's air vehicle survivability activity:

1980

W.P. Delaney

D.L. Briggs

X-band antenna for airborne test bed

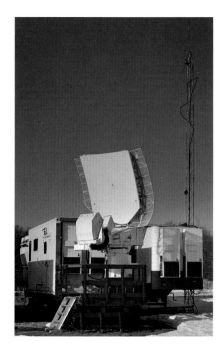

Figure 12-4
The L-X radar system in Lexington, Massachusetts.

"If you think you understand all the interactions, then plan a substantial-scale experiment and predict the results of the experiment beforehand. God won't change physics to make you look good."

Major experiments, participation in major tests and the development of critical field instrumentation have been a substantial part of the Laboratory's effort. Radar, IR and acoustic sensing have each been tested. Some instruments were built to the Laboratory's specifications; others were leased or borrowed for particular experiments. The military services made many weapon systems sensors available through cooperative ventures. The complete list of such initiatives is too great to cover in this brief chapter; only major initiatives and experiments are described here.

L-X Radar

The dual-frequency L-X radar was something of a radar of opportunity in the early 1980s. It was a derivative of a Raytheon AN/TPN-19 aircraft approach guidance radar that had been modified for a proposed artillery location role. Since L-band and X-band were of high interest in cruise missile survivability experiments, the Laboratory contracted with Raytheon in 1980 to modify the radar for a cruise missile testing role. Raytheon delivered the radar in 1982 (Figure 12-4). One of its contributions was early flight data on cruise missile signatures. The radar participated in twelve air-launched and ground-launched cruise missile tests at the Dugway, Utah, test range in 1983 and 1984. It was later used at Nellis Air Force Base, Nevada, and again at Dugway in 1989. The radar was decommissioned in 1990.

VHF Radar

VHF radars are an important element in field tests of the survivability of cruise missiles and other low-observable air vehicles. Even before the development of the modern cruise missile, the Soviets had deployed thousands of VHF ground radars. A particular concern to the United States was that cruise missile signatures tended to be higher at VHF than at microwave frequencies.

In 1983 the Laboratory initiated a competitive procurement for a VHF test range instrument, which was won by General Dynamics of Fort Worth, Texas. This radar, delivered in early 1985, is a very substantial but transportable radar featuring a 150-ft-wide antenna (Figure 12-5). It can emulate such Soviet VHF radars as Tall King and Spoon Rest (although it has superior electronic performance). The radar has undergone a number of modifications and upgrades to enhance its usefulness to the test community.

The principal contribution of the VHF instrumentation radar has been the development of realistic appraisals of VHF radar capability against advanced U.S. cruise missiles and aircraft. VHF radar performance predictions are rich in phenomenological questions relating to low-elevation-angle propagation and ground-clutter effects, and this radar has become the national test bed to explore and define these effects.

1990

ADS-18S antenna, White Sands Missile Range

IDPCA

Mountaintop equipment in Kauai

Figure 12-5
This VHF instrumentation radar could emulate such Soviet radars as Tall King and Spoon Rest.

Acoustic Instrumentation and Experiments

Air vehicles emit relatively loud acoustic signals from their engines and airframes. In the pursuit of low observability to all sensors, the acoustic signal became a concern. Until recently, little information was available on acoustic sensing systems and on their performance in an air defense mode. However, the Lincoln Laboratory Computer Technology Division had fortuitously developed substantial expertise with distributed arrays of seismic and acoustic instruments in support of DoD tactical battlefield initiatives. The staff had developed automated techniques for collecting signals from networks of sensors and establishing tracks on desired targets while rejecting unwanted noise and interference signals.

Between 1984 and 1988, under air vehicle survivability program sponsorship, the Computer Technology Division conducted and supported a variety of acoustic signature measurements on a wide range of military aircraft and cruise missiles. Processing techniques were developed for tracking such vehicles in backgrounds of natural noise and manmade interference. These experiments provided a realistic assessment of the potential threat of acoustic sensing to U.S. air vehicles.

FLEXAR Instrumentation

Essentially all weapons system radars are limited in performance against low-altitude, low-observable targets by ground-clutter residue signals in their receivers. This limitation engendered a seemingly everlasting argument among U.S. analysts (CIA, DIA, Air Force Intelligence, Army Intelligence, U.S. industrial contractors for radars or cruise missiles, military sponsors and government laboratories) on just how good the Soviet radar receivers were. Some postulated immense, others very limited Soviet capabilities.

Of great interest was the Soviet premier air defense SAM, the SA-10. The United States had no direct access to the SA-10, yet the fine details of its receiver and processor design had to be known to estimate its clutter rejection accurately. The next best thing was to look for existing U.S. systems to evaluate the technology limits.

The Hughes Aircraft Company had developed an experimental fire-control radar for Navy shipboard application called FLEXAR. Hughes was one of the world's leading companies in the field of clutter rejection, having pioneered the F-14 and F-15 look-down radars, so FLEXAR had state-of-the-art clutter rejection. The SA-10 and FLEXAR had similar origins; each was a surface radar system based on airborne radar technology.

The Laboratory conducted field experiments with the FLEXAR system from 1983 to 1986. It was first used to characterize the clutter rejection capability of high- and medium-pulse-repetition-frequency ground radars. It was later used at Eglin Air Force Base, Florida, and the China Lake, California, test range to evaluate U.S. electronic countermeasures against Soviet radars. Although FLEXAR did not settle the SA-10 clutter rejection arguments, it did add a healthy measure of real-world data to the debate.

Fuze Experimentation and Testing

Another element in the air defense chain is the RF proximity fuze, which is basically a short-range radar mounted in a guided missile that initiates a warhead detonation sequence when it detects a target. Because there was no consensus on the performance of existing fuzes against low-observable targets, an experiment was carried out in 1984 at an indoor fuze testing facility. This test was followed in 1987 by a larger measurement program with scaled targets and fuzes. A great number of missile flyby trajectories were simulated in this program and the extensive test results were used to validate a model developed at the Laboratory for assessing fuze performance. This model has since been used on a variety of targets.

Enhanced Insight

The phenomenological work by Lincoln Laboratory on clutter and propagation confirmed that the DoD can deduce and predict the fundamental effects underlying the success or failure of major weapons systems. The legacy of this critical phenomenological work was best captured by J. Barrie Billingsley, the Lincoln Laboratory principal clutter investigator, at the 1984 Cruise Missile Workshop, when he concluded his talk with an analogy concerning how high-quality, multi-frequency, multisite clutter and propagation data enhanced his insight:

"We had heard the violins and the horns and the woodwinds before, but now we could understand the whole orchestration — how frequency, terrain, propagation, resolution and polarization all operated together to produce the complex result we had witnessed but did not understand."

Technical talks seldom get spontaneous applause, but this one did!

signal and transmit back to the radar a signal that looked like a low-flying, low-observable target. This device immensely simplified the experiments; it could be placed in a wide variety of clutter scenes, from benign clutter (ocean or flat fields) to moderate clutter (farmland or forest) to severe clutter (mountains or cities). The actual size of the simulator's return could be varied from a large target to a quite low observable one. A detailed characterization of the AN/APG-68 radar was developed and compared with the predictions; the causes of differences were then determined. These results guided general assessments of look-down radars and supported airborne radar computer simulation. The success of this effort led to a similar one on the F-15 radars, the AN/APG-63 and the latest version called the AN/APG-70 (Figure 12-7).

The expertise acquired in the look-down radar test program has been shared with other members of the U.S. airborne fire-control radar community. The RADAIR computer simulation of look-down fighter capability (described earlier) has been distributed to a number of organizations investigating fire-control radar issues.

Airborne Seeker Test-Bed Experiments and Endgame Countermeasures Evaluation

Successful engagement of cruise missiles by enemy air defenses requires success in three distinct processes: (1) surveillance, for initial detection; (2) fire control, for track of the target; and (3) intercept, for kill of the target. Low-observable techniques attack all three of these processes, and overall enemy air defenses are limited by the weakest link.

In many situations the kill process is the weakest link. Because guns have very short effective ranges, a guided missile almost always makes the kill of the attacking cruise missile or aircraft. The missile is most often guided by a radar or IR seeker in its nose; thus the seeker must be small to fit in the missile's streamlined airframe. Therefore, in the interest of small size, low weight and reasonable cost, the seeker must be restricted to a small antenna (or optics aperture) and a limited amount of on-board electronics, constraints that often conspire to make the seeker the most vulnerable element in engagement of a cruise missile.

Assessing the performance limits of missile seekers and the impact of countermeasures is an important part of the air vehicle survivability program at Lincoln Laboratory. Early in the program the work was largely analytic, but in 1985 the Laboratory's efforts in analyzing the Improved HAWK SAM live firings and the Sparrow air-to-air missile live firings against cruise missiles, along with continued advances in countermeasure design, pointed to the need for an experimental mechanism to investigate missile seeker performance. Since firing actual missiles against targets would be an expensive and cumbersome way to gain this insight, the Airborne Seeker Test Bed (ASTB) effort was started.

The concept of the ASTB is to configure a jet aircraft to represent a missile. The nose of the jet houses the seeker sensor heads and the fuselage carries processing electronics and other antennas needed to emulate a surface-to-air or air-to-air missile. Many auxiliary sensors and extensive data recording equipment are carried, making the ASTB essentially a flying seeker laboratory. In 1986, Raytheon Missile Systems Division of Bedford, Massachusetts, received the contract to build the first major sensor, an X-band semiactive homing instrumentation head, which was then integrated with the other parts of the system developed at Lincoln Laboratory.

The ASTB design was kept as flexible as possible to allow it to collect data pertinent to a wide variety of U.S. and Soviet missiles, e.g., U.S. and Soviet IR-guided missiles, Improved Hawk, Patriot, Standard Missile, Sparrow, AMRAAM and Soviet SA-10. The somewhat bulbous nose of the aircraft, a Dassault Falcon 20 twin-engine jet, houses the radar missile seeker under test. The ASTB also carries other auxiliary sensors, including an IR camera and a global positioning system (GPS) receiver. Wing pylons support interchangeable pods that include a beacon tracker and various IR and RF seekers (Figure 12-8).

Figure 12-7
Test of the AN/APG-70 radar in an F-15 aircraft at Edwards Air Force Base, California. Vicki Melchior is standing next to the aircraft, Mark Wiener is sitting in the back seat and Jack Jones, a Hughes employee working at Edwards, is in the front.

Figure 12-8
Airborne Seeker Test Bed.

The first series of experiments was conducted in the spring of 1990. Early experimentation with the ASTB focused on clutter and target-scattering issues of importance in modeling missile seeker capability. These issues included the fluctuations of aircraft radar return strength and its polarization behavior, the characterization of ground clutter and the signal-propagation effects. These data are being used to ensure the accuracy of computer models of missile performance now under development.

The ASTB has also been used to evaluate the vulnerability of a variety of U.S. air vehicles to missile attack. In a typical survivability test, the target aircraft would fly at low altitude while the ASTB dived from above on a proportional navigation collision course. A look angle representative of an actual missile intercept would be maintained until the ASTB pulled out of its dive (prior to the collision point).

On its return from an extensive first measurement campaign in January 1991, the ASTB was able to respond quickly to a unique test opportunity in support of Operation Desert Shield. Eight missions were flown to help the U.S. Air Force prepare its air defense fighter forces for combat with the Iraqi Air Force. Although particulars of these tests are classified, the ASTB provided a unique source of insight for U.S. pilots training to combat potential Iraqi countermeasure tactics.

Countermeasures against missile seekers that operate in the last few seconds before intercept are often called endgame countermeasures. They tend to exploit the inherently poor angular resolution of the seeker caused by its small antenna. Endgame countermeasures are expensive to remedy, often requiring a multiple-mode seeker such as a radar/IR dual-mode sensor. Many efforts are under way to improve understanding of these countermeasures and to find economical ways to deal with them.

Since 1990 the ASTB has played a key role in the scientific characterization of endgame countermeasures and the rigorous investigation of counter-countermeasure techniques. The ASTB sensor suite is currently being upgraded to support experiments involving multispectral techniques that capitalize on the resolution capabilities of IR and millimeter-wave sensors to combat enemy countermeasures.

The Army Missile and Space Intelligence Center (MSIC) has the responsibility to characterize Soviet SAM seekers, and this agency, along with the Air Force, has contributed significantly to the funding of the ASTB development effort. The ASTB has become a national asset and has found use in programs for all the services and ARPA. Data have been widely distributed in the government and industry.

Lessons Learned

Field experimental work is difficult, and thousands of hours of hard work, travel, disappointment, argument, frustration and a few bright moments of success underlie this brief summary. The field workers are the heroes of the Lincoln Laboratory air vehicle survivability program, for it is they who provided the critical element of confidence via experimental verification of the Laboratory's analyses and predictions.

Advanced Air Defense Technology

The Lincoln Laboratory air vehicle programs between 1977 and 1984 focused almost exclusively on understanding and modeling the survivability of U.S. cruise missiles against existing or possible new Soviet air defenses. These in-depth investigations gave the Laboratory a substantial head start on the complementary question: how to develop advanced air defenses to counter enemy cruise missiles. A number of classified activities began in the mid-1980s, and the Laboratory has played an important part in their definition and execution. Two major activities can be discussed here.

The concept of the Mountaintop program was to use the UHF experimental radar on a mountaintop to emulate an airborne radar. Through the use of an ingenious technique developed at Lincoln Laboratory, stationary ground clutter seen by the radar can be made to appear to be moving at airplane velocity. Thus much of the initial experimentation on advanced techniques for airborne radar clutter mitigation can proceed without the cost burden of a large radar on a large aircraft.

Experimentation on adaptive space-time clutter processing and jammer mitigation techniques was carried out at White Sands in 1993. During 1994 the radar moved again, this time to Makaha Ridge on the island of Kauai, Hawaii, for a continuing series of tests with U.S. Navy assets.

National Leadership

In 1977 Lincoln Laboratory was challenged by DARPA and the office of the DDR&E to provide a strong scientific basis in survivability analysis to support the design and development of the new air vehicles known as cruise missiles. A corollary challenge was to improve the quality of the survivability analysis work throughout the national community. The approach that quickly evolved was to "raise the ante" on the quality of survivability analyses, predictions and experiments by setting the example.

A number of factors helped start this process. Cruise missiles were new, interesting and important to the nation. Many questions and problems needed to be addressed. DARPA was an enlightened sponsor with a reputation for independence and for taking the lead on national technical issues. Moreover, the technical challenges in this area attracted and motivated a cadre of exceptionally talented engineers and scientists from outside Lincoln Laboratory to interact with the Laboratory staff and provide independent and valuable augmentation to, and sometimes argument with, the Laboratory's perspective. All these talented individuals, more than any other factor, made for the success of the Laboratory's effort to enhance the national capability in the cruise missile survivability area. Later, the strong leadership of the Air Force sponsor consolidated the program and its activities became focused on survivability issues in major national efforts.

The Laboratory's goal of raising the ante on quality demanded that the staff find a means to interact with the community and publicize their work. Two initiatives instituted early in the program, and still followed, have accomplished this: the Cruise Missile Workshops and the Cruise Missile Technology series of technical reports.

The Cruise Missile Workshops

Lincoln Laboratory conducted its first Cruise Missile Workshop in the fall of 1979. It became an annual event and Workshop Number 16 was conducted in the spring of 1994. This annual meeting was renamed the Air Vehicle Survivability Workshop in May 1995.

The Workshop is an intensive three-day symposium typically featuring thirty half-hour technical talks by Laboratory staff on key results, ongoing work and new initiatives. (One visitor described it as a "core dump" on Lincoln Laboratory's work for the past year.) About ten outside speakers also give presentations, generally on such topics of interest as intelligence perspectives or recent cruise missile test results. Attendance is by invitation only, and the sponsors and Lincoln Laboratory invite only the members of the air defense technical community. In addition, since Room A-166, until recently the Laboratory's largest meeting room, holds a maximum of 125 people, deciding whom to invite can be an onerous task. And like airline flights, the meeting is always overbooked in anticipation of last-minute no-shows.

The Workshop quickly became *the* national meeting on survivability prediction, and it helped establish Lincoln Laboratory as a national entity in survivability analysis. There have a number of testimonies to the success of the Cruise Missile Workshop approach, the best of which are that each year for sixteen years the audience has reported, "This was the best workshop yet."

The Cruise Missile Technology Report Series

The Laboratory's protocol from the start included dissemination of all aspects of its work through technical reports. The Cruise Missile Technology, or CMT, report series was started for this purpose, and more than 180 CMT reports have been published to date. The report series by itself is a national archive on air vehicle survivability and advanced air defense.

Retrospective

This major national effort has had an important legacy: a healthy dose of the scientific method can keep complicated DoD weapons system efforts on a sound, credible track. And a federally funded laboratory like Lincoln Laboratory is ideally constituted to foster such an effort.

Another lesson from the success of this program is the importance of enlightened sponsor leadership. The program enjoyed continuous encouragement and support from the various Directors of Defense Research and Engineering over its seventeen-year history. DARPA had the vision to initiate the effort and the Air Force provided the strong commitment to sustain it and promote its growth into a national effort. The Air Force and DARPA program managers were all committed to a confident scientific understanding of the cruise missiles' strengths *and* weaknesses, and the Lincoln Laboratory team enjoyed the autonomy to "call them as they saw them." This activity is an example of how the DoD acquisition process is improved when government program managers assume the role of their own worst enemy, and thereby discover the shortcomings of their programs early in the acquisitions process, when time, money and the bureaucracy can accommodate substantial remedies and modifications.

The development of the modern cruise missile in the late 1970s opened another chapter in the evolution of weapons systems and the options for countering them. The Cruise Missile Detection Technology program provided Lincoln Laboratory the opportunity, and the privilege, to play a central national role. This role has included providing a national corporate memory for modern air offense penetration and modern air defense techniques. The continuing program is dedicated to supporting the DoD, all the services, ARPA and industry in these areas.

Notes

1 This section was contributed by Benjamin Lax.

2 A.L. McWhorter, "1/*f* Noise and Germanium Surface Properties," in *Semiconductor Surface Physics*, ed. R.H. Kingston. Philadelphia: University of Pennsylvania Press, 1957, p. 207.

3 R.H. Kingston, "Switching Time in Junction Diodes and Junction Transistors," *Proc. IRE* **42**, 829 (1954).

4 C.L. Hogan, "The Ferromagnetic Faraday Effect at Microwave Frequencies and Its Applications: The Microwave Gyrator," *Bell System Tech. J.* **31**, 1 (1952).

A nonreciprocal device is one that has different transmission properties in two directions. It can be used to separate signals that would otherwise interfere. In the case of radar, nonreciprocal devices separate the transmitted signal from the received signal so that the received signal goes into the receiver, but the transmitted signal does not. Because transmitted signals are many times more powerful than received signals, nonreciprocal devices are crucial to the operation of radar systems.

5 B. Lax, K.J. Button and L.M. Roth, "Ferrite Phase Shifters in Rectangular Wave Guide," *J. Appl. Phys.* **25**, 1413 (1954).

6 P.E. Tannenwald, "Ferromagnetic Resonance in Manganese Ferrite Single Crystals," *Phys. Rev.* **100**, 1713 (1955).

Indeed, it is in large part because of the close vertical integration of device physics with solid state science, materials and processing technology that the Solid State Division has established an international reputation as one of the premier participants in the field.

Early Solid State Physics and Device Research

Even during the early 1950s, when the work of every staff member was directed toward the goal of completing the design of the SAGE air defense system, basic research in solid state physics received strong support from Lincoln Laboratory management.[1] Professor Jerrold Zacharias, the first associate director of the Laboratory, was particularly interested in this area because he was among the first to recognize the potential of the transistor for fast, reliable computer operation. Therefore, he made the decision to create a group to study the physics and applications of semiconductors.

Zacharias recruited Richard Adler, then a young professor of electrical engineering at MIT, to head what became the Solid State and Transistor Group. Once Adler was on board, he began to recruit other physicists, engineers and chemists. In the summer of 1951 the first staff members joined the group which by the end of the year consisted of about twenty professional staff members. It grew to over fifty by the end of 1952.

The solid state programs began to take shape. The physicists and electrical engineers built and acquired equipment for measuring the properties of transistor devices. The chemists assembled equipment for growing crystals and for exploring the chemical and surface properties of semiconductors.

A visit by Lester Hogan of Bell Telephone Laboratories in 1952 excited the interest of Robert Fox and Benjamin Lax in the potential of ferrites for microwave radar applications. In the summer of 1953 they were authorized to form the Ferrite Group with Lax as group leader. He soon recognized that the program offered an extraordinary opportunity for basic research: the same microwave techniques that were being used for device development could be exploited to uncover the fundamental properties of ferrites and of semiconductors.

Thus began a highly successful program in resonance spectroscopy of solids. Most notable among the group's achievements were measurements of cyclotron resonance in germanium and silicon. These experiments measured for the first time the values of the tensor masses of electrons and the mass parameters of holes in these materials, and produced the first detailed models of the band structures of semiconductors.

The cyclotron resonance work triggered research in the United States, Europe and elsewhere that led to an understanding of the basic transport and optical properties of semiconductors. As an indication of the respect the international community had developed for Lincoln Laboratory's program, the American Physical Society awarded the 1960 Buckley Prize to Lax for the development of cyclotron resonance and magneto-optical spectroscopy (Figure 13-1).

Some administrative changes were made in 1953. Adler returned to his teaching duties on the campus, and MIT Professor Earl Thomas became leader of the Solid State and Transistor Group, a post he held for two years.

The year 1954 began a productive period for solid state research at Lincoln Laboratory. The Ferrite Group presented for the first time complete data about the energy band structures for both electrons and holes in germanium and silicon. The results stirred a great deal of excitement because the understanding of the carrier transport properties saw immediate application in device design. The Ferrite Group also began theoretical and experimental work on ferrite devices that soon replaced such World War II–era radar components as transmit-receive vacuum-tube switches, which allowed use of a common antenna for transmission and reception. Ferrite devices such as circulators and isolators were under development for such applications.

The Solid State Group began its work on surfaces, which ultimately led Professor Alan McWhorter to formulate a theory of the 1/*f* noise in semiconductor devices that tied it to fundamental physical processes at the semiconductor surface, and to publish a paper on the subject that became a classic in the field.[2] The group also developed a theory of the transient response of *p-n* junction and related devices that is still cited in the literature.[3]

Figure 13-1
Benjamin Lax explains the theory of cyclotron resonance in indium antimonide and bismuth.

Thomas left Lincoln Laboratory in 1955 and Lax was appointed as his successor. The two solid state groups were then merged into one, the Solid State Group.

With the merger of the two groups, interest began to broaden into magneto-optics and quantum electronics. In the spring of 1956, the Solid State Group announced its plan to use the Bitter magnet concept to produce extremely high dc magnetic fields, which would enable scientists to perform various experiments in solid state transport and spectroscopy that were difficult with pulsed fields. The goal was to produce a field of 250 kG, 2.5 times that achieved by Professor Francis Bitter in the basement of Building 6 at MIT. The results of this effort ultimately led to the creation of the Francis Bitter National Magnet Laboratory at MIT.

By 1958 the growing reputation and size of the Solid State Group made an administrative change imperative. The group, which had been a part of the Communications Division, was set up as a new division, the Solid State Division, with Lax as the head. From this point on, research expanded into a wide range of areas within the general solid state field, with particular emphasis on quantum electronics and solid state devices. Lax continued as division head until 1964, when he was succeeded by Harry Gatos. McWhorter was appointed head of the Solid State Division in 1965 and held the position until 1994, when he became the first division fellow and David Shaver became division head.

Ferrites

The Solid State Group first became aware of the possibility of using ferrites in microwave circuits when Lester Hogan of Bell Telephone Laboratories visited Lincoln Laboratory early in 1952. He explained how Faraday rotation could be used to make a nonreciprocal device that operated at microwave frequencies.[4]

Hogan was successful because he took advantage of the unique features of ferrites, materials that are magnetic yet are electric insulators. It was immediately apparent that the application of ferrites in microwave components was an essential and desirable activity for Lincoln Laboratory to undertake. Thus began a program to study the properties of ferrites and to develop devices for modern radars, including isolators, circulators and phase shifters.

Not long after Hogan initiated the use of ferrites by applying Faraday rotation, a new concept was introduced by a group at the Naval Research Laboratory. They proposed a circulator that utilized a single rectangular slab in a rectangular waveguide, and this device also exhibited nonreciprocal behavior.

The rectangular waveguide turned out to provide a seminal problem, and its solution was analytically obtained and numerically analyzed by Lax, Kenneth Button and Laura Roth.[5] Further analysis led to the invention of the twin-slab configuration, which is still used in phased arrays employing ferrite phase shifters.

Extensive experimental measurements of differential nonreciprocal phase shifts in rectangular waveguides containing ferrite slabs for various different ferrite parameters at a variety of microwave frequencies were investigated by Fox and compared with the theoretical results. These experiments led directly to the development of devices that could operate at frequencies of 500 MHz to 3 GHz.

The Solid State Group concurrently started a program to measure the microwave and magnetic properties of ferrites. A new staff member, Simon Foner, joined the group to concentrate on measuring the magnetic susceptibilities of a variety of ferrites and on developing instruments for such measurements. He invented the Foner magnetometer, which is still used in susceptibility measurements. His paper describing the magnetometer has been cited unusually widely in the technical literature.

On the microwave end, Peter Tannenwald extended the microwave resonant studies from the tensor properties of polycrystalline materials to those of single crystals.[6] From these measurements the anisotropy parameters of single crystals were deduced; in fact, all necessary microwave properties were made available to the device designers.

By 1956 the device research effort had moved into both lower and higher frequencies. The program now encompassed the electromagnetic spectrum from 600 MHz to millimeter wave.

Notes

19 B. Lax and Y. Nishina, "Interband Faraday Rotation in III-V Compounds," *J. Appl. Phys. Suppl.* **32**, 2128 (1961).

20 R.J. Keyes, S. Zwerdling, S. Foner, H.H. Kolm and B. Lax, "Infrared Cyclotron Resonance in Bi, InSb, and InAs with High Pulsed Magnetic Fields," *Phys. Rev.* **104**, 1804 (1956).

21 B. Lax, J.G. Mavroides, H.J. Zeiger and R.J. Keyes, "Infrared Magnetoreflection in Bismuth. I. High Fields," *Phys. Rev. Lett.* **5**, 241 (1960).

22 R.N. Brown, J.G. Mavroides and B. Lax, "Magnetoreflection in Bismuth," *Phys. Rev.* **129**, 2055 (1963).

23 H.E.D. Scovil, G. Feher and H. Seidel, "Operation of a Solid State Maser," *Phys. Rev.* **105**, 762 (1957).

24 A.L. McWhorter and J.W. Meyer, "Solid-State Maser Amplifier," *Phys. Rev.* **109**, 312 (1958).

25 A.L. McWhorter, J.W. Meyer and P.D. Strum, "Noise Temperature Measurement on a Solid State Maser," *Phys. Rev.* **108**, 1642 (1957).

26 R.H. Kingston, "A UHF Solid-State Maser," *Proc. IRE* **46**, 916 (1958).

27 S. Foner and L.R. Momo, "CW Millimeter Wave Maser Using Fe³⁺ in TiO₂," *J. Appl. Phys.* **31**, 742 (1960).

28 This section is taken from an article by I. Melngailis, "Laser Development at Lincoln Laboratory," *Linc. Lab. J.* **3**, 347 (1990).

The phenomenon was then investigated in indium antimonide, which led to the discovery of the anomalous magnetic moment of the electron for the first time. Laura Roth, who had just joined Lincoln Laboratory, used the theory created by Professor Joaquin Luttinger of the University of Wisconsin to explain the anomaly and developed a formula for it.

The next phase of the work was to study the Zeeman effect of impurities. The experimental work of Solomon Zwerdling and coworkers, together with theoretical work of Roth and Lax, made further contributions to the quantitative understanding of semiconductors. The spin-orbit splitting in silicon and the effective mass of the previously inaccessible valence band were measured for the first time.

Following this work, studies began on interband Faraday rotation in indium antimonide. Richard Brown, a graduate student at MIT working at Lincoln Laboratory, observed an anomaly as the wavelength approached the energy gap. This discovery, which was later explained theoretically and identified as the interband contribution,[19] led to the development of the interband Faraday rotation isolator, now used in the Firepond laser radar.

For his Ph.D. thesis, George Wright looked at the infrared magnetoplasma effect in such low-gap semiconductors as HgSe and InSb. He determined the masses of degenerate electrons in highly doped semiconductors, the densities and the relaxation time.

Interestingly, the first interband magnetoabsorption experiment was performed on the semimetal bismuth with pulsed magnets in 1956.[20] At that time, it was interpreted as cyclotron resonance. It was not until 1960 that Lax and coworkers reanalyzed the data and deduced that an interband phenomenon had been observed.[21] Subsequently, Brown performed much cleaner experiments using magnetoreflection in a Varian magnet at low temperatures, which confirmed the phenomenon in semimetals.[22]

Mildred Dresselhaus and John Mavroides later extended the studies to alloys of bismuth and antimony and to graphite. These elegant experiments and their interpretation established Dresselhaus as a prominent scientist.

The magneto-optical studies established another important tool for examining the energy band structure of semiconductors. The technique complemented cyclotron resonance when possible and replaced it when the other method was not feasible.

Masers

When Professor Nicolaas Bloembergen of Harvard University conceived of the three-level paramagnetic maser in 1956, he was serving as a consultant to the ferrite program. Since the facilities and equipment then in use for this program happened to be suitable for building a maser, when Bloembergen suggested prior to publishing his concept that Lincoln Laboratory embark on a project to build such a maser, the Solid State Group was in a good position to do so.

James Meyer was immediately assigned to the task of constructing a double-resonant cavity that would provide a pump frequency in the X-band and a signal frequency in the L-band. He was soon joined in the project by McWhorter and Stanley Autler. Their initial attempt used nickel fluorosilicate, but even at higher frequencies they were not successful.

In the meantime, a team at Bell Laboratories had demonstrated the operation of a three-level maser oscillator in gadolinium thiosulfate.[23] The race, however, was not yet lost. The Bell Laboratories crystal was not suitable for practical application as an amplifier.

After a search of the literature, McWhorter came up with the fortunate choice of potassium cobalt cyanide doped with chromium for the maser crystal. The crystal was immediately grown by Harry Gatos, who directed the chemistry work, and it proved to be highly successful.[24]

The maser operated both as an amplifier and as an S-band oscillator at a temperature of 1.25K and a frequency of 2800 MHz. This accomplishment proved for the first time that the maser could meet the objective of providing a low-temperature, low-noise amplifier (Figure 13-2).

Figure 13-2
Robert Kingston and Alan McWhorter demonstrate the first maser amplifier.

The program soon adopted a practical objective: to make the maser into an operational low-noise amplifier. A ferrite circulator was incorporated into the system and an apparatus was constructed to measure the noise temperature. McWhorter and coworkers established an upper limit of approximately 20K as its equivalent noise temperature.[25]

Robert Kingston joined the maser team and began work on pushing the frequency range of the maser into the L-band portion of the UHF.[26] Among other advantages, a maser frequency of 1400 MHz would permit the hydrogen line in space to be observed with greater sensitivity. A unique feature of the L-band maser was that it incorporated a superconducting loop to provide the resonant circuit inside the microwave cavity.

The maser effort proliferated in several directions, including such projects as the construction of a maser radiometer, an S-band maser radar and one of the first uses of a ruby crystal for a tunable L-band maser. The ruby-based tunable L-band maser incorporated a novel technique: a superconducting coil of niobium provided a highly stable magnetic field in a persistent mode. Two decades later, interest in superconductors was reborn at the Laboratory in an effort conducted by the Analog Device Technology Group.

Higher frequencies now beckoned, and the next objective was millimeter-wave spectroscopy. The question of sources was the most difficult, so the group began to investigate techniques of harmonic generation. Staff members looked for harmonics in magnetrons, crystal multipliers, ferrite frequency multipliers and varactor diodes. They built such components as resonant isolators, three-port circulators and superheterodyne receivers.

Simon Foner and Lynn Momo extended the operation of the maser into the millimeter range. Fe^{3+} in a TiO_2 dielectric was found to be suitable, and a tunable maser pumped at 4 mm was operated at frequencies of 26 to 39 GHz.[27]

The millimeter-wave spectrometers were used to study cyclotron, ferromagnetic and antiferromagnetic resonances in a variety of solids. When these spectrometers were combined with the 50-kG Varian magnet, Lincoln Laboratory had equipment for spectroscopy that was unmatched in the world.

Lasers

Laser research at Lincoln Laboratory began in 1962, soon after the invention of the laser, and it has continued as a major component of several programs for three decades.[28] Initial work was centered on semiconductor lasers; a strong effort persists in this area, especially in the development of materials to produce emission in the broad wavelength range from 0.3 μm in the ultraviolet to 30 μm in the infrared. Applications of semiconductor lasers have included spectroscopy, pollution monitoring, radars and communications. In particular, the development of quaternary InGaAsP diode lasers for the low-fiber-loss wavelength range of 1.3 to 1.5 μm has been one of Lincoln Laboratory's most significant contributions.

Through publications, direct contacts and spin-off companies, work performed at Lincoln Laboratory has found its way into the commercial sector. Former staff members have used technologies developed in the Solid State Division to form two companies: Laser Analytics (now part of Laser Photonics), founded in 1974 for the commercialization of spectroscopic and pollution-monitoring devices; and Lasertron, created in 1980 for the manufacture of fiber optic communications components.

In the 1970s Lincoln Laboratory developed ionic solid state lasers, which serve as broadly wavelength-tunable sources. Chief among the achievements of this effort was the invention and development of the titanium sapphire ($Ti:Al_2O_3$) laser.

Tunable from 0.65 to 1.12 μm, $Ti:Al_2O_3$ lasers are versatile devices whose applications include agile-beam laser radars and laser medicine. $Ti:Al_2O_3$ lasers are now manufactured by a number of organizations, including Schwartz Electro-Optics, where ex–Lincoln Laboratory staff played a key role in the laser's commercialization. Closely linked to the solid state laser research has been the development of frequency mixing and doubling techniques to produce sources at new wavelengths.

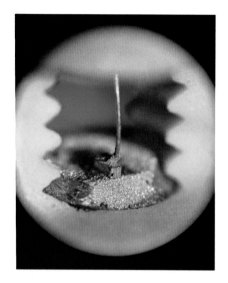

Figure 13-3
One of the first GaAs diode lasers fabricated at Lincoln Laboratory. The first Laboratory GaAs diode laser was developed in October 1962.

Notes

29 (a) P.L. Kelley, "Laser-Related Research at Lincoln Laboratory: A Historical Review — Part 1," *Laser Focus* **18**, 28 (August 1982); "Laser-Related Research at Lincoln Laboratory: A Historical Review — Part 2," *Laser Focus* **18**, 32 (September 1982); (b) R.H. Rediker, I. Melngailis and A. Mooradian, "Lasers, Their Development, and Applications at M.I.T. Lincoln Laboratory," *IEEE J. Quantum Electron.* **QE-20**, 602 (1984); (c) "Special Issue on Laser Technology," *Linc. Lab. J.* **3**, 347–500 (1990).

30 T.M. Quist, R.H. Rediker, R.J. Keyes, W.E. Krag, B. Lax, A.L. McWhorter and H.J. Zeiger, "Semiconductor Maser of GaAs," *Appl. Phys. Lett.* **1**, 91 (1962).

Research on gas lasers began in 1963. The work was aimed at achieving a new level of spectral purity and stability for applications in coherent laser radar and high-precision spectroscopy. These ultrastable devices enabled the demonstration of CO_2 laser radars at the Firepond site in Westford, Massachusetts, starting in the late 1960s. For the submillimeter portion of the spectrum, Lincoln Laboratory developed gas lasers that provided a large number of wavelengths in the range from 58 to 755 μm for use in spectroscopy and as sources for testing submillimeter-wavelength detectors.

Besides developing laser technology, Lincoln Laboratory has made important contributions to laser physics and to the science of laser materials. Fundamental studies were carried out on the band structure of semiconductor laser materials, nonlinear optics, light-scattering phenomena and high-resolution spectroscopy of gas molecules. The development of semiconductor epitaxial growth techniques and the study of ionic solid state crystals provided a base for advances in laser technology.

The numerous scientific and technological achievements in laser development at Lincoln Laboratory have resulted from a close collaboration of physicists, materials scientists and device engineers. More detailed descriptions of Lincoln Laboratory's lasers and their applications have appeared in several review articles.[29]

Semiconductor Lasers

Research on lasers at Lincoln Laboratory began in 1962, just after Hughes Research Laboratory's demonstration of the first laser in 1961. That first laser was a lamp-pumped ruby, but investigators at Lincoln Laboratory were speculating about the possibility of laser emission in other media, including semiconductors. The Solid State Division had extensive experience in semiconductor research, putting it in a good position to investigate such materials.

A key factor was Lincoln Laboratory's expertise in GaAs materials and device technology. In 1958 Robert Rediker, leader of the Applied Physics Group, decided to pursue GaAs, rather than silicon technology, which at the time was becoming the focus of semiconductor research at most other laboratories. Although the initial work on GaAs was aimed at high-speed electronic devices, it was soon discovered that GaAs diodes, in contrast to silicon and germanium diodes, were efficient light emitters. Thus early in 1962 Robert Keyes and Theodore Quist observed quantum efficiencies of 85% in spontaneous emission from GaAs diodes at 0.84 μm. This observation set the stage for a race to develop the first diode laser. By that fall, Quist and his coworkers at Lincoln Laboratory had demonstrated a diode laser (Figure 13-3),[30] but groups at GE and IBM had independently also developed GaAs diode lasers. At this same time, McWhorter, Zeiger and Lax developed a theoretical model of the semiconductor laser that identified some of its unique characteristics.

In the following years, work in the Solid State Division concentrated on developing lasers in other semiconductor materials to cover different parts of the wavelength spectrum (Figure 13-4). Although the motivation for the investigations during the early stage was primarily scientific, lasers fabricated from the different materials subsequently found application in numerous areas, including spectroscopy and fiber communications.

Several milestones are worth noting. In 1963, Ivars Melngailis observed laser emission at 3.1 μm in InAs diodes and in the ternary compound InGaAs at 1.8 and 2.1 μm. Robert Phelan obtained emission in InSb at 5.1 μm. In 1964 Rediker, Jack Butler and coworkers fabricated lasers in the IV-VI lead salts: PbTe at 6.4 μm and PbSe at 8.3 μm.

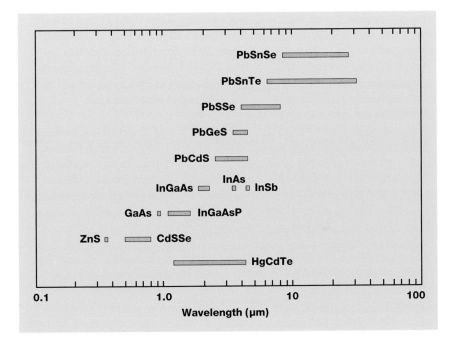

Figure 13-4
Wavelengths of semiconductor lasers that were developed at Lincoln Laboratory.

From Luminescence to the Diode Laser

"The thing that really set it off was going to a device conference and hearing a paper by Keyes and Quist."
— Robert Hall*

"I don't remember the junction luminescence reports at SSRDC of any group except that of Keyes and Quist. I think the reason for this was the impressive nature of the Keyes and Quist report of GaAs *p-n* junction luminescence, its high efficiency, and the fact that GaAs junctions had already been used to transmit signals."
— Nick Holonyak**

On July 9, 1962, Robert Keyes presented a paper coauthored with Theodore Quist to the Solid State Device Research Conference held at the University of New Hampshire that reported a luminescence efficiency for GaAs diffused diodes approaching 100%. This was an extraordinary result; previous estimates of the efficiency of light-emitting diodes had been in the range of 0.01%. The audience was astounded. In the questions following Keyes's talk, a conference attendee from Bell Laboratories questioned the measurement by arguing that it might violate the second law of thermodynamics. To this challenge Keyes replied that he was truly very sorry, drawing gales of laughter from the listeners.

A number of researchers immediately recognized that a material this efficient could meet the requirements for a semiconductor laser. Robert Hall, a conference attendee from the General Electric Research and Development Center in Schenectady, New York, began planning an experiment on the train home. Nick Holonyak, then working at the General Electric Laboratory in Syracuse, New York, and also an expert in the field, promptly set out to develop a GaAsP diode that could emit radiation in the visible. Marshall Nathan, working in the field at the IBM Research Center in Yorktown Heights, New York, had not attended the conference, but his management clipped an article about it from the next day's *New York Times* and urged him to develop a semiconductor laser as quickly as possible.

The race was on. Each of the researchers knew that someone would develop a semiconductor laser before the year was over, and each was determined to be first. Hall had not been working specifically on semiconductor lasers before the Keyes and Quist talk, yet he was the first to succeed, reporting the development of a semiconductor laser in a paper received on September 24. Nathan's group at IBM followed closely, reporting their laser on October 6. Holonyak announced a GaAsP semiconductor laser on October 17. At Lincoln Laboratory, lasing of GaAs was demonstrated during the first part of October and results were reported to *Applied Physics Letters* on October 23.

Four groups, each working independently, had produced a semiconductor diode laser within a single month. And all were inspired to action by a report of highly efficient luminescence given at a small conference in New Hampshire.

* R.N. Hall in J. Hecht, ed., *Laser Pioneers*. New York: Academic Press, 1992, p. 181.
** N. Holonyak, Jr., "Semiconductor Lasers — 1962," *IEEE J. Quantum Electron.* QE-23, 684 (1987).

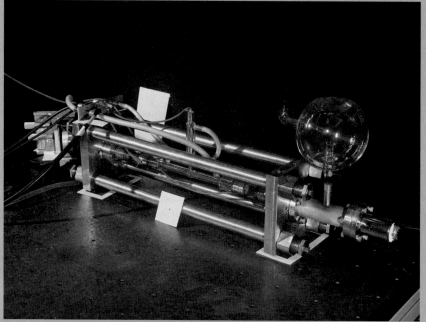

Progress in epitaxial growth techniques and the use of quantum-well active regions (thin [≈100 Å] layers sandwiched between other layers of materials with wider energy gaps and smaller indexes of refraction) has in recent years produced dramatic improvements in the performance of diode lasers. Current thresholds as low as 50 A/cm^2 and power efficiencies exceeding 50% are now commonplace for diode lasers. Nonetheless, high-power applications such as laser radar require large arrays of lasers. Consequently, a major portion of the diode laser research at Lincoln Laboratory since the 1980s has been devoted to the development of arrays. To date these arrays have been used primarily as pump sources for solid state lasers, and diode-array lasers have been found to be both more reliable and more efficient than lamp pumps.

A remaining major challenge in the diode laser field is the achievement of coherence among elements of large (≥1 cm^2) high-power multi-element arrays. Such coherent combining could produce near-diffraction-limited beams at high (≥100 W) power levels and thereby greatly expand the scope of both military and civilian applications of lasers. Research at Lincoln Laboratory is helping to realize this goal by developing monolithic diode laser arrays in which individual elements are fabricated on a wafer by lithography and etching. Arrays of this kind are candidates for establishing coherence when they are used in external-cavity configurations in conjunction with matched arrays of microlenses. Significant initial demonstrations in the coherent combining of diode lasers in small arrays have been performed in the Optics Division, where James Leger and coworkers have obtained a near-diffraction-limited beam.

In 1991 Walpole, Emily Kintzer and Christine Wang demonstrated a tapered semiconductor laser amplifier that provided a major increase in the laser power available from a single semiconductor laser while maintaining high beam quality (i.e., near-diffraction-limited beams at CW power levels up to 3.5 W, which is approximately an order of magnitude improvement over previous results). This advance yielded a simple structure that achieved many of the goals of the previous efforts aimed at combining the outputs from an array of many low-power lasers.

Another direction of current research is toward the development of high-performance lasers for room-temperature operation in the 2-to-5-μm wavelength range. Using GaInAsSb as the active material, Hong Choi and Stephen Eglash have recently developed lasers near 2 μm with excellent performance at room temperature (Figure 13-5). Han Le and George Turner have developed an optically pumped laser at 4 μm that generates 0.35 W average power at 80K, and have implemented a compact laser for IR countermeasures applications.

Ionic Solid State Lasers

Research on ionic solid state lasers at Lincoln Laboratory has been aimed at the development of efficient, compact sources with broad wavelength tunability. In 1964 Keyes and Quist were the first to demonstrate the use of diode lasers as pump sources for ionic solid state lasers by using a bank of GaAs diodes to pump a U^{3+}:CaF$_2$ laser rod. However, extensive employment of this technique did not take place until two decades later, when diode lasers had achieved the wavelength control, high efficiency, room-temperature operation and long lifetime that gave such pumping an advantage over lamp pumping.

More examples of pumped lasers developed at Lincoln Laboratory include the Co:MgF$_2$ laser, which operates in the CW mode when pumped with a 1.06-μm Nd:YAG laser, and is tunable from 1.63 to 2.08 μm. Daniel Ehrlich and coworkers demonstrated the first ultraviolet laser in 1979 with Ce-doped YLiF$_4$ (Ce:YLF), which is tunable from 300 to 325 nm. In 1980 emission at 286 nm was obtained from Ce:LaF$_3$. These were also the first observations of laser emission produced by 5d–4f transitions in trivalent rare earths.

Lincoln Laboratory's most notable accomplishment in solid state (non-semiconductor) lasers was Peter Moulton and Aram Mooradian's initial demonstration and subsequent development of the Ti:Al$_2$O$_3$ laser, which is broadly tunable between 0.65 and 1.12 μm and can be designed for efficient and stable operation at room temperature.[32] Fundamental materials studies carried out in the 1980s identified and reduced the parasitic defects in Ti:Al$_2$O$_3$ crystals. As a result, CW operation was achieved at room temperature and slope quantum efficiencies of 86% were measured with a frequency-doubled (0.53 μm) Nd:YAG laser as a pump source.

Notes

32 P.F. Moulton, "Titanium-Doped Sapphire: A New Tunable Solid-State Laser," in *Physics News in 1982*. New York: American Institute of Physics, 1982, p. 89.

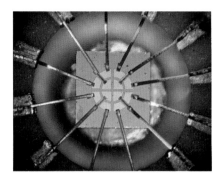

Figure 13-7
Twelve-element array of high-sensitivity 2-GHz-bandwidth HgCdTe heterodyne detectors developed in 1977 for the Firepond CO_2 laser radar.

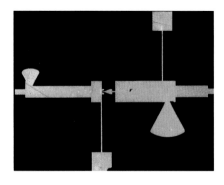

Figure 13-8
Monolithic K_a-band frequency doubler. A varactor diode is integrated with microstrip transmission lines, radial stub tuners and bias lines.

The very high (near ideal) detector sensitivity that Malvin Teich, Keyes and Kingston demonstrated in 1966 at 10.6 μm with a liquid-helium-cooled Cu-doped Ge detector operating as a photomixer proved that infrared heterodyne detection was both feasible and very sensitive.[38] In fact, the demonstration verified the feasibility of the concept of CO_2 laser radar. Because of the difficulty of liquid-helium operation, Cu-doped Ge detectors never became practical, but Pb-salt diodes operating at 77K were soon developed and were also found to give good heterodyne performance.

In 1970 Melngailis and Harman showed that, because the dielectric constant of HgCdTe is much lower than that of lead-based salts, diode photomixers could be made that operated at very high (0.5 GHz) bandwidths. Later that year, the Société Anonyme de Télécommunications (SAT) published results indicating bandwidths above 1 GHz in 10-μm HgCdTe photodiodes. However, when the Optics Division tried to purchase these devices for the Firepond laser radar, SAT responded with a very high price, a year for the delivery time and no guarantee of sensitivity. Since the Solid State Division had already developed a capability to make these detectors, staff members were asked to stay involved with the technology.

Over the next few years, David Spears and coworkers produced a number of advances,[39] including high-sensitivity multigigahertz-bandwidth quadrantal arrays and twelve-element arrays; both types of arrays went into the Firepond monopulse CO_2 laser radar facility (Figure 13-7). Twelve-element linear arrays were also developed for the Infrared Airborne Radar Program.[40]

In the course of this work, measurements to determine photodiode heterodyne performance characteristics were developed. The high heterodyne quantum efficiency of the Lincoln Laboratory HgCdTe photodiodes enabled astronomers at NASA and the University of California at Berkeley to use heterodyne radiometry effectively for numerous astronomical measurements. In the 1980s Spears developed special p-type HgCdTe photoconductors with good heterodyne performance at temperatures over 200K, making these detectors compatible with thermoelectric cooling.

Optoelectronic detector development began with work on avalanche photodiodes (APD) initiated by William Lindley and coworkers, who used the newly developed proton isolation process to eliminate edge breakdown in Schottky-barrier and ion-implanted GaAs devices. Wolfe and Stillman extended their pioneering work on GaAs vapor-phase epitaxy (VPE) and developed InGaAs APDs, the first devices with high gain and high speed at 1.06 μm. They also demonstrated a unique electroabsorption APD with greatly enhanced response near the GaAs absorption edge.

In 1977, following Hsieh's development of liquid-phase epitaxy (LPE) InGaAsP/InP, Hsieh and Hurwitz demonstrated the first APDs in that system. Later, Vicky Diadiuk and coworkers developed a polyimide passivation process that led to higher gains and significantly lower dark currents. Diadiuk and Groves continued to work on InP-based LPE detector technology and developed a unique lateral p-i-n detector structure. In the late 1980s Diadiuk, Groves and Calawa developed sensitive ultrawide bandwidth (5 to 10 GHz) 830-nm AlGaAs/GaAs heterodyne detectors and n^+-p InP epitaxial structures that were used in the satellite communication programs in the Communications Division.

High-Speed Electronic Devices
The high-speed electronic device effort grew out of the APD program because successful APD performance demanded that the dimensions of the active device be precisely defined. Lindley instituted the first photolithographic definition of devices at Lincoln Laboratory to achieve this objective.[41] Photolithography and proton isolation were shortly thereafter applied to advantage in the fabrication of GaAs IMPATT (impact-ionization avalanche transit time) diodes, and in 1972 R. Allen Murphy developed high-efficiency K_a-band GaAs IMPATT diodes with long extrapolated lifetimes.

New lithographic processing procedures were developed in the course of the IMPATT diode development effort. The IMPATT effort also made the importance of microwave packaging and characterization abundantly clear. Because of the need for good GaAs material, Carl Bozler designed and built a VPE system for microwave device material.

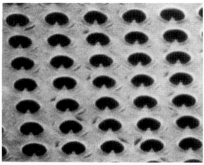

Figure 13-9

High-density gated cone array for a vacuum microtriode. The cones shown in the scanning electron micrograph have a density of 10^9 cones/cm^2 and a gate-tip spacing of 800 Å.

Notes

38 M.C. Teich, R.J. Keyes and R.N. Kingston, "Optimum Heterodyne Detection at 10.6 μm in Photoconductive Ge:Cu," *Appl. Phys. Lett.* **9**, 357 (1966).

39 D.L. Spears, "Theory and Status of High Performance Heterodyne Detectors," *Proc. SPIE* **300**, 174 (1981).

40 Lincoln Laboratory's binary optics program originally evolved from the task of making a holographic grating to form matching CO₂ local oscillator beams to this linear detector array.

41 This section was contributed by R. Allen Murphy.

42 C.O. Bozler, G.D. Alley, R.A. Murphy, D.C. Flanders and W.T. Lindley, "Permeable Base Transistor," *Proc. 7th Biennial Cornell Electrical Engineering Conf. Active Microwave Semiconductor Devices and Circuits.* Ithaca, New York: Cornell University School of Electrical Engineering, 1979, p. 33.

43 T.C.L.G. Sollner, W.D. Goodhue, P.E. Tannenwald, C.D. Parker and D.D. Peck, "Resonant Tunneling through Quantum Wells at Frequencies up to 2.5 THz," *Appl. Phys. Lett.* **43**, 588 (1983).

In the mid-1970s Brian Clifton developed GaAs mixer diodes for K_a-band operation on the LES-8 and -9 satellites. These Schottky-barrier devices were contacted by exquisitely crafted tungsten whiskers, and conversion losses were less than 4 dB, as was required for the satellites. The mixer technology was extended to a monolithic antenna/mixer circuit that eliminated the fragile whisker contact and provided a conversion loss of 4 dB at 100 GHz. A number of organizations have since used the planar mixer technology for mixer and varactor-diode applications.

A concurrent program to develop components for a monolithic millimeter-wave integrated circuit was set up by Alejandro Chu. Planar mixer technology was combined with selective epitaxy to fabricate a 32-GHz heterodyne receiver that consisted of a planar mixer and a field-effect transistor (FET) intermediate-frequency amplifier. Other millimeter-wave components later fabricated by Chu and Chang-Lee Chen for the Radar Measurement Division's monolithic millimeter-wave transceiver development program included phase shifters, monolithic power distribution networks and a 16-to-32-GHz doubler (Figure 13-8).

One of the early applications of VPE was a technique in which large regions of epitaxial GaAs films were grown over photoresist and subsequently removed from a reusable substrate, a process known as CLEFT. During the CLEFT development effort, it was observed that GaAs films of high crystallographic quality could be grown over metallic tungsten gratings. This observation led to the conception of the GaAs permeable base transistor (PBT) by Bozler and colleagues in 1978.[42]

In contrast to conventional planar FETs, where the current flow is parallel to the wafer surface, the current flow in PBTs is normal to the wafer surface. This feature provides the PBT with a number of advantages for high-speed operation, which Gary Alley quantified in numerical simulations performed in 1980.

The key elements in the PBT fabrication process are the definition of the submicron-periodicity control electrode, first accomplished by Dale Flanders with X-ray lithography, and the encapsulation of the control electrode within a single crystal of GaAs. The latter element requires the use of organometallic chemical vapor deposition as the overgrowth process and the careful elimination of sources of contamination prior to overgrowth. Mark Hollis performed a comprehensive set of secondary ion mass spectrometry experiments on the PBTs; this analysis technique turned out to be the only method that revealed exactly what was going on in the active region of the device.

In 1985, as a result of this extensive research effort, reproducible fabrication of PBTs with maximum frequencies of oscillation exceeding 200 GHz was demonstrated. More recently, Richard Chick and Robert Actis, through careful microwave characterization and power combining of monolithic GaAs PBT cells, demonstrated PBT power amplifiers that provided 1.8 W with 30% efficiency at 20 GHz.

A silicon version of the PBT was developed by Dennis Rathman to provide an alternative high-performance microwave device. The Si PBT demonstrated very low $1/f$ noise and excellent performance in low-phase-noise oscillators up to 20 GHz. The technology developed in the GaAs and Si PBT efforts led directly to current work in developing a vacuum microtriode, essentially a PBT in which vacuum is the transport medium (Figure 13-9).

Resonant-tunneling diodes (RTD) offer the potential for even higher operating speeds. The resonant-tunneling mechanism was proposed by Leo Esaki and Raphael Tsu of IBM Research in 1970, but interest in the field was low until 1983, when William Goodhue, T.C.L. Gerhard Sollner, and Peter Tannenwald collaborated to demonstrate a high-quality GaAs/AlGaAs RTD.[43] Conductance measurements indicated that the devices were capable of operating at frequencies as high as 2.5 THz.

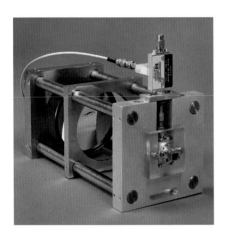

Figure 13-10
A quasi-optical resonant-tunneling diode local oscillator constructed for use in 200-GHz radiometric measurements.

Notes

44 G.M. Metze and A.R. Calawa, "Effects of Very Low Growth Rates on GaAs Grown by Molecular Beam Epitaxy at Low Substrate Temperatures," *Appl. Phys. Lett.* **42**, 818 (1983).

45 This section was contributed by Ernest Stern.

Elliott Brown and Sollner developed circuit models that incorporated parasitics, time delays involved in resonant-charge accumulation, and shot-noise cancellation arising from quantum-mechanical feedback. They then used the implications of the models to optimize devices and to design a microwave circuit that produced fundamental oscillations as high as 712 GHz. More recently, a quasi-optical 200-GHz RTD local oscillator was developed for the superconducting-insulator mixers that the Harvard-Smithsonian observatory is using in a prototype receiver intended for astrophysical measurements (Figure 13-10). In addition, the RTD is being investigated as the load element for a high-speed, low-power-dissipation digital logic circuit and as the bimodal element in a high-speed shift register.

A fundamental advance in materials research — the development of low-temperature-grown (LTG) GaAs — led to a significant advance in device performance. In 1983, a series of fundamental molecular-beam epitaxy (MBE) growth studies by George Metze and Robert Calawa led to the discovery that MBE at low temperatures (<400°C) produced GaAs layers that had high resistivity, showed good crystallographic quality and were stable at normal MBE temperatures ($\approx$600°C).[44]

In 1988 Frank Smith demonstrated, as part of an MIT Ph.D. thesis carried out at Lincoln Laboratory, that this new material, when used as a buffer, eliminated backgating in GaAs FET integrated circuits. In the early 1990s Chang-Lee Chen demonstrated that LTG GaAs, when used as a gate insulator, provided high FET power densities and, when used as a passivation layer, increased FET operating voltage. Femtosecond time-resolved-reflectance measurements indicated that LTG GaAs has a very short carrier lifetime ($\approx$150 fsec), permitting its application as a photoconductive switch and as a photomixer for the generation of signals up to 100 GHz. LTG technology has been transferred to numerous industrial organizations and is currently being used in a variety of applications, including high-speed analog devices.

A higher breakdown voltage makes InP potentially better than GaAs for microwave devices with high output powers. In the 1980s, Donnelly and John Woodhouse developed InP ion-implantation technology and p-channel InP FETs. Chen subsequently fabricated InP MISFETs with high power densities and analyzed the effect of interface traps on MISFET characteristics. Optimizing InP-based microwave devices remains an area of active research.

Surface-Acoustic-Wave Technology

When the ARPA-Lincoln C-Band Observables Radar (ALCOR) in the Kwajalein Atoll became operational in 1970, existing solid state signal processing devices were unable to handle all-range processing of the radar's wide bandwidth of 512 MHz and time-bandwidth product of 5120.[45] A huge, unstable bridged-T network housed in seven 7-ft-high electronic cabinets was built to process the ALCOR waveform, but the cost — several million dollars — was a major impediment to obtaining a second such system. However, the U.S. Army was just then planning a series of missile discrimination tests for which ALCOR needed to have two pulse-compression subsystems.

A team from the newly formed Analog Device Technology Group in the Solid State Division stepped in and made a daring proposal. Ernest Stern and associates believed that they could develop a SAW device that could perform the wideband signal processing task, and that the device could be small and inexpensive.

Jerome Freedman, then the assistant director responsible for strategic defense efforts, decided to call their bluff. Instead of ordering a second bridged-T pulse-compression subsystem, Freedman helped Stern obtain funding to develop the SAW device, called the reflective array compressor (RAC). With the funding, however, came a warning that the discrimination tests were scheduled to take place in two years and that the Solid State Division would be held responsible if the RACs failed to work properly.

The pressure was intense. The group had only two years to develop all necessary technologies and fabricate an operational device. A team was established that included Richard Williamson (for device modeling and design), Henry Smith (for fabrication technology development) and Barry Burke (for acoustoelectric amplifier research).

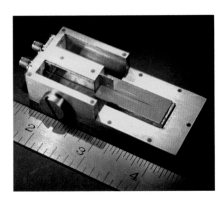

Figure 13-11
SAW reflective array compressor for ALCOR at KREMS.

The SAW wavelength of the ALCOR RAC had to be approximately 3 μm, which required the fabrication of 0.8-μm-wide metal lines and spaces and of thousands of precisely positioned 1.25-μm-wide grooves with a controlled depth of a few hundred angstrom. Because these requirements were well beyond the state of the art at the time, new fabrication processes and tools had to be invented and developed.

The most difficult part of the program was the requirement for submicron lithography. Smith converted one of the first available scanning electron microscopes into a pattern generator tool. Smith and Andrew Hawryluk, a graduate student, analyzed high-energy electron exposure of resist systems and used that knowledge to develop polymethyl methacrylate (PMMA)-based electron resists and exposure procedures, which are still in use throughout the electronics industry.

Because the photomask for defining the grating pattern could not be obtained from commercial sources, Williamson collaborated with the D.W. Mann Company to develop a laser-controlled pattern generator capable of producing the desired pattern. The pattern generator later became a commercial product. And because no existing tools were capable of transferring this grating pattern to a substrate, Smith devised a conformable mask technique that produced optical contact between a thin glass mask and the photoresist-coated LiNbO$_3$ substrate. The absence of a gap between mask and substrate controlled diffraction sufficiently to permit replication of the pattern with excellent fidelity.

It was not clear that the submicron transducer pattern could be transferred to the LiNbO$_3$ substrate with the conformable optical printing process, so a backup technique, X-ray lithography, was conceived by Smith, David Spears and Stern. Spears and Smith developed a soft X-ray source (a modified electron-beam evaporator) and an X-ray mask consisting of a transparent (to soft X rays), 5-μm-thick silicon membrane and a gold absorbing pattern. PMMA was effective as X-ray resist. By early 1973, both the conformable optical and the X-ray lithography concepts worked sufficiently well to produce submicron transducers on LiNbO$_3$; conformable printing, however, gave better results for both the transducer and grating patterns and was the method selected for device fabrication.

An etching system consisting of a French-designed ion-beam spacecraft thruster mounted on a vacuum chamber was modified by Williamson for etching the groove pattern into the exposed LiNbO$_3$ surface. A significant modification allowed the gratings to be etched with spatially varying depth.

The phase error of the ALCOR RACs could not be greater than one part in 10^6, a requirement that exceeded the intrinsic uniformity of LiNbO$_3$ SAW devices by an order of magnitude. There were no commercial instruments that could perform phase measurement on a device of this type, so Williamson led an effort to develop an automated instrument. The deviation of each RAC from ideal was measured, a compensatory phase-correction pattern was generated and applied to the substrate surface and a matched pair of RACs were produced in time for the 1973 real-time ALCOR demonstration (Figure 13-11).

When the program started in 1970, losses in RACs could not be predicted with confidence. Therefore, Burke developed a SAW acoustoelectric amplifier, previously conceived and analyzed by Kjell Ingebrigtsen at the Norwegian Institute of Technology, that could double (in dB) the available dynamic range. The amplifier consisted of a strip of silicon immediately adjacent to the LiNbO$_3$ surface on which the fringing piezoelectric field of the SAW interacted with drifting carriers in the adjacent silicon. By 1972 devices without amplifiers possessed a dynamic range sufficient for ALCOR, causing a shift of emphasis in acoustoelectric device research.

The RACs met all performance goals. They replaced the bridged-T network, and the full development cost of the RACs was less than the projected purchase price of even one bridged-T network. Moreover, the SAW technologies developed during the RAC program received wide acceptance in industry and defense communities. The submicrometer technologies created a separate legacy that led to the formation of the Submicrometer Technology Group.

RACs were installed in several Lincoln Laboratory systems, including MASR and FEP, forerunners of JSTARS and Milstar, respectively. RAC technology was transferred successfully to Texas Instruments, Hughes Aircraft and TRW.

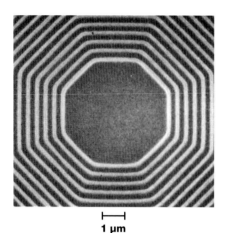

├─┤
1 µm

Figure 13-12

Scanning electron micrograph of single-layer resist imaged with conventional chrome-on-quartz photomasks and a 193-nm optical stepper.

Notes

50 This section was contributed by Barry Burke and Bor-Yeu Tsaur.

51 B.E. Burke, R.W. Mountain, D.C. Harrison, M.W. Bautz, J.P. Doty, G.R. Ricker and P.J. Daniels, "An Abuttable CCD Imager for Visible and X-Ray Focal Plane Arrays," *IEEE Trans. Electron Devices* **38**, 1069 (1991).

Interest in electron-beam lithography at Lincoln Laboratory had, in any event, already superseded X-ray lithography because X-ray lithography, though it can replicate patterns already on masks, cannot actually pattern a mask. For mask fabrication, therefore, the group turned to focused electron-beam lithography.

This first electron-beam lithography system was a modified microscope used to fabricated submicron SAW structures. A commercial electron-beam lithography system was purchased in 1979, and David Shaver used this tool to fabricate diffractive lenses (zone plates) for X-ray imaging applications. Cumbersome holographic techniques requiring custom optics had previously been used to fabricate such lenses, but the electron-beam system proved to be more flexible and more accurate.

The electron-beam system was also used to fabricate GaAs transistor devices and X-ray masks. Shaver and Theodore Lyszczarz used the system to test and customize digital integrated circuits by directly injecting charge on floating-gate devices. In 1986, the electron-beam system was retired when a more capable system was purchased, one that can fabricate devices 0.1 µm and smaller, with good pattern registration and automation.

An independent effort within the group investigated masked ion-beam lithography, which has the advantages of high throughput, robust processing and high resolution. Techniques for ion-beam etching and reactive-ion etching to transfer the patterns into a semiconductor or metal were developed, and Stella Pang explored the impact of etching on the quality of the semiconductor surface.

Technologies developed within the Solid State Division have permitted the fabrication of numerous electronic devices and optical elements at Lincoln Laboratory. The heart of the permeable base transistor, for instance, was a 320-nm-period base grating that was patterned with a combination of X-ray lithography, electron-beam lithography and reactive-ion etching.

While the Microelectronics Group was working on electron-beam and X-ray lithography, a parallel effort within the Quantum Electronics Group was laying the foundation for advanced optical lithography techniques. In the

fall of 1979 Thomas Deutsch, Daniel Ehrlich and Richard Osgood performed the first experiments in high-resolution patterning by laser-induced photochemistry, a technique that soon proved to be a new and exciting area of research. Tightly focused argon-ion lasers (typically at 488 and 514 nm or frequency doubled at 257 nm) were able to deposit thin films selectively or etch materials with submicron definition.

The early pioneering work of Jeffrey Tsao and Ehrlich was followed by more careful and applications-oriented studies performed by Ehrlich, Jerry Black and Mordechai Rothschild. Although conceptually simple, laser photochemistry demanded fine balances in gaseous, adsorbate and solid state phases, frequently augmented by photothermal reactions. The applicability of the technique to the prototyping and repair of photomasks, semiconductor devices and integrated optics drew immediate worldwide attention, and whole symposia were devoted to this topic.

Lincoln Laboratory's leadership role in laser-based processing was reaffirmed in 1988 when DARPA funded a major effort to develop techniques for efficient patterning of 0.25-µm semiconductor devices by optical projection with pulsed 193-nm excimer lasers. The submicron effort had become large enough by this time to warrant the establishment of a new group, the Submicrometer Technology Group.

The excimer program successfully addressed several issues in parallel: the stability of optical materials under prolonged 193-nm irradiation, the development of planarization technologies to alleviate depth-of-focus problems during patterning and alternative photoresist strategies. Construction of the world's first 193-nm exposure tool was subcontracted to SVG Lithography, with delivery to Lincoln Laboratory during 1993. Numerous advances positioned the Lincoln Laboratory group as the center of U.S. work in 193-nm lithography. Mark Hartney, Mark Horn and Roderick Kunz developed spun-on resists and plasma-deposited films necessary for 193-nm lithography. Rothschild studied the failure mechanisms of optical materials exposed to 193-nm radiation and, in collaboration with materials suppliers, improved the damage resistance of these materials. The technology, which is expected to be implemented in industrial fabrication lines around the

2 INCHES

Figure 13-13
Array of four CCD imagers for the space-based-visible experiment. The four chips are precisely aligned and contain a total of 700,000 pixels.

turn of the century, is already providing Lincoln Laboratory with semiconductor fabrication capabilities unique in the world (Figure 13-12).

The Submicrometer Technology Group was also active in related semiconductor materials and microstructures. In 1984, Michael Geis began developing techniques for etching diamond to form a heat sink for a microwave device. He constructed a system for growing diamond films and used the seeded-growth technique that he had pioneered to produce device-quality material. High-quality diamond diodes and a diamond permeable-base-transistor device were fabricated in the late 1980s. In 1992 Geis and Jonathan Twichell demonstrated an efficient field-emission diamond cathode that showed promise for application in flat-panel displays and RF devices.

Charge-Coupled Imagers

The charge-coupled device (CCD) technology activity within the Microelectronics Group has produced major performance improvements for the Laboratory's systems groups.[50] The first instance of this was the problem of detecting and tracking space objects (satellites and debris) with telescopes equipped with low-light-level imaging devices. This task required large-area imagers with both low noise and high quantum efficiency; in short, CCDs.

By 1978 the Microelectronics Group had produced 100×400-pixel devices and had assembled a precisely positioned array of six such chips on a ceramic board. The performance of these early devices confirmed the superiority of CCDs over the vacuum-tube sensors then being used in the Air Force GEODSS system, but device sizes were well below system requirements. Nevertheless, the unique capabilities of CCDs and the clear trend toward larger chips and improved performance prompted a long-range Laboratory investment in the technology. By 1984 a 420×420-pixel imager had been demonstrated. This device was the first designed to be closely abutted on two sides of the imaging area, and it was the basis of a 2×2 array of chips mounted on a common substrate and positioned to an accuracy of a few micrometers. In a technology demonstration of the system, the arrays were mounted on tapered fiber bundles to compress the 80-mm GEODSS focal plane size to match the CCDs. The devices set a new record for low noise when researchers at the Jet Propulsion Laboratory measured 1.6-electrons rms noise at a 50-kHz data rate.

Continued improvements in process technology and the need for faster frame rates led to a larger frame-transfer version of the 420×420 array in 1987.[51] This device was, for the first time, abuttable on three sides of the imaging area, and this feature, together with its very low noise (fewer than 6 electrons at 1 MHz) led to the development of a 1×4 array of the devices for the space-based visible experiment on the missile experimental (MSX) satellite (Figure 13-13).

Strong interest in CCDs also came from the MIT Center for Space Research, where George Ricker and his group were seeking high-performance detectors for space-based astronomy that were customized for soft X-ray imaging and spectroscopy. A collaboration with this group led to the development of 2×2 arrays of the 420×420-pixel devices for the Astro-D satellite. This satellite, a joint U.S.-Japanese effort launched in February 1993, incorporated the first Lincoln Laboratory CCDs and the first CCD X-ray imaging spectrometers in space. Future planned efforts in this line include the NASA-sponsored AXAF observatory, scheduled to be launched in 1998.

The Microelectronics Group began to develop back-illuminated CCDs in the 1980s. Although back illumination offered the potential of attaining the highest visible-band quantum efficiencies and of extending the usable spectral range of the devices into the ultraviolet and extreme ultraviolet, it required the development of a process to thin a chip chemically to a membrane. A process was developed in 1992 that produced devices with unequaled quantum efficiency, stability and uniformity across the near ultraviolet and visible. A new, larger CCD, with 1024×1024 pixels, was demonstrated.

Back-illuminated versions of a chip that has been optimized for the ultraviolet (200 to 350 nm) are to be used in the High-Energy Transient Experiment (HETE) satellite, which has been designed to use ultraviolet emissions to pinpoint the location of gamma-ray bursts. This satellite is currently scheduled to be launched in 1995.

Although most of the imager work has centered on large-area devices, an important application emerged for small, high-frame-rate devices that could be used in adaptive optics for laser-beam compensation. A 64×64-pixel, back-illuminated imager operating at 2000 frames/sec was included in a wavefront sensor the Optics Division used in active atmospheric compensation experiments on the island of Maui in Hawaii in 1991.[52] The devices are now being supplied to the astronomy community for adaptive optics to remove atmospheric turbulence effects from telescope images. An outgrowth of this work was the invention of a fast (50-nsec turn-on and turn-off times) integrated electronic shutter for back-illuminated CCDs, which allowed the sensor to be gated on only during the arrival of selected portions of a pulsed laser beacon, and eliminated the need for a Pockel cell for this function.[53]

In 1988, a separate activity was initiated to develop large-area infrared focal-plane arrays that combined Schottky-barrier detectors and CCD readout circuitry in support of the Aerospace Division's space-surveillance mission. This activity was based on earlier pioneering work conducted at the Rome Air Development Center. Significant efforts were devoted to the development of ultrahigh-vacuum processing for production of high-sensitivity detectors and to the development of improved CCD processing to achieve high-efficiency operation even at cryogenic temperatures. These two major technical advances, accomplished by Bor-Yeu Tsaur and Chenson Chen, led to the demonstration of large two-dimensional PtSi focal plane arrays with state-of-the-art performance in terms of sensitivity, uniformity and noise.

In early 1990 the emphasis of the electro-optical surveillance effort shifted toward missile surveillance and interceptor seeker applications for application to strategic and theater missile defense. Lincoln Laboratory's advanced PtSi focal plane arrays played a key role in enabling the development of several advanced ground-based and airborne sensor platforms, and of the Theater High-Altitude Area Defense (THAAD) interceptor seeker. In addition, to extend the wavelength range of the IR focal plane arrays beyond the 3-to-5-μm limit of PtSi, Lincoln Laboratory has demonstrated large arrays incorporating IrSi Schottky-barrier and GeSi heterojunction detectors, which operate at wavelengths out to 10 μm.

Charge-Coupled Signal Processors

CCD technology was soon recognized at Lincoln Laboratory and elsewhere as having substantial potential for electronic signal processing, and an active period of exploration of digital, analog and mixed analog-digital architectures began.[54] In the initial effort at Lincoln Laboratory, the analog tapped-delay-line techniques that were successfully implemented in SAW technology by Ernest Stern, Richard Williamson and their group were adapted to the charge domain, and resulted in the 1976 demonstration by Barry Burke and William Lindley of a transversal filter with 32 taps and 2-bit programmable weights.

The tapped line has been an important element of most architectures throughout the evolution of CCD signal processing at Lincoln Laboratory over nearly two decades. Indeed, during the late 1970s the SAW and CCD groups together demonstrated several processor functions with hybrid SAW/CCD acoustoelectric devices. This coupling of a LiNbO$_3$ delay line and a Si tapping circuit across a narrow air gap extended both the bandwidth and the programmability of the devices, but at the expense of custom fabrication and packaging.

It soon became clear that the promise for CCD signal processors could be realized only by mixing increasingly sophisticated weighting, programming and support circuits, both analog and digital, onto a monolithic integrated-circuit chip. This combination, though not achieving the bandwidths of either the SAW or superconductive signal processors, yielded far more flexible signal processors in very compact, low-power forms. Alice Chiang and Scott Munroe separately had this early vision. They each invented techniques and circuits that established the Laboratory as the unchallenged leader in charge-domain signal processing.

Chiang extended the filter architecture to six parallel tapped lines as a means to implement 6-bit weights, then invented a far more compact method based on multiplying digital-to-analog converters (MDAC),[55] one for each 8-bit tap weight. Using multiple MDACs, Chiang demonstrated a wide variety of computationally efficient circuits operating at up to 10 million samples per second.

Notes

52 H.T. Barclay, P.H. Malyak, W.H. McGonagle, R.K. Reich, G.S. Rowe and J.C. Twichell, "The SWAT Wavefront Sensor," *Linc. Lab. J.* **5**, 115 (1992).

53 R.K. Reich, R.W. Mountain, W.H. McGonagle, J.C.M. Huang, J.C. Twichell, B.B. Kosicki and E.D. Savoye, "Integrated Electronic Shutter for Back-Illuminated Charge-Coupled Devices," *IEEE Trans. Electron Devices* **40**, 1231 (1993).

54 This section was contributed by Richard Ralston.

55 A.M. Chiang and B.E. Burke, "A High-Speed Digitally Programmable CCD Transversal Filter," *Government Microelectronics Applications Conf. Digest, 1980*, p. 182.

Figure 13-14
Diffusion area in a Class 10 clean room.

The matrix-matrix-product chip implemented a conventional algorithm for radar waveforms, provided eighteen variable-frequency Doppler bins for each of sixteen range cells and could resolve multiple simulated targets 42 dB below dc clutter. The image feature extractor chip used a neural network algorithm for 128×128-pixel analog images and performed a 7×7-pixel correlation with twenty programmable 8-bit feature templates. These chips, and others, with their arrays of MDACs, outstrip pure digital approaches and achieve more than 10^9 multiply-accumulate operations per second per watt.

As a member of the Laboratory's Tactical Communications Group, Munroe was involved in overseeing RCA's production of a CCD-based programmable matched filter in an effort begun by Freeman Shepherd of the Rome Air Development Center. Shepherd and Munroe were both strong advocates of CCDs and convinced of the usefulness of CCDs for signal processing, and the filter was successfully demonstrated within prototype jam-resistant secure-voice aircraft radios developed by the Laboratory. Munroe subsequently joined the Analog Device Technology Group and, working with Duane Arsenault and others, implemented a succession of increasingly integrated analog-signal/binary-reference programmable transversal filters that were easy to interface to standard CMOS subsystems. Prototype chips with 256 taps in each of two channels were provided to the NASA sponsor and then embedded in receivers by Stanford Telecommunications. These ICs will provide synchronization and demodulation functions over a wide range of data rates in the ground segment of the Tracking and Data Relay Satellite System. Integrated circuit designers at Boeing Aircraft have also been taught the methods of CCD design.

The demand for compact and efficient wireless communications services has brought new opportunities for applications. Chiang is targeting a single-chip adaptive filter for canceling video ghosts as a convincing means of validating performance in a wireless application. This device will exploit the charge-domain A/D converter demonstrated by Susanne Paul as well as an array of MDACs.

Overall, interest in industry continues to grow. In addition to the active technology transfer to Boeing, a strong effort was established at Analog Devices, when Munroe joined them in 1990. Working jointly with industry to combine innovation in architecture with new processes from the Microelectronics Laboratory should enable the CMOS/CCD technology to achieve power efficiencies that will ensure its broad application within this decade.

Current Trends
The solid state program is seeing significant changes in the present decade. The end of the Cold War, the resultant reduction in the military budgets and the increased role of the government in strengthening the civil sector are encouraging greater development of dual-use technologies and collaborations between government-funded laboratories and industry through such mechanisms as Cooperative Research and Development Agreements. As a consequence, less funding is now available for exploratory and component demonstration projects, and an increased fraction of the Solid State Division's program is being devoted to engineering development. However, since most solid state technologies have both military and civilian uses, the Solid State Division is in a good position to meet the challenges posed by present national priorities and to support current Laboratory activities.

Of particular importance is the Microelectronics Laboratory, which became operational during 1993 and now provides state-of-the-art facilities for semiconductor device fabrication (Figure 13-14). Lincoln Laboratory's pioneering work in sub-0.25-μm lithography is expected to provide enabling technology for future generations of integrated circuits for military and civilian applications. Other major themes will most likely include sensors, displays and communications. In all these areas, the Solid State Division's efforts in electro-optical devices, lasers, microwave devices and materials will provide an excellent and enduring technology base.

14   Computers and Signal Processing

Computer technology has always played a central role in the Laboratory's activities.[1] Lincoln Laboratory developments in computer technology have helped to spawn new industries and new technical disciplines, and have profoundly influenced the worldwide digital revolution in the second half of the twentieth century.

At the Laboratory computer technology developments have followed four major threads: seminal developments from the first digital computers to the minicomputer; digital signal processing; speech processing; and pattern recognition.

Numerous contributions and spin-off companies from Lincoln Laboratory have helped to create and shape the modern computer and digital signal processing industries. Examples of Laboratory spin-off companies include Digital Equipment Corporation (DEC), which invented the minicomputer, and Applicon, which developed software for computer-aided design of integrated circuits. Other influential developments include interactive computing; computer graphics; wafer-scale restructurable very large scale integration (VLSI); secure digital voice communications; voice communication in packet networks; robust speech recognition for DoD applications; and artificial neural network technology. In fact, the emergence of Massachusetts as a center of the computer industry derives in large part directly from the Lincoln Laboratory computer technology program, its spin-off companies and their descendants.

From Whirlwind to TX-2

The Whirlwind computer was developed initially in the 1940s in the MIT Servomechanisms Laboratory, and subsequently in the MIT Digital Computer Laboratory and Lincoln Laboratory in the 1950s to perform real-time tasks, originally as a flight simulator and later for the SAGE system. Real-time performance was obtained by building the computer as a 16-bit parallel system and employing a random access memory.[2] The replacement of Whirlwind's small and unreliable storage-tube memory by a magnetic-core memory in 1953 was an epochal event in the history of computers. Equally important was the linking of computer and man through displays and light pens. The story of Whirlwind and magnetic-core

memory and its importance for the SAGE system and the early history of Lincoln Laboratory are found in chapter 1, "Beginnings," and chapter 2, "The SAGE Air Defense System."

The early emphasis on real-time applications, memory systems and man-computer interaction continued through the development of several generations of new computer technologies and systems at the Laboratory.

Whirlwind in 1952 had about 5000 vacuum tubes and 11,000 diodes in its logic circuits. A preliminary design for a transistorized computer for SAGE, the TX-1, was developed but not implemented because the transistor was too immature. The AN/FSQ-7, the first SAGE computer, used about 25,000 tubes in each computer of the duplexed system. Transistor circuit development was pursued, however, and in 1955 a double-rank shift register of eight stages was built with 100 surface-barrier transistors manufactured by Philco. Later that year, an 8-bit multiplier with about 600 transistors was produced.

During this time Lincoln Laboratory built a 64k-word (256×256) magnetic-switch-driven core-memory array. The memory drive currents were generated by vacuum tubes, 425 in total, but it also used 625 transistors. To test both the memory and the transistor logic circuits, Lincoln Laboratory built the TX-0 computer.[3]

TX-0 was an 18-bit machine built with about 3600 transistors. Gates and flip-flops were packaged as individual plug-in units. Each flip-flop was composed of ten transistors and operated at 5 MHz; the instruction rate was 80,000 instructions per second. Sixteen address bits were required in each single-address instruction word, which left only 2 bits for instructions. Three of the four instructions — add, store and conditional jump — used an address; the fourth used the address bits for controlling such functions as clearing and complementing the accumulator, transfers between registers and input/output (I/O) operations. I/O was provided by a Flexowriter, a paper-tape reader and a cathode-ray tube (CRT) display system. Marginal checking was implemented by varying a positive bias voltage on the base of the *p-n-p* transistors.

The next computer to be constructed was the TX-2 (Figure 14-1), which was a much more complete implementation of transistor technology than TX-0. Many of the concepts in the design of TX-2 came from the TX-1 design; the core memory, however, came from TX-0. The TX-2 was a constantly evolving machine; each week one day was devoted to maintenance, improvements and changes.[4] In what would turn out to be a highly successful innovation, all circuits for TX-2 were packaged in a single type of standard pluggable module.

In 1957 Kenneth Olsen and Harlan Anderson, who had worked on the matrix core switch for core memories, the AN/FSQ-7 design and the circuit design for the TX-0 and TX-2 computers, left Lincoln Laboratory to found Digital Equipment Corporation. Their first product was a line of pluggable logic modules based on TX-2 circuits. The first DEC computer, the PDP-1, was introduced in 1960 and was oriented to the type of interactive computing that Whirlwind, TX-0 and TX-2 had pioneered. The minicomputers developed by DEC soon revolutionized the computer industry.

By 1958 TX-2 had three core memories: the large 64k-word system, a transistor-driven 4k-word memory and a fast 64-word index memory (Figure 14-2). Many additional registers, including the arithmetic registers, were addressable in the memory address space. The separate memory units could operate in parallel so that faster operation was possible if instructions and data were in separate memories. TX-2 implemented a single-instruction architecture with an 18-bit address and 6 bits to specify an address index from the index memory.

The arithmetic element could be reconfigured on each instruction into one 36-bit, two 18-bit or four 9-bit sections, all executing the same instruction. All data in and out of the arithmetic element flowed through an exchange element where data could be shuffled among the four 9-bit registers. The configuration was specified by five instruction bits that accessed a set of thirty-two 9-bit registers, twenty-eight fixed and four settable; later the configuration registers were implemented in a small read-write magnetic-film memory.

All I/O processing was handled by the central computer through a multiple-program-sequence technique. There were thirty-two sequences, each of which had its own program counter, organized by priority. Three were assigned to main programs and the others to alarm conditions and I/O devices. Each instruction had control over whether it would allow switching to another sequence at its completion. Therefore, each I/O device could be controlled with the full power of the computer, even though several slow devices could be operating at the same time. Multisequence architecture was more efficient for programmed I/O than the widely used interrupt-vector approach. Direct memory access hardware was added to TX-2 later. Almost twenty years later, Xerox's Alto computer used a similar multiple-sequence technique.

New I/O devices were relatively easy to interface to TX-2 and many were connected, including standard tape drives, a very large magnetic drum, a Stromberg-Carlson Charactron-driven xerographic-process printer, an x-y plotter, light pens, several different tablets, a 3-D wand input device, two keyboard workstations and several different display devices. There was a plan for building a tape library system for TX-2 with 100 transports with a total capacity of 10^{10} bits and an access time of 30 sec. Although only one such transport was ever built, the scheme illustrates the innovative thinking that characterized the engineering of TX-2.

Address transformation hardware to provide both segmentation and paging was added when operation moved to a time-sharing mode. In 1966, the tube-driven 64k-word memory was replaced by commercial core memories; both magnetic-film and semiconductor memories were added later. By the end of the program, TX-2 had evolved to about the size and power of the DEC PDP-10. The TX-2 computer was retired in 1975 (Figure 14-3).

Notes

1 Material in the chapter was provided by Allan Anderson and James Forgie (early computers), Charles Rader (digital signal processing), Clifford Weinstein (speech technology) and Richard Lippmann (neural networks).

2 K.C. Redmond and T.M. Smith, *Project Whirlwind.* Bedford, Mass.: Digital Press, 1980, p. 237. This book provides a fascinating history of the technological and the political issues surrounding the development of Whirlwind.

3 J.L. Mitchell and K.H. Olsen, "TX-0, a Transistor Computer with a 256 by 256 Memory," *Proc. 1955 Eastern Joint Computer Conf.,* p. 93.

4 A set of articles describe the TX-2 computer in detail in *Proc. 1957 Western Joint Computer Conf.*

Figure 14-1
The TX-2 computer was often used in a time-sharing mode. Carma Forgie is working at a dual-storage scope station with a custom color-coded keyboard; Alan Nemeth is using a graphics display. On the left is a small part of the logic frame.

Figure 14-2
Don Ellis removes one bit plane from the 64k-word memory that was used first with TX-0 and later with TX-2. Each bit plane was a 256 x 256 array of ferrite cores.

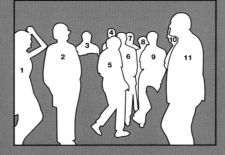

Figure 14-3
The TX-2 computer was retired from service on June 27, 1975. The ceremony brought together many luminaries in the computer field.

1 Mary Allen Wilkes, 2 Ivan Sutherland,
3 Omar Wheeler, 4 Richard Best,
5 Unidentified, 6 Jack Gillmore,
7 Harry Forsdick, 8 Unidentified,
9 Wesley Clark, 10 John Laynor,
11 Kenneth Olsen

Hands-On Computing and Interactive Graphics

Batch operations were standard for most computers of the 1960s, but the TX-2 was designed for hands-on use from its inception. The accessibility and convenience of interactive computing eventually made the batch mode obsolete, and TX-2 had a major impact on the rapid acceptance of interactive operation. Two sponsored programs, one from the Air Force and the other from ARPA, facilitated the development and rapid evolution of the tools of hands-on operation.

The Air Force asked Lincoln Laboratory to develop software to support hands-on use of the computer to perform a variety of frequently required computations without the need to master the details of a programming language. This effort produced a time-sharing system for the TX-2 called APEX that supported multiple concurrent users. It also led to the development of a software system called Reckoner that operated in a coherent environment so the output of one program could serve as the input to another program. Files of data used by Reckoner had descriptors, allowing the programs to interpret input data appropriately.

In the early 1960s Ivan Sutherland developed the Sketchpad system,[5] often called the first interactive graphics program (Figure 14-4). Although the Sketchpad user could create drawings on a display with a light pen, the emphasis was not so much on drawing as on serving as a tool for education and design. Sketchpad included a sub-picture capability for including arbitrary symbols on a drawing, a constraint capability for relating the parts of a drawing in any computable way, and a definition copying capability for building complex relationships from combinations of simple constraints. The topology of a drawing was described in a ring structure that permitted rearrangement of the data storage structure during editing of pictures with a

minimum of file searching and rapid constraint satisfaction and display file generation. Example applications included moving mechanical linkages, loaded truss bridges with display of computed forces and various artistic pictures.

In this same time period Lawrence Roberts used TX-2 in his research on machine perception of three-dimensional solids and introduced the use of homogeneous matrix representations and manipulation to computer graphics, a technique now universally employed.

The second sponsored effort, the ARPA Graphics program, was aimed at enhancing the state of the art of interactive graphics in a time-sharing environment. This program was started in 1965 to support the development of successively more sophisticated display hardware, the enhancement of APEX to provide operating-system support for display outputs, the demonstration of a variety of input devices and the creation of new languages to facilitate the writing of application programs that could take advantage of the interactive graphics capabilities.

Hardware development for the ARPA program took display generators from early point-by-point capabilities through straight-line vectors to conic sections. Because the desire was to time-share a single generator among a number of displays while maintaining an acceptable flicker rate, speed was a major objective. It became clear that this objective could not be achieved with the available technology, so storage scopes were added to the system to handle applications such as text editing that did not require the full performance of the refreshed displays.

Much attention was given to the input side of interactive graphics. Light pens were used, and some work was done with an ultrasonic acoustic wand as a 3-D input device, but the principal graphics input device under study was the tablet. Both commercial tablets and laboratory-built units were connected to TX-2.

Notes

5 I.E. Sutherland, "Sketchpad: A Man-Machine Graphical Communication System," *Proc. 1963 Spring Joint Computer Conf.,* p. 329.

6 Wesley Clark gave a history of the development of LINC, with additional notes on TX-0, TX-2 and ARC, in his article, "The LINC was Early and Small," in A. Goldberg, ed., *"A History of Personal Workstations."* New York: ACM Press, 1988, p. 347.

1950

1955

Memory Test Computer

TX-0 computer with TX-2 in background

Figure 14-4
Ivan Sutherland using the Sketchpad graphics program at the TX-2 console. On the display is part of a bridge, with numbers calculated by Sketchpad that show the forces in the structural members.

One useful capability based on the tablet was a simple and very fast stroke-following character recognizer that operated as part of APEX. It allowed the user with a simple hand motion to point to an object on the screen and specify an operation to be performed on that object. A trainer program was provided so that the user could customize the alphabet of characters. Modern technology uses the mouse and its buttons for this function, but the tablet and recognizer provided a wider range of choices for the action to be taken with respect to an object selected by pointing.

The ARPA program supported the development of a compiler-compiler called VITAL that was used to create a number of other languages. The most widely used language was one known as LEAP, a high-level language based on ALGOL, and having in addition associative data structuring operations, reserved procedure forms for display and input manipulation and real-time variables. A RECOGNIZE statement was available to retrieve a character from the tablet recognizer. LEAP was used to create a number of application programs, including the Mask Maker.

The Mask Maker program was written in the late 1960s to perform computer-assisted layout of photomasks for the fabrication of integrated circuits. In this program, the user could call up predefined components from a library or define new components from smaller parts, instead of working with individual rectangles on the different layers of the integrated circuit. A unique aspect of Mask Maker was its user input of commands through characters drawn on the tablet. The program was used to lay out a number of integrated circuits that were fabricated both at Lincoln Laboratory and by a subcontractor. The designers of Mask Maker—Harry Lee, Gary Hornbuckle, Richard Spann and Fontaine Richardson—left Lincoln Laboratory to found Applicon, an early and highly successful manufacturer of computer-aided design equipment.

Between the late 1950s and the early 1970s, TX-2 was used in a wide range of applications. The computer processed image and audio data (including Caruso recordings), simulated neuronlike nets and evaluated graphical design in mechanical engineering. Professor Amar Bose of MIT, who later founded Bose Corporation, used the TX-2 to process data taken in a sound chamber and to develop a novel type of loudspeaker. TX-2 was used in early experiments on packet switching between computers and was an early host on the ARPAnet. Other applications that made use of TX-2 included simulations of air traffic control problems at dual-runway airports, analysis of speech processing techniques and modeling of logic circuits.

ARC and LINC

Wesley Clark was a user of Whirlwind and the Memory Test Computer and one of the principal architects of TX-0 and TX-2.[6] As a proponent of the idea that computers are tools and that convenience of use is the most important single design factor, he believed that computers should be affordable and compact. Whirlwind, of course, was neither. Clark's Laboratory Instrument Computer (LINC) was both; in fact, it prefigured the workstation computer revolution of the 1980s.

Working with Belmont Farley, also a Laboratory staff member, Clark began a collaboration on the use of computers in biomedical research with the MIT Communications Biophysics Laboratory. The Average Response Computer (ARC), built in 1958, was an 18-bit machine with TX-2 circuit modules and a 256-word memory. It had an analog-to-digital (A/D) converter so that computations could be performed in real time on analog signals. The ARC was hardwired to perform in any of three modes: response averaging, amplitude histogram compilation and compilation of time histograms of single-neuron activity. The success of ARC and the conviction that a programmable machine would be even more useful led to the design of LINC.

Magnetic thin-film array

J.M. Frankovich and D.C. Wheeler with TX-2 computer

Notes

7 I.S. Reed, "Symbolic Design of Digital Computers," *Lincoln Laboratory Technical Memorandum No. 23*, Lexington, Mass.: MIT Lincoln Laboratory, 19 January 1953.

8 J.I. Raffel, "Operating Characteristics of a Thin Film Memory," *J. Appl. Phys.* **30**, 60S (1959).

9 C.T. Kirk, Jr., "A Theory of Transistor Cutoff Frequency (f_t) Falloff at High Current Densities," *IRE Trans. Electron Devices* **ED-9**, 164 (1962).

Since LINC was to be an affordable laboratory tool, a driving force in its design was a $25,000 cost goal. (The team came close to its goal; the first machines actually cost $32,000.) LINC was a 12-bit parallel machine with a 1k-word memory, an A/D converter and a small CRT display made from a modified laboratory oscilloscope. It had two block-addressable tape drives that were miniature versions of the experimental tape drive that had been built for TX-2. The tape reels were small enough to put in a pocket. The logic sections were built with DEC logic modules; the computer filled one relay rack plus a separate console box and was quite easily moved. The LINC architecture was simulated on TX-2 and the first assemblers were also written on TX-2.

The first machine was demonstrated at the National Academy of Sciences Conference on Engineering and the Life Sciences in Washington in April 1962. After the conference, LINC was moved to a National Institutes of Health laboratory, where its A/D input channel was connected to a multiple-electrode array implanted in the brain of a cat; the average responses were computed and displayed.

In January 1963 the LINC effort moved from Lincoln Laboratory to a new center at MIT and then in 1964 to Washington University in St. Louis. Twenty LINCs were built for biomedical researchers in 1963 and more than 1200 LINC or LINC variants were manufactured commercially. DEC sold about 150 copies of the LINC-8, a combination of the LINC and the PDP-8, and about 1000 PDP-12s, which incorporated a modified LINC design. A small start-up company called Spear subsequently produced an integrated-circuit version of the LINC, called the micro-LINC.

CG-24 Computer

The CG-24 computer was being built in the Laboratory's Group 24 (the name, CG-24, stands for Computer Group 24) at the same time that Group 63 was building the TX-2. CG-24 was a 25-bit parallel machine with an 8k-word core memory driven by transistor circuits (Figure 14-5). It was the first all-transistor machine; TX-0 and TX-2 had vacuum-tube-driven memories.

The transistor and diode circuitry was capable of operation at clock rates up to about 0.5 MHz, and the computer operated with a 0.33-MHz clock. Considerable parallelism was employed to improve the computation rate. The addition time was 24 μsec and multiplication time 84 μsec, both including the access time of the 12-μsec cycle time memory. Its I/O included three input registers for transfer of real-time data, a Flexowriter and two CRTs for display of alphanumeric data. CG-24 was packaged quite compactly in a three-quarter circle arrangement of low cabinets.

Perhaps the greatest innovation in the design of CG-24 was Irving Reed's development of a register-transfer language, which enabled the designers to simulate the logic design of CG-24 before the machine was built; this technique achieved wide acceptance within the computer industry.[7] The register-transfer description of the machine was simulated on TX-0, and a CG-24 program was executed by the simulation. The control element was implemented as a read-only diode memory, but the concept of a read-write control memory was recognized and described.

The CG-24 computer was built in 1956 and 1957 and moved to Millstone in 1958. The Millstone staff used the machine to process radar data in real time until it was replaced by a commercial computer in 1966.

Magnetic-Film Memory

Lincoln Laboratory mounted a large effort in the 1950s in the development of methods of ferrite-materials preparation with the objective of building smaller and faster memory systems. Engineering efforts were made to reduce the cost of testing and construction, and the results of all these development activities had a major influence in the industry. Magnetic-core memory had become a very big business; by 1970 IBM was producing more than twenty billion each year. However, as transistor circuitry and higher levels of integration permitted the construction of faster and cheaper computers, two drawbacks of ferrite-core memories became apparent: switching speeds were too slow and the production costs of threading three wires through each core were too high.

John Goodenough led an extensive program in the physics of magnetic materials, and under Donald Smith's leadership this activity was extended to magnetic thin films in 1956. Magnetic films have much shorter switching times than ferrite cores and are suitable for batch fabrication. For a while it seemed that magnetic films might replace ferrite cores, and a film memory project was started.

In 1959 a 32-word × 10-bit film memory was installed in TX-2 to store configuration control words.[8] It used two 16 × 16 arrays of magnetic film spots and had a cycle time of 0.8 μsec. A small 50-megapulse computer, the FX-1, was constructed with transistor circuitry to conduct a realistic exercise of film memory with a 0.3-μsec cycle time. A film memory was also installed in TX-2 as a Page Address Memory, and in 1968 a million-bit film memory was installed as part of the main memory.

For the million-bit memory, magnetic film and copper were evaporated onto 10 × 1.6-in glass substrates and then etched into continuous word lines in the long dimension. Digital lines were formed as long copper lines on flexible substrates that were pressed onto the glass pieces. A storage element was formed at the intersection of a word line and two digit lines. Each substrate had 100,000 bits, and spare word lines were wired in to replace lines with defective bits. The memory had the unusual feature of reading or writing 352 bits per cycle; this, potentially, gave a very high data rate, though TX-2 could not take advantage of it. The memory was bench tested at a 1.2-μsec cycle time, but it was limited to a slower speed by the computer. A cross section of a tenfold larger memory was built, but by that time advances in integrated-circuit memory devices had outstripped all other technologies for computer storage in speed, packing density and cost.

Integrated Circuits and Wafer-Scale Integration

In cooperation with the research division of Philco, a program in the design and characterization of switching transistors was pursued in parallel with the design of transistor circuits for TX-0 and TX-2. In 1962 Charles Kirk, Jr., published a paper that explained why high collector current limited the frequency response of bipolar transistors.[9] This mechanism, the spreading of the base layer into the collector region at high current density, was thereafter known as the "Kirk effect."

Fabrication of digital integrated circuits at Lincoln Laboratory began in 1970 with equipment that had been used in the magnetic-film program. Over succeeding years research was conducted in materials, circuits, systems and design methods in support of general research and specific projects.

In the mid-1970s a monolithic circuit to perform 3-bit A/D conversion was built. It comprised an array of eight comparators with a bias network and output encoders. Eight of the devices were used to build an experimental 6-bit A/D converter with a sampling rate of 200×10^6 samples per second. A version of this circuit was also built by Westinghouse.

The ultrahigh-density memory project attempted to make a semiconductor memory that was comparable in cost to such bulk memories as magnetic disk, yet provided higher speed and reliability. The storage element was made as simple as possible; it was a capacitor formed by the crossing of a metal line over a silicon line with a silicon-nitride/silicon-dioxide sandwich as an insulator to achieve the highest bit density. Information was stored in the metal-nitride-oxide semiconductor (MNOS) device by storing a charge in the nitride, and was maintained even without an applied voltage.

A 64k-bit chip with partial on-chip decoding and off-chip sensing was built, and writing and reading in several microseconds was demonstrated. A megabit chip was designed but not built, because ultimate density was more likely to be limited by material properties than by lithography.

The Lincoln Laboratory project in restructurable VLSI, headed by Jack Raffel, took circuit integration to the wafer level through the use of defect avoidance and customization. In this scheme, wafers were fabricated with arrays of circuits and uncommitted wiring. After testing of the circuits, interconnections were modified or restructured to connect only the good circuits into the system. It was proposed initially to use MNOS transistors for the restructuring, but laser restructuring proved to be the more area-efficient method.

Making Perfect Music

Compact discs are magnificent devices. Their sound is flawless, their range immense. Not even scratches affect their quality. Yet compact discs, hard disk drives and other forms of digitally recorded information do contain errors, and error-correcting codes are necessary to provide insurance against these flaws. In the simplest form, an error-correcting code just repeats each piece of data several times. That means that if n errors are anticipated, then repeating all information $2n + 1$ times will compensate for the errors. However, this brute force approach to error correcting defeats the purpose of high-speed, high-density information processing. What is needed is an error-correcting code that adds only a few bits to the length of a message. And this is exactly what a concept proposed by two Lincoln Laboratory staff members, Irving Reed and Gustave Solomon, did.

In 1960, Reed and Solomon published a five-page paper that introduced the idea of coding groups of bits, rather than individual zeros and ones. This feature made the Reed-Solomon code particularly good at dealing with bursts of errors. Just as the eye can recognize and correct for a few bad points in what is otherwise a smooth curve, the Reed-Solomon code can spot incorrect values and recover the correct message.

No one could have predicted in 1960 that this short, highly mathematical paper would solve a crucial problem in the development of high-density digitally recorded data. Information densities were not very high in 1960; moreover, the technology to implement the code was not yet available.

The technology did catch up and an efficient algorithm for decoding the Reed-Solomon code was invented. Today, more than three decades later, products that rely on the Reed-Solomon code appear in almost every home and office. Reed and Solomon received the 1995 IEEE Masaru Ibuka Consumer Electronics Award "for contributions to basic error-correcting codes, specifically the Reed-Solomon Codes, which led to the compaction of data and made possible a generation of consumer compact optical disk products."

Figure 14-5
CG-24, the first all-transistor
computer.

Figure 14-6
Computer-controlled laser in the
process of manufacturing a wafer-
scale adaptive-nulling system using
restructurable VLSI.

Notes

10 A.H. Anderson, J.I. Raffel and P.W. Wyatt, "Wafer-Scale Integration Using Restructurable VLSI," *Computer* 25, 41 (April 1992).

11 See, for example, B. Gold and C.M. Rader, *Digital Processing of Signals.* New York: McGraw-Hill, 1969.

12 C.J. Weinstein, "Quantization Effects in Digital Filters," *Lincoln Laboratory Technical Report No. 468.* Lexington, Mass.: MIT Lincoln Laboratory, 1969.

Restructurable VLSI technology was demonstrated by the construction of nine different wafer-scale systems (Figure 14-6).[10] The most ambitious system was the Matrix Update Systolic Experiment (MUSE), built in 1991. It was an array of thirty-two processors on one wafer, and it performed real-time adaptive antenna nulling computations with sixty-four degrees of freedom. The device executed about 1.4 billion real operations per second.

The technology and computer-aided design programs were transferred to the National Security Agency and the University of South Florida. Restructurable VLSI technology was also used to build a 4000-gate logic array that was customizable after fabrication for use in rapid application-specific integrated-circuit prototype development.

Digital Signal Processing

Analog processing of a waveform can be simulated by using a computer to process the digital sequence that represents the waveform; this procedure is called digital signal processing. Many of the key advances in the development of digital signal processing began at Lincoln Laboratory, and staff members played an important role in spreading the basic concepts throughout the technical community.

The vocoder (voice coder) research in the Laboratory's Speech Systems Technology Group, for example, took sampled-data signal representations of speech and developed algorithms to determine voiced pitch, and then used the resulting pitch to excite an experimental vocoder. The bulk of the vocoder hardware was in the narrowband bandpass and low-pass filters, so digital signal processing offered the potential of producing a more effective vocoder design by simulating the filters. In 1960, however, digital filtering involved discrete convolution of a filter's sampled input with its sampled impulse response, which required hundreds of multiplications and additions to simulate just one filter accurately.

In 1962 Charles Rader and Bernard Gold came up with the idea of using recursive digital filters, and they increased the speed of computation of filter outputs by two orders of magnitude. This result led them to develop many techniques for the design of recursive digital filters with prescribed frequency responses, and to analyze the effects of finite word-length arithmetic for digital filters.

But even the recursive filter designs of that era required about ten seconds of computer time to simulate vocoder processing of one second of speech. During the 1960s, however, circuit speeds increased and circuit costs decreased, so real-time digital simulation became possible. In fact, the digital signal processing implementation was simply an alternative realization of the system, and mathematical simulations of vocoder designs eventually replaced the analog hardware.

Computers were also being used for spectrum analysis of speech signals, but the computations ran slowly until 1965, when two mathematicians, James Cooley of IBM and John Tukey of Princeton University, developed an algorithm for the fast Fourier transform (FFT). Charles Rader, Norman Brenner and Thomas Stockham took the concept of the FFT, improved the algorithm, implemented it on a computer and used it to accelerate vastly the computation of correlations and convolutions.

With the availability of the FFT technique, digital signal processing was ready to make the transition to a practical technology. Numerous tutorial publications by Lincoln Laboratory authors introduced digital signal processing to the electrical engineering community.[11]

The FFT was of major importance, but its use was initially limited to computing discrete Fourier transforms for the relatively few data sequence lengths that were highly composite numbers and preferably powers of two. Then, in 1968, Lincoln Laboratory developed the chirp z-transform algorithm, which allowed the FFT to be applied to sequences of any length. At the same time, a second scheme, employing permutations based on number theoretic principles, allowed the FFT to be used on sequence lengths that were prime numbers. In addition, an analogy to the FFT algorithm called the Fermat number transform was developed to compute convolutions and correlations without any errors due to numerical round-off. Research at the Laboratory also developed fundamental analyses of the performance limitations resulting from finite word-length computations in digital filtering and the FFT.[12]

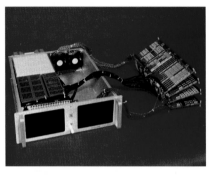

The requirement for high-speed computation led to the development of specialized parallel computing systems that were optimized for digital signal processing. The Fast Digital Processor (FDP), completed in 1970, carried out signal processing tasks about a hundred times faster than the general-purpose computers of that time.[13] Approximately a tenfold increase in computing speed came from using the fastest available circuits; another tenfold speedup came from the FDP architecture. The FDP could simultaneously perform four instructions and compute the addresses of data to be used in subsequent instructions.

Subsequent processors built on the ideas about specialized hardware that came out of the FDP effort (Figure 14-7). The Lincoln Digital Voice Terminal (LDVT), for example, was a flexible signal processor that was programmed to realize any of a wide variety of speech compression systems in real time; modern integrated-circuit digital signal processor designs are architectural descendants of this system.[14]

The Laboratory made use of digital signal processing techniques in a number of applications besides speech processing, most notably in radar. The high bandwidths common in radar introduced some challenging requirements; huge rates of arithmetic operations per second were necessary for real-time processing.

The pipelined FFT, a highly parallel organization of processing elements for FFT computation, was developed at several laboratories during the early 1970s. Lincoln Laboratory researchers then generalized the pipeline concept to apply to the most efficient FFT algorithms of the era. A high-speed FFT pipelined processor built in the late 1970s for radar applications was able to compute a 16,384-point transform of complex data every 136 μsec.

Lincoln Laboratory had been developing a large radar digital signal processor known as the Advanced Digital Signal Processor (ADSP) that was intended to be integrated with the System Technology Radar, a phased-array radar located on Meck Island in the Kwajalein Atoll. The installation of the ADSP was canceled when the System Technology Radar operation was discontinued in late 1980. Work to evaluate the technology continued and a major ADSP subsystem, the Digital Convolver System, was tested at the Laboratory. The Digital Convolver System used approximately 27,000 integrated ECL 10K series circuits with a large multiplexed MOS memory to achieve a high throughput data rate for the FFT.

In many ways, radar is the perfect application area for digital signal processing, and Lincoln Laboratory has been preeminent in both proving and applying this technology to radar. In a periodically pulsed radar, the gated returns from each range (after digitally filtering for pulse compression) comprise sampled signals that can be digitally processed to extract information about the objects under study. This analysis can be carried out in many creative ways. First, clutter can be eliminated by digital filtering, leaving only the reflections of moving targets. Second, a Fourier analysis can give the distribution of velocities of scatterers at any range. Finally, the radar returns from objects with known rotational motion can be analyzed in both range and Doppler to give two-dimensional images, because the cross-range displacement of a scatterer is proportional to its Doppler frequency. Alternatively, the known motion of a radar can be used to produce a synthetic aperture, enabling all-weather mapping of any area with high resolution.

Digital signal processing is finding a new application in phased-array radar. The antenna pattern of a phased-array radar can be redirected in microseconds, giving this type of radar a significant advantage over mechanically steered

J.E. Laynor with FX-1

W.A. Clark, Jr., with LINC computer

B. Gold

C.M. Rader

Figure 14-8
This early channel vocoder built at Lincoln Laboratory included a bank of twenty analog Bessel filters and an implementation of the Gold pitch detector in digital hardware.

Notes

13 B. Gold, I.L. Lebow, P.G. McHugh and C.M. Rader, "The FDP, a Fast Programmable Signal Processor," *IEEE Trans. Comput.* **C-20**, 33 (1971).

14 P.E. Blankenship, "LDVT: High Performance Minicomputer for Real-Time Speech Processing," *EASCON '75 Record.* IEEE Publication 75CH0998-5 ECON. New York: IEEE, 1975, p. 214-A.

15 C.M. Rader, "Wafer-Scale Integration of a Large Systolic Array for Adaptive Nulling," *Linc. Lab. J.* **4**, 3 (1991).

16 B. Gold, "A History of Vocoder Research at Lincoln Laboratory," *Linc. Lab. J.* **3**, 163 (1990).

conventional antennas. Analysis of data from a phased array, however, requires the ability to weight and sum the received signals, which could not be done digitally at the necessary data rates until recently. Digital phased-array radars, such as the Radar Surveillance Technology Experimental Radar (RSTER), have now been demonstrated successfully, and many more are proposed.

Sometimes the optimum signal processing for a given signal is not known when the system is designed or programmed. Adaptive systems solve this problem by using statistical properties of a signal to create a digital filter. A dramatic example of such an adaptive system was Lincoln Laboratory's multiple-antenna surveillance radar, which used an adaptive spatial-temporal digital filter to suppress clutter with the same Doppler frequency as the target under study.

The MUSE (Matrix Update Systolic Experiment) system,[15] completed in 1991, can compute optimum adapted weights for a sixty-four-antenna phased array in the presence of as many as sixty-three jamming sources impinging on the antenna sidelobes. The entire MUSE design was realized as a single wafer-scale integrated circuit.

Digital signal processing is now well established as an important tool for electrical engineering. Hundreds of companies manufacture products that make use of the techniques of digital signal processing. And within Lincoln Laboratory, the concepts of digital signal processing continue to be refined and to be incorporated in a wide range of applications.

Speech Technology

Lincoln Laboratory's contributions in speech technology began in the 1950s with development of pioneering computer-based systems for speech coding, pitch detection and speech recognition. Since that time, Lincoln Laboratory has sustained a speech technology effort that has yielded major contributions in speech coding, recog-

nition, enhancement and networking. The program has produced new algorithms, hardware/software implementations and system applications. Speech studies at the Laboratory have also served as a focus for development of technologies that subsequently proved to be important in other areas. Speech applications were the initial focus for Laboratory work in digital signal processing, for example, and speech applications were a key early focus for Lincoln Laboratory work in artificial neural networks.

Speech Coding and Networking

The purpose of a vocoder is to analyze and synthesize speech in terms of a set of parameters (characterizing the pitch and spectrum) that can be encrypted and transmitted at a much lower bit rate than the original speech waveform. Vocoders have a rich history, including the SIGSALY system that allowed President Franklin Roosevelt and Prime Minister Winston Churchill to converse freely over a highly secure transatlantic telephone. The SIGSALY system comprised a room full of equipment at each side, and the transmitted speech, though reasonably intelligible, was not very good in quality. Today's secure telephones provide significantly higher quality than SIGSALY in units the size of a typical telephone desk set.

Lincoln Laboratory has played an important role in the advancement of vocoder technology. The Laboratory's entry into the vocoder field was initiated in the early 1960s by Bernard Gold's development of a computer-based pattern-recognition algorithm for pitch detection on the TX-2 computer. The unreliable performance of pitch detectors had been a limiting factor in vocoder performance, and Gold's algorithm yielded significant improvements over previous techniques; it was one of the first successful applications of computer technology to an important problem in waveform processing. The algorithm later became a key part of various vocoders developed at Lincoln Laboratory and elsewhere over the next thirty years (Figure 14-8).[16] In the mid-to-late 1960s, Lincoln Laboratory designed and built channel vocoders

J. Tierney evaluating speech vocoder

Coordinate Rotation Digital Computation (CORDIC) cell of approximately 54,000 transistors

MUSE system array of 130 CORDIC cells on a 5-in wafer

Air Traffic Control Technology

The Laboratory has been able to apply its surveillance expertise to air traffic control by developing system technology for the Federal Aviation Administration. Principal technical activities include collision avoidance, hazardous-weather detection and enhanced safety and efficiency for terminal areas.

Left: Aerial view of Boston's Logan International Airport.

Lincoln Laboratory's program in civil air traffic control (ATC) began because one man — Herbert Weiss — became exasperated by delays in air travel. Back in the late 1960s, Weiss, as head of the Radar Division, was flying to Washington frequently. As he later recalled it, the experience was "horrendous." Flights were almost invariably late.[1]

Weiss was not alone. In the late 1960s the U.S. ATC system faced a crisis. The introduction of jet aircraft in the late 1950s had led to a rapid expansion of scheduled air carrier traffic, and the booming economy had stimulated enormous growth in general aviation. Flight delays increased and the current system appeared to be on the verge of breakdown. Moreover, the projected growth of aviation made substantial improvements in the quality and efficiency of the ATC system imperative.

In the course of waiting for his many delayed flights, Weiss had plenty of time to think about improving ATC. The system needed better radars, computers and communications — exactly Lincoln Laboratory's areas of expertise. As he considered the problem further, he also realized that the SAGE program had essentially been an exercise in air traffic control — detecting enemy aircraft and vectoring fighters to intercept them. Although the Laboratory's program had broadened substantially over the years, and in fact no longer included air defense, considerable interest and expertise in ATC remained among Lincoln Laboratory personnel.

Lincoln Laboratory had another reason for becoming involved with ATC. By the late 1960s a sense had developed that the U.S. government was placing too much national research and development talent into defense-related areas and was neglecting important needs in the civilian economy. Therefore, the DoD was encouraging its laboratories to demonstrate the applicability of DoD-developed technology and resources to nondefense problems. In particular, the Air Force was willing to permit the Laboratory to use research funds as seed money to develop programs in selected nondefense areas. ATC was particularly appropriate since the Air Force had decided to reduce its own ATC research and development and give the responsibility for joint-use ATC/air defense sensors to the Federal Aviation Administration (FAA).

Weiss began a personal campaign with the FAA. The centerpiece for his crusade was a technical note published in 1968 that proposed a new approach, the "spaghetti tube," to en route traffic management.[2] Weiss's proposal was that the FAA create a set of preplanned routes between various American cities, which he called spaghetti tubes, instead of allowing pilots to create their own flight plans. Although pilot objections to the spaghetti tubes ended this proposal, Weiss did succeed in stimulating the FAA's interest in Lincoln Laboratory.

In late 1968 an Ad Hoc Committee on Air Traffic Control was formed within Lincoln Laboratory. The committee was charged with carrying out a broad study of the ATC system and its problems and with recommending a program to develop solutions. The committee met over a period of several months, and in May 1969 published its report, including a proposal, based generally on Weiss's concept, for a Laboratory program in the ATC area.

In September 1969 a study group chaired by Walter Morrow, then an assistant director of Lincoln Laboratory, was convened to examine further the possibility of new programs in air traffic control. In addition to Lincoln Laboratory personnel, members of this group were drawn from the MIT Flight Transportation Laboratory in the Department of Aeronautics and Astronautics, the Electronic Systems Laboratory, the Measurement Systems Laboratory and the Draper Laboratory, then part of MIT. Over a three-month period the study gave its participants a broad education in the various disciplines related to ATC and validated the idea that an ATC program should be pursued.

Both the committee and the study group concluded that the Laboratory had the right mix of capabilities to make a unique contribution to ATC research and development.

To give a focus to the development of an ATC program at Lincoln Laboratory, the Laboratory restructured the Radar Division in early 1970 and named it the Air Traffic Control Division. Ongoing defense-related activities were moved to other divisions, and the Air Traffic Control Division became the nucleus for the development of the ATC program. A small number of interested staff members from other parts of the Laboratory joined the

Air Traffic Control Division at this time to work with Weiss on the development of an ATC program. Paul Drouilhet, Jr., was appointed Group Leader of the newly formed Air Traffic Control Group.

During the same time period, the Department of Transportation formed a national committee, the Air Traffic Control Advisory Committee (ATCAC), to examine all aspects of the national air traffic control system, to project the demands on the system for at least the next twenty years and to recommend a national ATC program. The committee reviewed and was influenced by the Lincoln Laboratory study, but proceeded independently and with a broader scope. The ATCAC report, dated December 1969, proposed an architecture for an evolving system to meet projected ATC needs, and outlined a development program to realize the proposed architecture.[3]

A key element of the ATCAC plan was to upgrade the existing Air Traffic Control Radar Beacon System (ATCRBS) to allow expanded data communication with individual aircraft and to add an integral data link for two-way communication between ATC facilities and aircraft under control. The upgraded surveillance system would support Intermittent Positive Control (IPC), an automatic ground-based collision-avoidance concept. IPC ground facilities tracked otherwise uncontrolled aircraft and issued conflict-resolution commands via the data link to resolve potential conflicts.

The principal technologies necessary to bring the concept to reality — radar, signal processing, digital communications, data processing — were well matched to the capabilities and interests of Lincoln Laboratory. Thus the Discrete Address Beacon System (DABS) became the Laboratory's initial foray into air traffic control.

The Early Years

In early 1971 the FAA established its first sponsored program at Lincoln Laboratory, a six-month effort to prepare a technical development plan for DABS. The original FAA contract totaled $140,000, a pittance compared to the defense-related funding. In fact, the size of that first contract convinced many within Lincoln Laboratory that nondefense work should not be pursued. Fortunately for the Laboratory and for ATC, however, the FAA program was continued.

The FAA's key concern with the design of DABS was compatibility: since most aircraft would continue to be equipped with ATCRBS transponders, signals from DABS could not be permitted to interfere with ATCRBS. Lincoln Laboratory's technical development plan addressed this problem in detail, and the plan convinced the FAA that it was possible to design a new beacon system that would not only be compatible with the old system, but could employ the same aircraft antennas and operate in the same frequency band.

The successful completion of the technical development plan led to a greatly expanded program to develop, test and demonstrate DABS and its associated IPC capability (Figure 15-1). The execution of this program included the development of a DABS experimental facility adjacent to the Laboratory and a transportable measurement facility for testing DABS around the country. Several aircraft were outfitted to make airborne measurements and to test the IPC concept. A number of pilots from the local community, as well as airline flight crews, participated in these flight tests (Figure 15-2).

Lincoln Laboratory completed the basic design of DABS in the mid-1970s. Walter Wells and Stanley Miller directed the early development; Vincent Orlando and David Karp headed the later work. Paul Drouilhet was overall project leader. Subsequently, the Laboratory assisted the FAA and Texas Instruments in developing and testing three commercial prototype DABS sensors. These prototypes were completed on time, performed well and demonstrated that Lincoln Laboratory's design could be readily reduced to commercial practice. The three Texas Instrument sensors interrogated and tracked airborne transponders in the South Jersey and Philadelphia airspace for a number of years and conclusively demonstrated the compatibility of the DABS waveforms with existing ATCRBS equipment.

While prototype testing was under way, Lincoln Laboratory was active as the FAA's principal technical agent in generating national and international standards for the DABS waveforms and transponder protocols. This painstaking and complex work was led by Vincent Orlando and Jerry Welch. As a result of this effort, the International Civil Aviation Organization (ICAO) adopted the design and changed the name of the system from DABS to Mode S, where the "S" stands for Select.

Notes

1 This chapter is taken in part from P.R Drouilhet, "Air Traffic Control Development at Lincoln Laboratory," *Linc. Lab. J.* **2**, 331 (1989).

2 H.G. Weiss, "A Concept for Air Traffic Control," *Lincoln Laboratory Technical Note 1968-29.* Lexington, Mass.: MIT Lincoln Laboratory, 17 October 1968, DTIC AD-678060.

3 *Report of the Department of Transportation Air Traffic Control Advisory Committee, Vol. 1* (December 1969).

The Day All Hell Broke Loose

Certainly one of the most rewarding of the Laboratory's programs has been the Terminal Doppler Weather Radar effort. The TDWR has had a major impact on aviation safety, but never more so than on July 11, 1988, the ninth day of the first operational test of the system's detection capability.

It was a hot and humid afternoon in Denver, Colorado, perfect weather for microbursts. At 4:07, the TDWR reported the presence of microbursts near the approach end of the runway.

Traffic was heavy; five United Airlines aircraft were on the approach. A few days earlier, United had issued a bulletin to its pilots that instructed them to not take off or land if a microburst was reported. But out of the five pilots approaching Denver, only one remembered the portion of the bulletin dealing with microburst advisories.

Within the next six minutes, two of the pilots who attempted to land during the microburst lost altitude in a critical phase of flight. Flight 395 dropped to less than 100 ft above ground level, at a distance of more than a mile from the end of the runway. A second aircraft, Flight 236, lost almost 3000 ft, but remained safely above the airport surface. Only Flight 862, flown by the one pilot who responded correctly to the microburst advisory with an avoidance maneuver, was unaffected.

A transcript of the exchanges between Denver air traffic control and the pilots is given below. The printed word, however, cannot convey either the icy calmness of the air traffic controllers or the fear in the voices of the pilots. It was, as a film produced by the FAA and the National Center for Atmospheric Research was called, *The Day All Hell Broke Loose.*

862: Denver tower, United 862 just outside Altur, visual to the right, say your winds please, and we're going to alpha 8.

ATC: United 862, Denver tower. Runway two six right, cleared to land. Microburst alert, center field wind two two zero at niner, a four zero knot loss, one mile final, reported by machine, no pilot report.

395: United 395 inside Altur.

ATC: United 395, Denver tower. Runway two six left, cleared to land. Wind two one zero at five, a four zero knot loss, one mile final. Microburst alert, not substantiated by aircraft.

395: United 395.

ATC: United 395, say your gate.

862: Missed approach. We don't want to make the approach with a microburst alert.

ATC: Who wants to go missed?

862: United 862. We'd like to go to the right here if we can.

ATC: United 862, change to runway to three five right, cleared to land. I do have a microburst alert for that runway. Wind three five zero at fifteen, a four zero knot loss on three mile final.

862: We don't want to make *any* approach. We'd like to go ahead and hold somewhere until you stop having the microburst alerts.

395: United 395, we're missing.

ATC: United 395, fly runway heading, climb, maintain 7000.

395: Seven thousand.

[At this point, United 395 is roughly twenty to seventy feet above ground level. Passengers later report seeing the ground just off the end of the wing. The pilot follows correct microburst avoidance procedure, but his anxiety is evident.]

ATC: United 395, turn right, heading zero one zero, climb, maintain 8000.

395: Okay, say that heading again?

ATC: Turn right, heading zero one zero, climb, maintain 8000, United 395.

395: Zero one zero, 8000, United 395.

236: United 236 heavy. Sky Ranch for the left one, we have Buffalo 9 for gate.

ATC: United 236 heavy, Denver tower, microburst alert threshold wind one four zero at five, expect a five zero knot loss, two mile final, runway two six left. Cleared to land.

236: Cleared to land.

395: And you say 8000 for United, uh, 395?

ATC: Yeah, 395, affirmative, climb, maintain 8000, heading zero one zero. United 395, fly heading zero three zero for right now, please.

395: Okay, zero three zero, 395.

ATC: United 395, contact Denver Approach, one two eight point zero five.

395: One two eight zero five.

236: We're going around, United 236 heavy.

ATC: United 236 heavy, fly runway heading, climb, maintain 7000.

236: Seven thousand.

949: Hey, tower, United 949 is marker inbound.

ATC: United 949, caution wake turbulence from the heavy DC-8 going around. Microburst alert, threshold wind zero nine zero at three, expect a seven zero knot loss on a three mile final.

305: United 305.

949: United 949, we're going around.

ATC: United 305, microburst alert, threshold wind one six zero at six, expect an eight zero knot loss on a three mile final, say request.

305: Did you say *eight zero* knots?

ATC: Affirmative, United 305.

Unknown: He's correct.

Second unknown: And we can confirm it.

ATC: United 305, what is your request?

305: United 305 is going *around.*

The plan had been to remove the Lincoln TDWR test-bed equipment from the Denver airport at the end of the summer so that further tests could be conducted at another site. However, the FAA Air Traffic Service made the decision to continue protection at Denver by operating another experimental radar with the Lincoln Laboratory wind shear detection software until a production TDWR system became available.

Based on a suggestion made by engineers at the MITRE Corporation, a special characteristic of the existing ATCRBS transponders was used to prevent overlapping replies. The interrogator could temporarily desensitize the ATCRBS transponder's receiver by means of a special pulse-code sequence. This capability, used in conjunction with the natural variation in air-to-air transmission losses to the nearby aircraft, permitted the target transponders to be divided into small groups and interrogated separately, thereby reducing the likelihood that their replies would garble one another.

BCAS (like most of the proposed ACAS designs) warned pilots of equipped aircraft that they were in a threatening encounter and provided a climb or a descend command to resolve the encounter. However, test flights revealed that pilots were uncomfortable with a command to execute an avoidance maneuver without an explanation of the conflict. This problem was alleviated by adding a traffic display to BCAS that provided the pilot with a picture of the range, bearing and relative altitude of nearby aircraft. After addition of this feature and other enhancements necessary to operate the system in the highest projected traffic densities in the United States (seven hundred aircraft over the Los Angeles basin), the system was renamed the Traffic Advisory and Collision Avoidance System (TCAS).

The BCAS/TCAS program was a cooperative effort between Lincoln Laboratory and the Virginia division of MITRE. Lincoln Laboratory developed the surveillance and communication subsystem, which detected and tracked nearby aircraft and exchanged information with other TCAS-equipped aircraft. MITRE was responsible for the conflict-resolution subsystem, which acted on the surveillance data to determine the warnings and commands and to suggest appropriate avoidance maneuvers.

During the early years of the BCAS program, IPC development proceeded in parallel. BCAS was seen as a service primarily for air-carrier and similar high-cost/high-performance aircraft, and IPC as a service primarily for general-aviation aircraft. In 1981, FAA Administrator Lynn Helms discontinued the development of IPC and selected TCAS (which operated independently of the ground-based ATC system) as the single FAA-supported backup to the ATC system.

As with the DABS/Mode S system, Lincoln Laboratory supported the BCAS/TCAS development all the way from the basic surveillance concept through the publication of final international standards. This development included initial design and test, technology transfer to industry and limited implementation program testing (Figure 15-6). Several avionics manufacturers now produce TCAS equipment for airlines, and all large air-carrier aircraft flying into U.S. airports are now equipped.

In the late 1970s the Department of Transportation's Transportation System Center undertook an examination of the use of satellite-based ATC systems for communications, navigation and surveillance. Lincoln Laboratory participated in this effort by examining the application of satellites to each of the principal ATC functions. The study concluded that consideration of satellites for the communications and surveillance functions of air traffic control in the continental United States was premature. Since then, interest in satellite-based communications and surveillance has grown, particularly for application over the ocean and over remote areas. In principle, an accurate satellite navigation system and a digital communications link — acting as a so-called automatic dependent surveillance (ADS) system — can augment or replace conventional radar surveillance equipment. Recently, interest in the ADS concept has been encouraged by the growing availability of low-cost civil navigation receivers using the military Global Positioning System (GPS). Several current programs at Lincoln Laboratory actively exploit this technology.

The first fifteen years of the Lincoln Laboratory program for the FAA focused primarily on issues of surveillance. In 1987 the Laboratory began broadening its focus to include the development of techniques and algorithms to improve air traffic management (Figure 15-7). With FAA support the Laboratory initiated two major automation programs that have continued to the present. These programs, directed at increasing the efficiency and capacity of aircraft operations in the terminal area, are the Terminal Air Traffic Control Automation (TATCA) program and the Airport Surface Traffic Automation (ASTA) program.

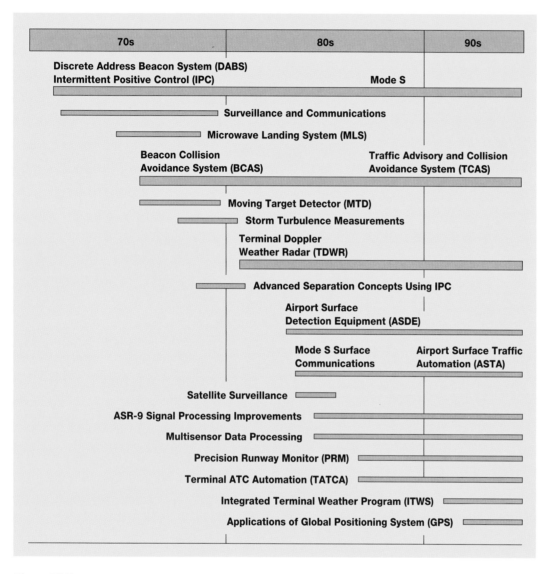

70s	80s	90s

Discrete Address Beacon System (DABS)
Intermittent Positive Control (IPC)   **Mode S**

Surveillance and Communications

Microwave Landing System (MLS)

Beacon Collision   **Traffic Advisory and Collision**
Avoidance System (BCAS)   **Avoidance System (TCAS)**

Moving Target Detector (MTD)

Storm Turbulence Measurements

Terminal Doppler
Weather Radar (TDWR)

Advanced Separation Concepts Using IPC

Airport Surface
Detection Equipment (ASDE)

Mode S Surface   **Airport Surface Traffic**
Communications   **Automation (ASTA)**

Satellite Surveillance

ASR-9 Signal Processing Improvements

Multisensor Data Processing

Precision Runway Monitor (PRM)

Terminal ATC Automation (TATCA)

Integrated Terminal Weather Program (ITWS)

Applications of Global Positioning System (GPS)

Figure 15-7
Principal Lincoln Laboratory programs
for the FAA from 1971 to the present.

The TATCA Program Office was established in late 1990. Its objective was to increase the ATC system's capacity through the use of new automation technology as an alternative to the more expensive construction of new airports or runways.

Early in the program, the TATCA Program Office elected to adopt the Center-TRACON Automation System (CTAS), which had been under development at the NASA Ames Research Center. CTAS provided an integrated set of tools to assist both Center and terminal controllers in optimizing terminal traffic flow. The system prototype was implemented on a network of engineering workstations.

Since 1990 the TATCA Program Office has continued to develop CTAS. A rapid prototyping approach has been taken, in which a set of automation tools are incrementally developed and further refined in operational field sites at the Denver and Dallas–Fort Worth airports. In parallel with these activities, the Program Office has been developing a strategy for deploying systems based on CTAS to additional sites.

In the field, CTAS uses auxiliary workstation processors interfaced to existing ATC computers. In its final form, it will be an integrated system comprising four tools: the Traffic Management Advisor (TMA), the Descent Advisor (DA), the Final Approach Spacing System (FAST) and the Expedite Departure Path (EDP). The TMA prototype has been installed in the Denver International Airport (Figure 15-8). The Laboratory has been active in the development of the interfaces to be used in the field to connect CTAS to the existing ATC systems, and has also been responsible for reengineering of prototype software to improve its modularity, robustness and maintainability.

The goal of the ASTA program is to improve surveillance and communication on the airport surface, and to develop automation aids that enhance the safety and efficiency of surface operations. The program especially addresses operations during periods of bad weather and limited visibility. ASTA includes (1) an upgrade of the capabilities of the ASDE (airport surface detection equipment) radar to include tracking and enhanced target identification, (2) a safety system to alert controllers and pilots

Figure 15-8
A TMA prototype display at the Denver International Airport.

Figure 15-9
Real-time ASTA demonstration at Boston's Logan Airport. The runway-status lights were not installed on the airport surface but were displayed on a scale model of the airport, located in the demonstration room in the airport control tower.

of runway incursions and other unsafe conditions and (3) automation aids to assist the controller in efficiently managing traffic movements on the airport surface.

The ASTA program was very successful. Under the leadership of Ervin Lyon, in a period of less than two years, a proof-of-concept system was developed at Logan International Airport that used a low-cost commercial marine radar to drive an automatic runway-status light system for warning pilots of unsafe conditions on the airport surface. The demonstration system performed extremely well and substantiated the concept of runway-status lights (Figure 15-9). The system achieved a 99% probability of detection of aircraft in movement areas within the radar's line of sight. Had actual runway-status lights been installed on the airport surface, pilots would have observed light illuminations impeding normal safe traffic flow only about once every fifty operations. Lights would have provided the intended safety backup with negligible impact on airport capacity or controller and pilot workload. Furthermore, these performance measures could have been improved significantly in an operational system.

During the same period, the Precision Runway Monitor (PRM) program was begun to increase the use of closely spaced parallel runways in bad weather. Because controllers find it difficult to detect and respond in a timely fashion when an aircraft strays from its intended approach path if parallel runways are spaced too closely, ATC procedures previously permitted independent operation of parallel runways in reduced visibility only when the lateral spacing between the runways was 4300 ft or greater. Thus those airports with parallel runways closer than 4300 ft suffered a severe capacity penalty in reduced visibility.

To alleviate this problem, the FAA initiated the PRM program to develop high-update-rate, high-accuracy sensors augmented by a computer-assisted blunder detection capability for use in monitoring parallel-runway operations. PRM technology went into operational use at the Raleigh-Durham airport for dual-parallel runways in 1993 and will support the triple-parallel approaches at the new Denver airport in 1995. This program, under the direction of Raymond LaFrey, has seen substantial success within a short time.

A transportable monopulse beacon sensor that was originally used in the Mode S program was employed for the PRM sensor. The update rate of the sensor was doubled by the use of back-to-back antennas. In addition, improved displays and computer-assisted blunder detection features were provided to the controllers. With this new equipment, it is now possible to carry out independent operations safely even on parallel runways spaced as closely as 3400 ft (Figure 15-10).

The Ongoing Program
Currently, Lincoln Laboratory is involved in more FAA programs than at any other time in the past. The Laboratory has three groups working on FAA projects. The Air Traffic Automation Group (Group 41) focuses on automation tools to help air traffic managers and controllers work more safely and efficiently. The Air Traffic Surveillance Group (Group 42) focuses on communication, navigation and surveillance systems for improved air traffic management. The Weather Sensing Group (Group 43) focuses on weather phenomena, fusion of data from diverse weather sensors and automatic prediction of hazardous weather events for air traffic controllers and traffic managers.

Although the largest automation activities have been the TATCA and ASTA programs, Lincoln Laboratory has recently begun an important new automation activity to support the FAA's oceanic program office. The goal of the oceanic program is to develop modern surveillance processing and display capabilities for controllers handling oceanic airspace, where radar surveillance is not available.

In the mid-1980s the Laboratory began to develop radar system refinements to permit data from both primary and secondary radars to be input into a multisensor data processing capability. The use of this capability to improve aircraft tracking for ATC has continued.

Lincoln Laboratory has also recently begun an important program to develop an automatic dependent surveillance system based on GPS and Mode S. This so-called GPS-Squitter system uses GPS for determining the position of aircraft and uses the Mode S data link as a means of transferring data on each aircraft's GPS position to the air traffic management system. The transfer of the position data

Figure 15-10
Experimental PRM sensor with back-to-back Mode S antennas at the Memphis Airport.

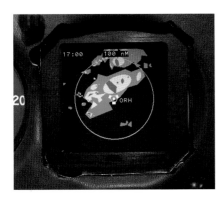

Figure 15-11
The Graphical Weather Service displays complex weather information for use on the civil-aviation flight deck.

Notes

4 Reviews of these programs were published in the Fall 1989 and Fall 1994 issues of the *Lincoln Laboratory Journal.* Both issues were devoted entirely to air traffic control.

is accomplished via spontaneous (squitter) transmissions from the Mode S transponder. This technique holds great promise as a practical and effective means of providing reliable surveillance and identification for aircraft on the airport surface. It has the advantage that it utilizes existing Mode S transponders and does not require new frequency allocations or signal-in-space standards.

The work on data-link applications for transport-category and general-aviation aircraft has continued with the development of the Traffic Information Service and the Graphical Weather Service. When requested by an aircraft, the Traffic Information Service uses the processing capability inherent in the Mode S sensor to determine the range, azimuth and relative altitudes of nearby aircraft and sends a Mode S data-link message to the requesting aircraft with that information. On board the aircraft, the traffic information is displayed to the pilot in a format similar to that used for TCAS.

Graphical Weather Service provides a means to deliver complex graphical weather products via data link for display on the flight deck. An initial Graphical Weather Service product is derived from a ground-based weather-radar mosaic. On a request from an aircraft, an image is extracted from a weather database, compressed, transmitted and displayed in the aircraft (Figure 15-11). Because Graphical Weather Service is derived from ground-based sensors and is applicable to such other graphical weather products as turbulence and icing, it offers significant benefits to all categories of aircraft, regardless of the presence of on-board weather avoidance equipment. General-aviation groups will participate in field evaluations of these and other data-link applications by using industry-built Mode S data-link avionics prototypes. Selected airlines will use air transport data-link avionics to make a parallel field evaluation of the Graphical Weather Service.

An important activity is under way to fuse data from all available weather sensors in the airspace surrounding major airports to improve terminal efficiency and capacity when adverse weather is present. Terminal weather is the principal cause of significant (greater than fifteen minutes) delays in the air system. The Integrated Terminal Weather System (ITWS) seeks to reduce these delays by providing information on hazardous cells in the terminal area as well as planning information (for example, on route impacts and changes in ceiling, visibility and snowfall rate) for use by traffic managers, pilots, controllers and airlines. The ITWS will support TATCA by providing wind information for flight trajectory computations and by identifying terminal routes and/or runways that will not be usable because of adverse weather. Initial ITWS testing at Orlando and Dallas–Fort Worth has shown a significant benefit in maintaining an orderly traffic flow and reducing delays when thunderstorms are present. The FAA is planning to commence full-scale development in the near future.

For more than twenty-five years Lincoln Laboratory has carried out research and development for the FAA.[4] Major outputs of these programs are beginning to reach fruition and enter nationwide service in support of air traffic control. These outputs include systems for the Mode S sensor (for improved surveillance), the Mode S data link (for better communications), TCAS (for collision avoidance), the ASR-9 radar (for improved detection of aircraft in the presence of clutter) and TDWR (for severe-weather sensing).

As the current programs are completed, new programs are being undertaken. These efforts focus on the use of new technical capabilities to enhance the efficiency and capacity of aircraft operations in the terminal area and on the airport surface. Through these programs Lincoln Laboratory will continue to play a major role in providing the FAA with critical technology in the coming years.

16   Technology for Other Government Agencies

National concerns arising during the Vietnam War prompted the Laboratory to expand its efforts into a wide range of non-DoD activities in the 1970s. The president of MIT during that turbulent period, Howard Johnson, made the announcement in 1970 that the Institute would divest itself of one of its two large defense-oriented laboratories, the Charles Stark Draper Laboratory, but would retain management of Lincoln Laboratory. However, Lincoln Laboratory was strongly encouraged to find wider uses for its research and development resources. Chapter 15, "Air Traffic Control," describes what has become the Laboratory's largest non-DoD activity. This chapter covers other non-DoD activities, in areas including health care, education, energy, support for manned space flight and recent efforts for NOAA and NASA.

Manned Space Flight

The Soviet launch of Sputnik-I on October 4, 1957, spurred the United States into beginning a manned-space-flight effort. Just one year later, the creation of the National Aeronautics and Space Administration (NASA) and the start of Project Mercury — the program to put an American into space — were concurrently announced.[1]

Project Mercury was carried out in a hurry. The first of two manned suborbital flights took place on May 5, 1961, about two years after NASA assigned the prime contract for the capsule to McDonnell Aircraft. Five manned orbital flights followed in short order.

The several streams of data coming from and going to the capsule had to be integrated on the ground so that the Mercury Control Center at Cape Canaveral, Florida, could make good decisions about the progress of a mission and could implement them reliably. There was also an urgent need for expertise in acquiring and tracking the capsule by radar from various stations in the range and for transmitting the tracking data to the Goddard Space Flight Center in Greenbelt, Maryland.

The overall task of developing the Mercury worldwide ground tracking range was similar in many ways to the SAGE tracking problem. The Project Mercury task was easier than SAGE, because there was only one target. SAGE, however, was designed to detect objects moving much more slowly than the Mercury capsule. Because Lincoln Laboratory certainly had more experience in

tracking than any other organization, NASA awarded a contract to the Laboratory to study all phases of tracking and computation for Project Mercury.

Lincoln Laboratory predicted radar-tracking problems for the Mercury capsule long before the first suborbital flight, and a number of remedies were suggested and implemented. Because of the time pressure on the Project Mercury effort, the tracking range was made up from radars that were already available. For the most part, the worldwide ground tracking range comprised C-band AN/FPS-16 radars and S-band very-long-range trackers (VERLORT).

Lincoln Laboratory improved the C-band AN/FPS-16 radar in Bermuda with a larger, higher-gain antenna, a more powerful transmitter and a more sensitive receiver. The S-band VERLORT located there was given a more sensitive receiver.

Antenna deficiencies in the C-band tracking-radar beacon transponder in the capsule were identified and remedied. In the face of widespread opinion to the contrary, Lincoln Laboratory predicted unacceptably low-quality radar tracking during the crucial period of measuring the orbital-insertion parameters. The Laboratory implemented a suggestion made by A.E. Hoffman-Heyden of RCA Service Company and developed a system design for a time-varying ferrite phase shifter, which turned out to be of great importance when the prediction of poor tracking was fulfilled during the first unmanned Mercury-Atlas orbital flight.

The phase shifter was placed in series with the C-band antenna elements, filling in the interference nulls between the main lobes of the elements. The first orbital flight with a chimpanzee on board, November 29, 1961, carried a single RF phase shifter in series with a C-band antenna element. Radar tracking was much improved. The first manned orbital flight, of astronaut John Glenn on February 20, 1962, carried the full two RF phase shifters, as did the remaining Mercury missions. Performance was excellent and the phase shifters were also used on the two-man Gemini flights. At Lincoln Laboratory's recommendation, the orientation of the capsule in flight was changed to give better antenna-pattern performance in the direction of the tracking radars.

Notes

1 Material for this section was contributed by William Ward. Background material is taken from H. Sherman, "Lincoln Laboratory Participation in the Apollo Program May 1961–May 1963," *Lincoln Laboratory Memorandum 65L-0001*. Lexington, Mass.: MIT Lincoln Laboratory, 22 May 1963.

2 For a further description of this program, see H.E. Sherman and A.L. Komaroff, *Ambulatory Care Project, Final Contract Report 14A, 30 June 1969 to 29 February 1976*. Lexington, Mass.: MIT Lincoln Laboratory, 1976.

Operator performance was another problem area. Because flights were separated by several months, the individuals in charge of tracking and acquisition needed assistance in maintaining their skills between missions. At the urgent request of NASA, and on an extremely short time schedule, Lincoln Laboratory developed and tested the VAT and RAZEL simulators and installed them at three of the tracking stations in the worldwide ground tracking range.

Lincoln Laboratory accurately predicted that, as a result of ground reflections and end-on capsule antenna patterns, communications at most tracking stations would be inadequate as the capsule came over the horizon. The contractor for this part of the capsule electronics, the Collins Radio Company, changed the antenna design and solved the problem.

The original design of the computation complex had substantial problems. An alternative design was formulated, and it formed the basis for a substantial revision in the unified Goddard computer system.

In May 1961 President John Kennedy announced Project Apollo, the mission to land an American on the moon by the end of the decade. A year later a small Laboratory effort, which had been advising NASA on communications problems encountered during atmospheric reentry by the Mercury and Gemini manned orbital space capsules, was expanded to study spacecraft telecommunications and associated ground support for Project Apollo. The focus of the Lincoln Laboratory effort was on combining all the telemetry functions, the voice communications and the ranging code onto a single S-band carrier. This approach was demonstrated to NASA with prototype equipment constructed in the Radar Division and became the basis for the communications approach used in Project Apollo.

As Project Apollo moved into the implementation phase, NASA support for the Lincoln Laboratory activity declined. A gallium arsenide laser radar was developed for possible application on the moon prior to the end of the Laboratory role in Project Apollo in 1964.

Ambulatory Health Care

Two Lincoln Laboratory engineers, Herbert Sherman and Barney Reiffen, initiated a program on health care in 1969. The program focused on the delivery of ambulatory health care, that is, caring for nonhospitalized patients.[2]

Ambulatory visits can be classified into two categories: acute and chronic. Sherman and Reiffen observed that most acute-care ambulatory visits were due to a small number of complaints, such as colds, headaches or abdominal pain. Similarly, most chronic-care ambulatory visits were for a small number of conditions, for example, hypertension or diabetes. These visits were usually straightforward and routine. Sherman and Reiffen proposed that through the use of standardized protocols, one for each of the most common acute complaints and chronic diseases, health practitioners other than physicians could handle the majority of medical visits.

Each protocol was an algorithm that described the appropriate data to be taken during an ambulatory visit for a given problem. These data derived from the history, physical examination and laboratory tests. Once the data were collected, the protocol gave precise rules for action. The protocols incorporated branching logic, so that the data collected and the medical action recommended could be adapted to each patient's clinical picture. And, of course, the protocols always called for physician intervention whenever a patient's condition failed to fit within the standard parameters.

One of the most useful applications for the protocols was in well-child care. For healthy children, a health-care practitioner with only a high school diploma could use the protocols to provide the same care as a pediatrician — allowing the pediatrician more time to devote to patients whose problems were serious and complex.

In 1969, when the ambulatory care project began, computers and on-line service were expensive. Therefore, the protocols were not implemented as software; they were printed on paper (Figure 16-1).

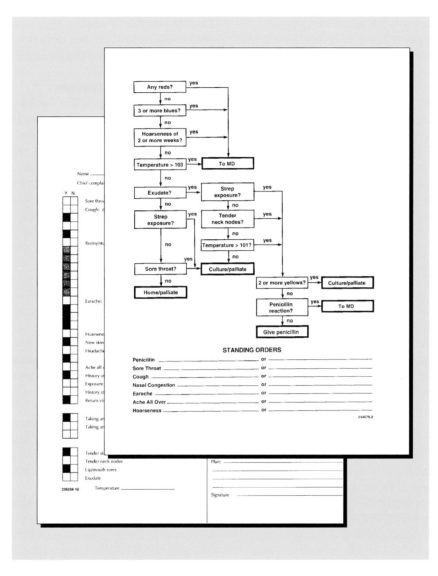

Figure 16-1
Protocol developed in 1972 for the diagnosis of upper respiratory complaints.

The most attractive feature of the protocols was that their use supported the role of health aides in the effort to address the problem of the maldistribution of physicians. Although the United States as a whole had an ample supply of medical doctors, many parts of the country, particularly in rural areas and inner cities, had severe shortages. The Laboratory-developed protocols gave health aides the tools they needed to increase the availability of medical care to patients in those areas.

The ambulatory care project was conducted by Lincoln Laboratory under a contract with the Department of Health, Education and Welfare. Beth Israel Hospital of Boston was a full collaborator, its work supported by a subcontract. Lincoln Laboratory staff developed the concepts; the Beth Israel staff provided the medical contents of the protocols and tested their reliability.

The development of each protocol involved an intensive review of the medical literature, consultation with experts on the ailment under study and interviews with physicians in primary care practice. When the protocol content and medical logic were finalized, a validation study was performed. Typically, this study involved the random allocation of patients with a particular medical problem into an experimental group in which they were cared for by health aides using the protocols with physician consultation, or into a control group in which they were managed only by physicians. Thoroughness of the recorded evaluation, accuracy of diagnosis, relief of symptoms, expressed patient satisfaction and the development of unrecognized illnesses were evaluated by medical record review and telephone follow-up.

The ambulatory health care project was a technical success. Follow-up studies evaluated the time spent by the health practitioner, the physician and the patient in each group. Depending upon the medical problem being addressed, a physician time saving of 20 to 90% was achieved.

Figure 16-2
Charles Ciacera, Philip Jarvinen
and Frederick DiGregorio install a
1/10-scale flywheel system to evaluate
the feasibility of a kinetic-energy
storage proposal.

Figure 16-3
Solar-photovoltaic power station at
Natural Bridges National Monument,
Utah.

The Laboratory built a fully operational 1/10-scale proto-type energy storage unit that incorporated a flywheel developed at Sandia Laboratory (Figure 16-2). In-out storage efficiency of the utility-interactive inverter fly-wheel unit was 80%. For a flywheel equipped with a stand-alone cycloconverter, the efficiency was 65%, al-most exactly the same as that of a battery-inverter system. The difference in efficiency between the two systems was partly due to the increased complexity of the stand-alone system and partly to design deficiencies in the filter, where most of the losses occurred.

Even though residential applications were recognized early to be extremely important, Lincoln Laboratory conducted its first field tests on nonresidential systems. The Department of Energy had requested that Lincoln Laboratory delay the study of residential systems until the National Photovoltaic Program as a whole was ready to deal with the relatively large number of experimental systems involved. During the nonresidential phase of the program, Lincoln Laboratory designed and constructed systems for a farm, a museum display, a commercial radio station and a national park.

The first nonresidential field test was carried out on an experimental farm in Nebraska. The test began in the spring of 1977 when Lincoln Laboratory installed a 25-kW photovoltaic system at the University of Nebraska's Agricultural Research Station in Mead, Nebraska. The study looked at energy management strategies, monitored system performance and evaluated the match between the agricultural load and the available solar energy.

The Mead experiment established a concept that Lincoln Laboratory would substantiate in all subsequent photovol-taic projects: utility-interactive operation was preferable to stand-alone operation. Stand-alone operation provided the advantage of being able to operate through a utility outage. However, the need for a storage battery in a stand-alone system meant that the system either had a complicated start-up sequence or a large inverter and control subsystem.

Operation in parallel with the electric utility provided a considerable advantage by eliminating the costly bat-tery-storage subsystem and its attendant system-control functions. It also allowed the utility to absorb the motor-starting transients, thereby obviating the need for a vari-able voltage/frequency motor-starting sequence.

Lincoln Laboratory's second project was a 1.6-kW system to power a display in the Chicago Museum of Science and Industry. System reliability was outstanding — between 1977 and 1983 there were no module failures. No other system at the time demonstrated comparable reliability.

In November 1978 Lincoln Laboratory initiated a project with WBNO, a daytime AM radio station in Bryan, Ohio, to power their transmitter. Nine months later a 15-kW photovoltaic system began operation. The system was designed to be economically attractive and to supply power primarily to dc loads requiring minimal energy storage. During two years of operation, the Bryan system provided approximately 19 MW-hr of energy, or about 80% of the total energy required by the transmitter.

The final nonresidential project was the most ambitious. In this effort, the Laboratory worked with the National Park Service to set up a photovoltaic power station at a remote site. The project began with a study of sixty-three sites for their photovoltaic potential. Laboratory personnel then visited the ten most promising locations. Natural Bridges National Monument in Utah — offering both insolation and isolation — was chosen as the optimum site for a test of the usefulness of photovoltaics for the National Park Service.

At the time of its completion in June 1980, the 100-kW Natural Bridges unit was the largest photovoltaic system in the world (Figure 16-3). Because the system was lo-cated in a remote corner of the Southwest, it had excel-lent insolation, but connection to the utility grid was not available. Therefore, despite poor results in earlier tests of energy storage, the Laboratory included a backup diesel generator and a battery-storage unit in the system. Even though these elements increased system complexity con-siderably, unattended operation was successful.

Figure 16-4
Solar-photovoltaic-powered residence in Carlisle, Massachusetts.

Lincoln Laboratory turned to a study of residential systems in late 1978. The first systems were prototypes in uninhabited structures. Two Residential Experiment Stations were built, one in the northeastern and one in the southwestern region of the United States. The stations were complete in the technical details of their photovoltaic systems and in their integration into a residence-like structure, but only the portion of the structure needed to effect the integration was constructed. The Northeastern Station, located on Virginia Road in Concord, Massachusetts, included five prototype systems; the Southwestern Station, on the grounds of the New Mexico State University campus in Las Cruces, New Mexico, had eight.

Each Residential Experiment Station included a rooftop photovoltaic array, sized to meet at least 50% of the annual electrical demand of an energy-conserving house, and an enclosed structure for the remainder of the photovoltaic equipment, test instrumentation and work space. Each building was the minimum size that could accommodate the photovoltaic system.

Photovoltaic systems for two additional uninhabited residences, one in Florida and the other in Arizona, were constructed in 1980. The Florida system was located at the Florida Solar Energy Center in Cape Canaveral, Florida; the Arizona system was installed in a model house built by John F. Long Properties in Phoenix.

The annual ac energy output of the Florida residential system was approximately 8000 kWh, with an average system efficiency of 6.4%. Reliability was excellent; only two out of 168 photovoltaic modules failed during sixteen months of operation.

1990

A.J. McLaughlin

D.H. Staelin

H. Kottler

The Arizona structure was the first test of a batten-and-seam photovoltaic module developed by ARCO Solar. During two years of operation, problems arose with both the photovoltaic array and the inverter. Changes to the installation scheme for the photovoltaic modules and corrections to the power-conditioning system improved the reliability, and these modifications were carried over into subsequent designs.

Lincoln Laboratory's first test of an inhabited structure was in a grid-connected residential system installed at the University of Texas Solar Energy Research Facility in Arlington, Texas. The house featured an integrated solar system that combined solar-photovoltaic and solar-heating collectors. The most significant contribution of this project, however, was its success in integrating photovoltaics with the electric utility grid.

Although the Texas house was inhabited, it was still an experimental effort. In the next project, however, Lincoln Laboratory brought photovoltaics into the real world. The Laboratory participated in the design of a fully solar house located on Monroe Hill Road in Carlisle, Massachusetts (Figure 16-4).

Energy-conservation features, passive solar heating, solar hot-water collectors, heat-pump space heating, a wood stove and a photovoltaic power system made this house an energy-self-sufficient residence. Designed by Solar Design Associates of Lincoln, Massachusetts, it included a living room, dining room, kitchen, family room and four bedrooms. The living area, excluding the two-car garage, was 3100 sq ft.

Lincoln Laboratory installed the largest residential photovoltaic system of its time: a 1000-sq-ft array with utility-interactive dc-to-ac power conditioning equipment to eliminate the need for on-site storage. Peak power capacity was 7.3 kW, about ten times larger than that of any previous solar home. The house was completed in May 1981 and a family of four moved into it the following March. Over an average year, the house generated about 9500 kWh, about half the family's annual energy consumption.

Three other photovoltaic residential systems were installed in Hawaii, which was ideally suited for photovoltaics. The warm and sunny climate gave abundant insolation, and the cost of electricity was high. Moreover, being composed of a group of islands with scattered population centers, Hawaii used isolated utility plants, not a power grid.

Lincoln Laboratory arranged with the Hawaii Natural Energy Institute to retrofit three occupied residences with photovoltaic systems. The three houses were of various types and in different locations. One was a two-story duplex in the Kalihi section of Honolulu, the second was a quadruplex in a public housing area in Pearl City and the third was a forty-year-old ranch house on the island of Molokai. Because these homes were already occupied, safety was of paramount importance. Each site was checked by an MIT safety officer and by a State of Hawaii safety inspector. Peak power output from the Pearl City and the Molokai houses was 4 kW; the smaller Kalihi residence generated 2 kW. Each system became operational in June 1981.

NASA GOES-7 image of Earth

Lincoln Laboratory mechanical design for ITS

Figure 16-5
Louis Hallowell using LTS.

Notes

4 Material for this section is taken from two sources: R.C. Butman and F.C. Frick, *The Lincoln Training System: A Summary Report, Technical Note 1972-26, 3 October 1972*; and R.C. Butman and W.P. Harris, *Educational Technology Program, Final Report, 28 October 1980*.

5 W.P. Harris, *Guide to Computer-Text Training, 6 August 1980*. Lexington, Mass.: MIT Lincoln Laboratory, 1980.

In 1982, after six years of participation in the National Photovoltaic Program, shrinking budgets prevented Lincoln Laboratory from continuing its work on technology development. Therefore, the Laboratory made the decision to withdraw from the program.

During the course of the National Photovoltaic Program, Lincoln Laboratory installed more than 11,000 photovoltaic modules in thirty-three field sites. The total power output was 283 kW.

Educational Technology

Lincoln Laboratory initiated a program on educational technology in 1970 with the objective of developing an automated training system for self-paced instruction. The outcome of that effort was the Lincoln Training System (LTS), an interactive teaching machine (Figure 16-5).[4]

Jointly supported by the Air Force and ARPA, the Lincoln Laboratory educational technology group concentrated on computer-aided instruction for the military environment. By 1975 the usefulness of LTS for civilian applications had become apparent, and the Bureau of Mines began a program that supported development of instruction aids for safety training in the mining community.

The heart of the LTS concept was its use of microfiche (4 × 6-in film cards) as the storage medium (Figure 16-6). Work carried out at Lincoln Laboratory — principally by teams led by Frederick Frick, William Harris and David Karp and subsequently by Alan McLaughlin and Robert Butman — made it possible to integrate visual images, voice-quality audio and control logic on a single microfiche. Therefore, each LTS could provide lesson-specific information at each student's terminal; it was an interactive learning system at a time when interactive computers were complex and expensive.

LTS-3, the first system to undergo testing, consisted of a DEC PDP-8/I computer and five terminals for student instruction. The central computer held lesson material, interpreted student responses and recorded their performance. Each terminal comprised an Image Systems Model 201 CARD reader (modified to give improved

frame registration), a dual video/audio projection system, a solid state photodiode tracker-reader assembly for the audio and a keyboard. Audio for each frame was stored on a spirally recorded optical track that could contain up to twenty-eight seconds of speech.

Early in 1972 the 3380th Technical School of the Air Force Training Command conducted a field test of the LTS-3 at Keesler Air Force Base, Mississippi. Course material for the test was developed by a team of Air Force classroom instructors and consisted of thirty hours of material from the Standardized Electronic Principles Course. The authors prepared the visual display, audio script and specifications for control logic.

The LTS-3 reduced training time by 37% with no loss in student achievement. Students and instructors were uniformly enthusiastic about the system.

The success of the Keesler trial led to an effort to design a more economical system. The LTS-3 random access microfiche selector could hold 780 microfiches; for the LTS-4, a microfiche selector that could hold only thirty microfiches was chosen, still enough for an hour of learning.

To reduce costs, LTS-4 was designed to be a stand-alone system; the shared PDP-8 was replaced by state-of-the-art microprocessor-based hardware. The use of microprocessors provided another advantage: it permitted individual training at remote locations.

In 1975, at the end of the LTS-4 development period, the DoD ended its support of the educational technology program. The Bureau of Mines funded the program for an additional five years to develop stand-alone systems and instructional materials for training miners in safety procedures.

The last Bureau of Mines task, initiated in 1979, asked Lincoln Laboratory to produce a book to bring stand-alone teaching equipment into the mining community. The next year Lincoln Laboratory issued the *Guide to Computer-Text Training,* which taught instructors with little or no computer experience how to develop lesson materials.[5]

Figure 16-6
Audio/graphic fiche for the educational technology program.

Notes

6 This section was contributed by Harold Heggestad.

7 This section was contributed by John Andrews.

8 A.F. Hotz, C.H. Much and T.J. Goblick, eds., "Advanced Traffic Management Technology Development and Field Demonstration," *Lincoln Laboratory Project Report ACC-1*, Lexington, Mass.: MIT Lincoln Laboratory, 21 February 1992.

The commercial availability of the personal computer and video disks changed the computer-aided instruction field. Mass-marketed software became commonplace, and Lincoln Laboratory carried out no further work on educational technology for a decade.

The Partners in Manufacturing Education Project

In 1989, in the interest of enhancing American competitiveness in manufacturing, Lincoln Laboratory under the leadership of Alan McLaughlin, then head of the Computer Technology Division, and Harold Heggestad resumed its work on the development of training aids that make use of computer-assisted instruction techniques. The focus of the new Lincoln Laboratory initiative was on educating the workforce to perform well in the flexible, adaptable manufacturing environment of the 1990s. The chosen means to this end was the formation of a partnership including Lincoln Laboratory, educational institutions and industry, with the goal of developing a hands-on laboratory-based manufacturing technology curriculum that would produce graduates who could function efficiently, adapt to changing conditions, solve problems as they occurred and contribute to the evolution of manufacturing processes in the workplace.[6]

The school selected for this activity was the Minuteman Science and Technology High School in Lexington, Massachusetts. Minuteman Tech provides vocational and technical training to students in sixteen neighboring towns. Its students are typically hands-on, mechanically oriented and inclined to learning by doing.

On the basis of discussions with Minuteman Tech, the need for early industry involvement in the program was identified. The Partners in Manufacturing Education Working Group was formed, chaired by Heggestad, associate leader of Lincoln Laboratory's Machine Intelligence Technology Group, and currently including McLaughlin, now an assistant director at the Laboratory, and representatives from the MIT campus, Harvard University, Digital Equipment, Raytheon, Polaroid, Vermont Circuits, Minuteman Tech, Middlesex Community College and the University of Massachusetts at Lowell. These partners committed effort, expertise, personnel and equipment to the creation of a manufacturing training program at Minuteman Tech.

In 1990, as a result of collaborative proposal efforts by Minuteman Tech and Lincoln Laboratory, the school was awarded a National Science Foundation grant of $151,000 for a four-year project entitled "Math/Science Enhanced Manufacturing Center." The development effort was directed by Ronald Fitzgerald, Superintendent-Director of Minuteman Tech.

Lincoln Laboratory continues to coordinate industry/school activities. A teacher from the Acton-Boxborough (Massachusetts) Public Schools is working at Lincoln Laboratory on the project. Digital Equipment Corporation and Raytheon are providing teams of engineers to assist in designing the manufacturing curriculum and in teaching the students, and these companies are also providing modern equipment for a manufacturing line in a laboratory space newly refurbished by Minuteman Tech.

A three-year curriculum has been developed; it uses a real manufacturing facility and produces real products. The first manufactured output was completed in the spring term of 1993 — nine copies of a DEC voice-synthesis subsystem known as MULTIVOICE that is used by voice-impaired individuals.

Highway Management

The term Intelligent Vehicle/Highway Systems (IVHS) describes a broad range of concepts that apply new technology to problems of congestion and safety on road networks. Since Lincoln Laboratory has had an ongoing involvement in surveillance and control systems for military applications and air traffic control, it could make significant contributions to IVHS-related activities. IVHS work at the Laboratory also benefits from contact with researchers on campus, and joint projects with the MIT Center for Transportation Studies have proven productive.[7]

In 1991 the Laboratory undertook an investigation of emerging IVHS needs and identified items of technology necessary for the demonstration of IVHS capabilities.[8] In 1992 the Laboratory became a partner with the MIT Center for Transportation Studies in a project aimed at verifying and enhancing the sensing and control elements of Boston's Central Artery/Third Harbor Tunnel project. This project involved simulation of traffic flow, a study of efficient use of sensor data and analysis of the project control system.

17   Benefits of Laboratory Innovation

The regular transfer of Lincoln Laboratory's technology advances to the technical and industrial communities has been a source of widely ranging benefits to the nation. Because so much of Lincoln Laboratory's work is at the leading edge of technology development, it has found application in nondefense as well as defense industries. New uses in the commercial industrial sector for the innovative concepts, devices and systems developed at Lincoln Laboratory have established the Laboratory's role in promoting national economic development. In every Laboratory mission area, from radar systems to advanced electronic components, technological leadership has produced enabling technologies for the nation's defense, has improved capabilities in the scientific and technical communities and has promoted new enterprises in the commercial sector. The transfer of technology to new industries has provided a foundation for the creation of large numbers of jobs.

Contributions to Economic Security

Indirect, unanticipated transfers of technology to the commercial sector have often produced profound enhancements to the nation's economic competitiveness. Significant contributions to the nation's commercial industrial base have resulted from technologies developed for national defense in the areas of computers, communications and signal processing, radars, optics and solid state devices. This section gives examples of just a few of the contributions to the national economic security that have resulted when Laboratory developments have been used in the commercial sector in applications beyond the initial intended objective.

The SAGE air defense program at Lincoln Laboratory demonstrated real-time digital computer control of a large, geographically dispersed system for the first time. Many nondefense applications have been based on this technology, including the national air traffic control system, industrial process controllers and business inventory systems. In addition, Lincoln Laboratory's work with Bell Telephone Laboratories on transmission of digital data over telephone circuits for remote radars in the SAGE system led to the development of the modem and contributed to worldwide computer data networks.

The Laboratory also pioneered some of the earliest digital signal processors; the SAGE system was capable of processing radar outputs for automatic target detection so as to transmit only target reports to the central computers. One of the earliest books on digital signal processing was written by two Laboratory staff members,[1] who also taught some of the first courses on the subject. Digital signal processing techniques are now used extensively not only in military radars, but also in air traffic control radars and in numerous other applications ranging from oil prospecting to medical imaging.

Lincoln Laboratory's work with IBM as a contractor for the SAGE computer strongly influenced the development of the mainframe computer and the growth of the business computer industry.[2] The initial concepts for the first minicomputer were based on work in the development of transistorized computers carried out at the Laboratory, and led to the formation of Digital Equipment Corporation as an early spin-off from Lincoln Laboratory. The success of the first minicomputer led in turn to the formation of an entirely new industry and to the emergence of Massachusetts and neighboring states as a center of high technology. The Laboratory Instrument Computer (LINC), built in the late 1950s, was the first small computer, and the concepts behind this system established the foundation for the much later development of the personal computer. Computer graphics systems have a historical basis in the TX-2 interactive graphics interface demonstrated at the Laboratory in the early 1960s.

The Laboratory played a leading role in the development of computer algorithms, including efficient techniques for coding. The Reed-Solomon error-correction code, developed in the early years of the Laboratory, is widely used in a variety of commercial as well as military communications systems and is employed almost universally in such familiar applications as compact-disc players. In the 1980s the Laboratory developed the first truly compact speech-coding device that implemented a Linear Predictive Coder algorithm. The speech recognition work subsequently led to the development of the high-performance hidden-Markov-model algorithms that are becoming important in numerous industrial applications.

Figure 17-3
Kenneth Olsen left Lincoln Laboratory to found DEC in 1957.

Notes

3 E.B. Roberts, "Technological Entrepreneurship: Birth, Growth, and Success," *MIT Management* (Winter 1991), p. 21.

4 *MITRE: The First Twenty Years*, Bedford, Mass.: The MITRE Corporation, 1979.

5 Stanley Charren and Norman Moore were not Lincoln Laboratory employees.

1980

Additional research at Lincoln Laboratory led to the development of imaging radars. The range resolution of imaging radars is normally determined by the bandwidth of the radar transmission, the cross-range resolution by the length of integration time used to measure the Doppler frequency shift. In recent years mathematical techniques derived from super-resolution angle-of-arrival antenna systems have been applied to imaging radars, and these techniques have increased radar imaging resolution by almost a factor of three without an increase in the radar bandwidth. Nondefense applications of these developments in the future appear probable.

Although a microwave imaging radar can detect fixed ground objects in the open, it cannot detect objects hidden by foliage. UHF signals can penetrate foliage, but it was thought that the phase disturbances created by foliage would make it impossible to form radar images at such long wavelengths. Lincoln Laboratory has recently demonstrated, however, that objects can be detected through foliage with relatively high resolution. The Laboratory has also developed a variety of recognition techniques for ballistic missile defense, ship recognition and ground-target recognition. Recently, neural network concepts have been applied to recognition problems.

Communications

Lincoln Laboratory was the first organization to employ UHF, SHF and EHF bands for military satellite communications. Numerous current military satellites, including DSCS, FLTSAT and MILSTAR, now employ these frequency bands, as do international civil satellite communications systems. The Laboratory continues to develop lightweight equipment for space-based communications applications. Lightweight robust EHF ground terminals developed at the Laboratory have recently seen service in the field.

Air Traffic Control

In air traffic control work the Laboratory has already been effective in improving the availability of information to aircraft pilots with DABS or Mode S transponders. Improved short-term weather-prediction capability for airport terminal areas offers the potential for greater efficiency in protecting the nation's airlines and passengers from hazardous flying conditions. The Laboratory has worked closely with the FAA to apply its advanced technologies effectively to the development of a wind shear alerting capability. Currently, industry-built weather radars are being installed at selected sites.

Commercialization of Laboratory Technology

Lincoln Laboratory does not compete with the private sector; instead, it places a high priority on working with and encouraging technology transfer to the commercial industrial base through individuals and organizations. In some cases, employees who leave the Laboratory to set up their own firms are given advice and encouragement from the MIT Technology Licensing Office during the transition. In other cases, the Laboratory transfers new technologies to the private sector through government-sponsored arrangements, licenses or cooperative agreements.

Public Law 96-517, popularly known as the Bayh-Dole Act of 1980, has particular importance for MIT and Lincoln Laboratory. Because of this law, universities and small businesses can acquire the title to patents arising out of federally funded research. The Bayh-Dole Act allows universities to grant licenses and receive royalties, and thereby encourages the commercialization of federally funded research. The government retains the right to royalty-free use of the patents.

Lasertron founders J.J. Hsieh and K.W. Nill

Kopin founder J.C.C. Fan

Figure 17-4
A windpower farm built by U.S. Windpower, founded by Herbert Weiss, Stanley Charren and Norman Moore.

In recent years MIT's extensive technology licensing program has expanded Lincoln Laboratory's technology-transfer activities. Companies that have obtained Laboratory-licensed technology through the MIT Technology Licensing Office now also receive technical support from Lincoln Laboratory personnel to facilitate the transfer of technologies.

Spin-Off Companies

Spin-off companies are a powerful vehicle for technology transfer from the Laboratory to the commercial sector. Studies show that the success rate of high-technology companies in the first five years is roughly 70 to 85%, a figure far higher than for nontechnology companies.[3] Lincoln Laboratory's impact on U.S. industrial development is evident from the number of high-technology enterprises started by former staff members. More than sixty successful businesses have spun off from the Laboratory, ranging from small consulting firms to midsize manufacturers to corporate giants, and these companies have created over 100,000 jobs. This technical entrepreneurship has had a favorable influence on both the state and national economy.

A few of the technology-based commercial ventures created by former Laboratory employees are described here to indicate the breadth of technological expertise at the Laboratory and the range of companies spawned.

Digital Equipment Corporation: Kenneth Olsen (Figure 17-3) and Harlan Anderson founded DEC in 1957 to manufacture transistorized circuit boards and computers for engineers. Three years later DEC introduced the PDP-1, the first computer to offer interactive operation, and the company soon was on its way to becoming the world's second largest computer manufacturer.

MITRE Corporation: Established by Robert Everett, John Jacobs and others in 1958 to complete the system engineering of the Lincoln Laboratory–developed SAGE system, MITRE is a nonprofit corporation that provides systems engineering support in air traffic control, information systems, telecommunications and command, control, communication and intelligence.[4]

Electronic Space Systems Corporation (ESSCO): Founded by Albert Cohen and Joseph Vitale in 1961, ESSCO manufactures precision antenna systems and space-frame and composite radomes.

Signatron Acquisition Corporation: Formerly a subsidiary of Sundstrand Corporation, Signatron was founded in 1962 by Julian Bussgang. This company manufactures systems and components for defense and industrial electronics communications.

Applicon: Now a division of Gores Enterprises, Applicon was founded by Harry Lee, Gary Hornbuckle, Richard Spann and Fontaine Richardson in 1969. Applicon was one of the first organizations to develop computer-aided-design/computer-aided-manufacturing (CAD/CAM) software for commercial applications.

U.S. Windpower: Founded in 1979 by Herbert Weiss, Stanley Charren and Norman Moore,[5] U.S. Windpower is the world's largest wind energy company. Now known as Kenetech Windpower, it works closely with utility companies on technology and wind-farm development projects (Figure 17-4).

1990

Micracor founder
A. Mooradian

V.W.S. Chan

Teratech founder
A.M. Chiang

Integrated Computer Engines
founder I.H. Gilbert

Figure 17-5
Emanuel Landsman, Ervin Lyon and Neil Rasmussen (left to right), founders of the American Power Conversion Corporation.

Notes

6 Jess Belser was not a Lincoln Laboratory employee.

7 J.W. Forrester, "Multicoordinate Digital Information Storage Device," U.S. Patent No. 2,736,880, February 28, 1956.

8 L.M. Johnson, "Apparatus and Method for Reducing Modulator Nonlinearities," U.S. Patent 5,002,353, March 26, 1991.

9 C.A. Wang, R.A. Brown and J.A. Caunt, "Vapor Phase Reactor for Making Multilayer Structures," U.S. Patent No. 4,997,677, March 5, 1991.

10 Library and Information Services, *Bibliography of Patents and Licenses Issued to MIT Lincoln Laboratory (Third Edition)*. Lexington, Mass.: MIT Lincoln Laboratory, 1991.

Lasertron: Founded by J. Jim Hsieh and Kenneth Nill in 1980, Lasertron manufactures fiber optic telecommunications systems and components. The company has supplied tens of thousands of 1.3- and 1.55-μm lasers, detectors and light-emitting diodes for optical fiber communications. Manufacturers of telephone transmission equipment worldwide use Lasertron components to transmit signals over fiber optic cables.

American Power Conversion Corporation: Emanuel Landsman, Ervin Lyon and Neil Rasmussen founded American Power Conversion Corporation in 1981 (Figure 17-5). The company designs and manufactures electronic uninterruptible-power-supply products for personal computers, engineering workstations, file servers, communications equipment and other sensitive devices that depend on electric utility power. The company's products provide automatic, virtually instantaneous backup power in the event of a utility power failure.

Kopin Corporation: Founded by John Fan in 1984, Kopin was created to develop, manufacture and market advanced composite semiconductor wafers for the next generation of high-performance integrated circuits. Kopin's wafer engineering technique produces high-quality thin films of advanced materials, including GaAs-on-silicon and silicon-on-insulator. The company is also developing active-matrix liquid-crystal flat-panel displays.

Micracor: Founded by Aram Mooradian and Jess Belser[6] in 1990, Micracor manufactures advanced laser devices, including a miniature single-frequency solid state laser capable of optical pulses as short as 300 psec and a two-dimensional high-power solid state laser array. The company has benefited from federally supported technology-transfer programs and has successfully demonstrated the commercial benefits of military research.

Spin-off activity to new technical enterprises continues. In 1994 Alice Chiang formed Teratech Corporation to exploit the charge-domain processing technology she had developed at Lincoln Laboratory. Chiang's company will

initially develop and manufacture low-power medical imaging instruments for diagnostic applications. Also in 1994, Ira Gilbert sought to apply Laboratory technology for the building of high-performance workstations based on parallel-array architecture. Gilbert and three non-Lincoln Laboratory partners were brought together by the MIT Technology Licensing Office and formed Integrated Computing Engines. Their computers employ dedicated real-time signal processing and are intended to be used for medical imaging, engineering simulation, scientific computation and defense applications.

Cooperative Activities with Commercial Industries

The Stevenson-Wydler Act of 1980, as amended by the Federal Technology Transfer Act of 1986, has given federally funded research and development centers new mechanisms for technology transfer to industry on a precompetitive basis. In recent years, the Laboratory has been working extensively with industrial organizations to take advantage of these new opportunities for enhancing the nation's economic vitality and promoting job growth. Cooperative Research and Development Agreements (CRDA), for example, now allow Lincoln Laboratory to develop technologies with, and transfer technologies to, industry through cooperative arrangements.

In such industry-funded activities as CRDAs, a research agreement between Lincoln Laboratory and an outside company protects the confidentiality of proprietary information that the company shares with Lincoln Laboratory as well as proprietary information developed under the CRDA. Title to any intellectual property developed is negotiated as part of the CRDA, with Lincoln Laboratory rights retained by MIT, just as it is for government-sponsored research.

During 1993 and 1994 thirteen CRDAs were approved, and several more are being processed. Lincoln Laboratory receives no government funding for CRDA activities, and CRDA work at the Laboratory must be completely supported by the companies involved. Both small and large industrial companies have established CRDAs with Lincoln Laboratory and have funded Laboratory work at levels from tens of thousands to several millions of dollars.

The Laboratory has also participated in the formation of university-industry consortia for the development of advanced technologies. Working with MIT campus groups, Lincoln Laboratory played a central role in the establishment of two major consortia: the Consortium for Superconducting Electronics, directed by Richard Ralston, and the All-Optical Network Consortium, directed by Vincent Chan. With support from ARPA, the All-Optical Network Consortium, comprising MIT, AT&T Bell Laboratories and DEC, is seeking to demonstrate a wideband optical network that will increase light-fiber communications network capacities by orders of magnitude over existing systems.

Patents and Licensing

The first patent that came out of work conducted at Lincoln Laboratory was one of the most important: the magnetic-core memory, patented by Jay Forrester in 1956, which became the standard memory device for high-speed digital computers for more than two decades.[7] Recent examples of Laboratory technical innovations licensed to industry for commercialization include an apparatus to reduce modulator nonlinearities through a cancellation scheme based on operating a modulator in two optical polarization states simultaneously, which was developed by Leonard Johnson (Figure 17-6);[8] and a new vapor-phase reactor design to permit highly reproducible production of semiconductor epitaxial layers of GaAs, AlGaAs and InGaAs, developed by Christine Wang, Robert Brown and James Caunt (Figure 17-7).[9] By 1994 work at Lincoln Laboratory had received a total of 419 patents, of which 276 had been licensed to industry for commercial applications (Figure 17-8).[10]

Spin-Off Companies

One direct measure of the Laboratory's contribution to the nation's economy is its success in transferring technology to spin-off companies. The partial list of spin-off companies that follows indicates the range of industrial activities that have been generated and supported by ideas and techniques developed at the Laboratory.*

American Power Conversion
Amtron Corporation
Applicon
Arcon Corporation
Ascension Technology
Atlantic Aerospace Electronics
Carl Blake Associates
Catalyst
Centocor
Clark, Rockoff and Associates
Computer Corporation of America
Corporate-Tech Planning
Delta Sciences
Digital Computer Controls
Digital Equipment Corporation
Electro-Optical Technology
Electronic Space Systems Corporation
F.W.S. Engineering
Hermes Electronics
HH Controls Company
Hrand Saxenian Associates
Information International
Integrated Computing Engines
Interactive Data Corporation
Janis Research Company
Jerome A. Lemieux

John Ackley Consultants
Kopin Corporation
Kulite Semiconductor Products
Lasertron
L.J. Ricardi
Louis Sutro Associates
Man Labs
M.D. Field Company
Meeks Associates
Metric Systems Corporation
Micracor
Micrilor
Micro-Bit Corporation
MITRE Corporation
Object Systems
Photon
Pugh-Roberts Associates
QEI
Schwartz Electro-Optics
Signatron Acquisition Corporation
Sound/Image
Sparta
Spiral Software
Synkinetics
Tau-Tron
Technology Transfer Institute
Telebyte Technology
Telenet Communications
Teratech Corporation
Transducer Products
Tyco Laboratories
U.S. Windpower
Viewlogic Systems
VV Imaging
Wolf Research & Development
Xontech
Zeopower Company

* Additional information about these companies is available in the booklet *Spin-Off Companies from MIT Lincoln Laboratory (Fifth Edition)*. Lexington, Mass.: MIT Lincoln Laboratory, 1993.

Figure 17-6
Leonard Johnson demonstrates an
invention that improves the linearity
of integrated optical modulators.

Figure 17-7
Christine Wang developed this
vapor-phase-epitaxy reactor to
deposit semiconductor films with
exceptionally high uniformity.

A Continuing Commitment

The flow of enabling technologies in which interacting technical innovations lead to new commercial products can be difficult to trace. Researchers may develop similar ideas nearly simultaneously, and several organizations working in the same area may advance a technology rapidly by building on each other's earlier work. Even if a technical advance occurs with astonishing speed, the widespread application of the new idea or technology can take an agonizingly long period. The evolution of technology from innovation to application is impossible without the nation's most important resource — its technical talent. The nation's economic security, which depends on its technical competitiveness, requires the effective use of all sources of technical innovation in both the defense and commercial sectors. Engineering laboratories continue to play an essential role in producing, and demonstrating the usefulness of, technical innovations.

Lincoln Laboratory's ongoing technological leadership will ensure that it remains a source of innovative technology for the nation. In carrying out its primary mission of developing technology for application in the national defense, the Laboratory will continue to provide other benefits to the technical community and the nation. Lincoln Laboratory has demonstrated its commitment to the widest dissemination and application of technology advances. As a source of innovative research and development, it has provided enabling technologies for major new enterprises and created thriving companies. Today, global economic competition and the national policy promoting dual-use technology are compelling the Laboratory to continue to increase its support for commercialization of technical advances. The Laboratory has been involved in the transfer of innovative technology to industry since its establishment in the early 1950s, and it will persevere in this essential task.

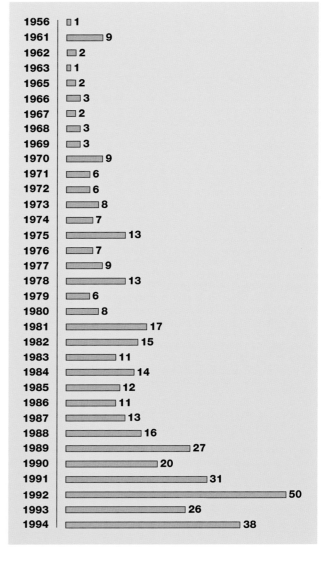

Figure 17-8

Through 1994 a total of 419 patents had been issued to MIT Lincoln Laboratory employees.

18   The Laboratory's Style of Operation

Lincoln Laboratory applies a consistent philosophy to each design effort. Highly qualified technical personnel are assigned, necessary support is provided and each project is followed systematically from concept development, through simulation and analysis, to the demonstration of an integrated system.

Left: Building A, shown in 1988, was the main entrance to Lincoln Laboratory for four decades.

The preceding chapters recount the diverse technical achievements of Lincoln Laboratory. But what is the source of this substantial, continuing productivity? The answer lies in the Laboratory's style — an approach to the management of research and technology development that encompasses every aspect of its operations.

The basic style of operation of Lincoln Laboratory can be traced to the World War II–era MIT Radiation Laboratory.[1] The Radiation Laboratory, known as the Rad Lab, was successful both in developing microwave radars for the war effort and in laying the groundwork to establish continuing relationships between the government and the nation's research universities. The Rad Lab had enormous independence: it maintained close working relationships with industry and the armed services, including forces in the field, and it was permitted intimate access to classified information in the United States and Great Britain. By the end of World War II the Rad Lab had 3500 employees, and they took their experience with them to influence the development of multidisciplinary research efforts at universities across the nation.

The Rad Lab ceased operations at the end of World War II, but many of the individuals who served there went on to participate in the Project Charles study and in Project Lincoln, bringing with them their ideas about how a laboratory should be run. Much has changed in Lincoln Laboratory's operations since 1951, but the heritage from the MIT Rad Lab remains strong.

Personnel, Organization and Facilities

The key ingredients in a successful research and development laboratory are its personnel, its organizational structure and its facilities. Lincoln Laboratory has long recognized the importance of these factors and that its excellence derives from its advanced technical facilities; its supportive organizational structure and administrative functions; its skilled technical support personnel; and its highly motivated, intelligent and creative technical staff.

Personnel

The association of Lincoln Laboratory with MIT, the nation's leading technical university, is an essential element in attracting the best scientific and engineering expertise. This affiliation gives assurance of quality research and technology development while providing access to the university's unique facilities and outstanding faculty.

The determining factor in maintaining excellence at Lincoln Laboratory is the quality and creativity of the approximately eight hundred principal technical staff members. The Laboratory recruits top graduates of the leading technical universities in the country. Emphasis is placed on hiring candidates with advanced graduate training, and currently over half of the staff hold doctorates (Figure 18-1). In recent years about one applicant out of sixty-five has been selected, principally from candidates with advanced degrees in physics, electrical engineering or computer science.

Because of the rapid pace of advances in science and technology, technical staff members need ongoing opportunities to maximize their capabilities through technical courses, self-education, professional contacts and peer reviews. The Laboratory environment respects and encourages cooperation among colleagues and free exchange of information. The contributions of each technical staff member are evaluated regularly in writing to assess performance on current assignments and guide staff members in planning their future at the Laboratory. Reviews based on these assessments, coupled with regular merit-based turnover, result in continual renewal of the technical staff. Recognizing the critical importance of retaining a superior technical staff, management devotes considerable time to staff development and evaluation of staff quality.

Organizational Structure

As the largest research laboratory of MIT, Lincoln Laboratory is accountable to the senior management of the Institute (Figure 18-2). The director of the Laboratory reports to the MIT provost, who has an advisory committee of academic and industrial leaders to assist in evaluating and guiding the operation of the Laboratory. This committee serves a function similar to that of a visiting committee to an academic department.

All research and development programs undertaken at the Laboratory must be approved by the DoD Joint Advisory Committee (JAC). The Laboratory was created as and remains a joint-service DoD facility with close ties to its sponsoring organizations. In its oversight role, the JAC ensures that the Laboratory adheres to federal policies for DoD Federally Funded Research and Development Centers and annually reviews the Laboratory's proposal for programs to be undertaken in the subsequent fiscal year. The JAC is advised in its oversight of the Labora-

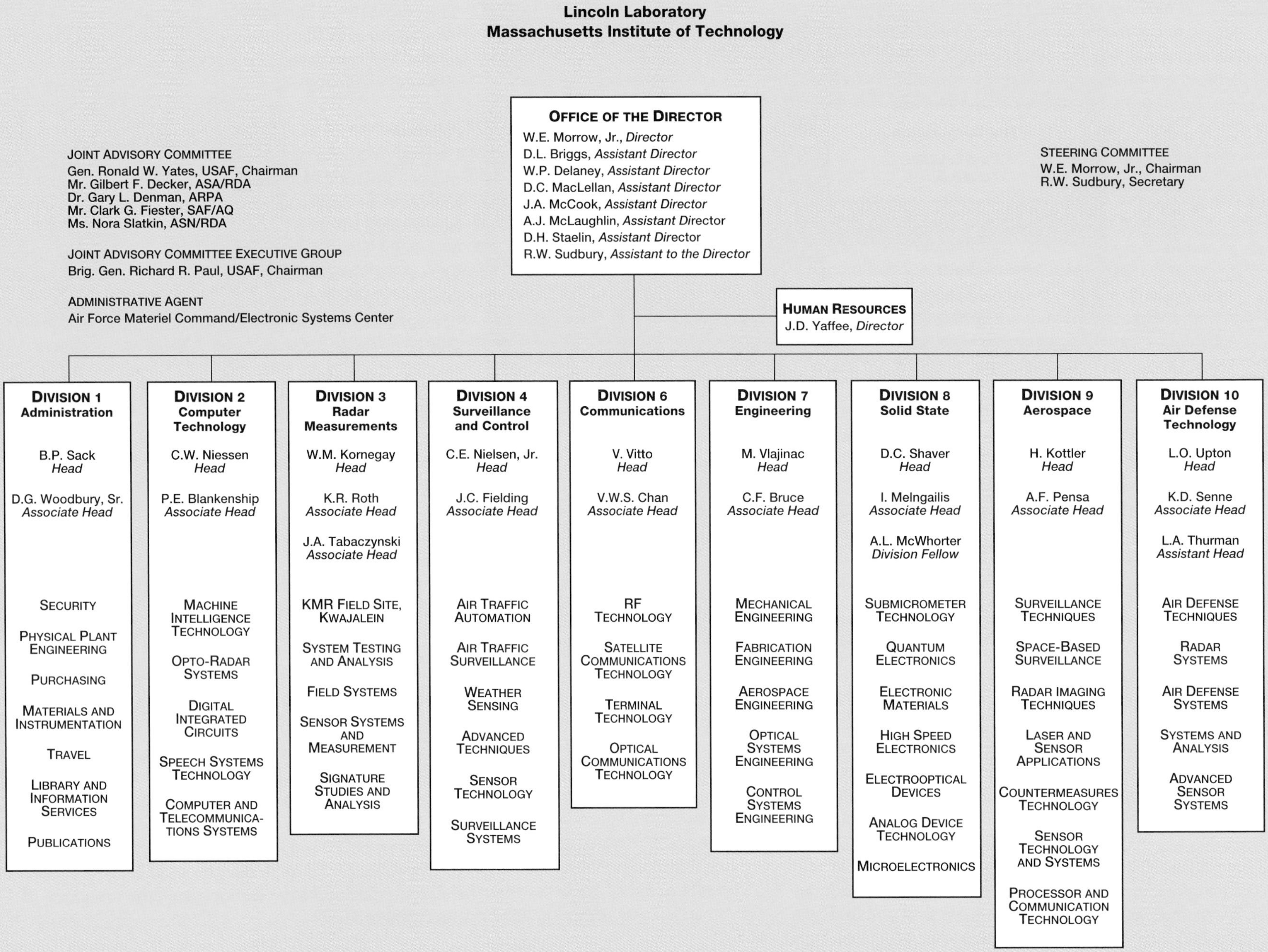

Lincoln Laboratory
Massachusetts Institute of Technology

OFFICE OF THE DIRECTOR
W.E. Morrow, Jr., *Director*
D.L. Briggs, *Assistant Director*
W.P. Delaney, *Assistant Director*
D.C. MacLellan, *Assistant Director*
J.A. McCook, *Assistant Director*
A.J. McLaughlin, *Assistant Director*
D.H. Staelin, *Assistant Director*
R.W. Sudbury, *Assistant to the Director*

JOINT ADVISORY COMMITTEE
Gen. Ronald W. Yates, USAF, Chairman
Mr. Gilbert F. Decker, ASA/RDA
Dr. Gary L. Denman, ARPA
Mr. Clark G. Fiester, SAF/AQ
Ms. Nora Slatkin, ASN/RDA

JOINT ADVISORY COMMITTEE EXECUTIVE GROUP
Brig. Gen. Richard R. Paul, USAF, Chairman

ADMINISTRATIVE AGENT
Air Force Materiel Command/Electronic Systems Center

STEERING COMMITTEE
W.E. Morrow, Jr., Chairman
R.W. Sudbury, Secretary

HUMAN RESOURCES
J.D. Yaffee, *Director*

DIVISION 1
Administration

B.P. Sack
Head

D.G. Woodbury, Sr.
Associate Head

SECURITY

PHYSICAL PLANT
ENGINEERING

PURCHASING

MATERIALS AND
INSTRUMENTATION

TRAVEL

LIBRARY AND
INFORMATION
SERVICES

PUBLICATIONS

DIVISION 2
**Computer
Technology**

C.W. Niessen
Head

P.E. Blankenship
Associate Head

MACHINE
INTELLIGENCE
TECHNOLOGY

OPTO-RADAR
SYSTEMS

DIGITAL
INTEGRATED
CIRCUITS

SPEECH SYSTEMS
TECHNOLOGY

COMPUTER AND
TELECOMMUNICA-
TIONS SYSTEMS

DIVISION 3
**Radar
Measurements**

W.M. Kornegay
Head

K.R. Roth
Associate Head

J.A. Tabaczynski
Associate Head

KMR FIELD SITE,
KWAJALEIN

SYSTEM TESTING
AND ANALYSIS

FIELD SYSTEMS

SENSOR SYSTEMS
AND
MEASUREMENT

SIGNATURE
STUDIES AND
ANALYSIS

DIVISION 4
**Surveillance
and Control**

C.E. Nielsen, Jr.
Head

J.C. Fielding
Associate Head

AIR TRAFFIC
AUTOMATION

AIR TRAFFIC
SURVEILLANCE

WEATHER
SENSING

ADVANCED
TECHNIQUES

SENSOR
TECHNOLOGY

SURVEILLANCE
SYSTEMS

DIVISION 6
Communications

V. Vitto
Head

V.W.S. Chan
Associate Head

RF
TECHNOLOGY

SATELLITE
COMMUNICATIONS
TECHNOLOGY

TERMINAL
TECHNOLOGY

OPTICAL
COMMUNICATIONS
TECHNOLOGY

DIVISION 7
Engineering

M. Vlajinac
Head

C.F. Bruce
Associate Head

MECHANICAL
ENGINEERING

FABRICATION
ENGINEERING

AEROSPACE
ENGINEERING

OPTICAL
SYSTEMS
ENGINEERING

CONTROL
SYSTEMS
ENGINEERING

DIVISION 8
Solid State

D.C. Shaver
Head

I. Melngailis
Associate Head

A.L. McWhorter
Division Fellow

SUBMICROMETER
TECHNOLOGY

QUANTUM
ELECTRONICS

ELECTRONIC
MATERIALS

HIGH SPEED
ELECTRONICS

ELECTROOPTICAL
DEVICES

ANALOG DEVICE
TECHNOLOGY

MICROELECTRONICS

DIVISION 9
Aerospace

H. Kottler
Head

A.F. Pensa
Associate Head

SURVEILLANCE
TECHNIQUES

SPACE-BASED
SURVEILLANCE

RADAR IMAGING
TECHNIQUES

LASER AND
SENSOR
APPLICATIONS

COUNTERMEASURES
TECHNOLOGY

SENSOR
TECHNOLOGY
AND SYSTEMS

PROCESSOR AND
COMMUNICATION
TECHNOLOGY

DIVISION 10
**Air Defense
Technology**

L.O. Upton
Head

K.D. Senne
Associate Head

L.A. Thurman
Assistant Head

AIR DEFENSE
TECHNIQUES

RADAR
SYSTEMS

AIR DEFENSE
SYSTEMS

SYSTEMS AND
ANALYSIS

ADVANCED
SENSOR
SYSTEMS

Figure 18-3
**Lincoln Laboratory organization chart
in 1994.**

designs and delineates a plan of attack. A defining study often reveals the need to gather specific environmental data such as radar clutter, noise backgrounds, electromagnetic propagation, infrared emission or acoustic levels. Or a study may call for a characterization of the properties of the system itself. Measuring and understanding the relevant phenomenologies provide information vital to the successful creation of new technical approaches and allow verification of the concepts underlying development efforts. Experience has shown that proceeding with equipment development without such studies can bring unfortunate surprises.

Quite often, technical challenges can be met through the development of new electronic or optical devices. Devices developed in the past include the core memory, the laser diode, surface-acoustic-wave devices, electro-optic devices and high-sensitivity optical and infrared sensors — and these are just a few examples of devices developed at Lincoln Laboratory. The Laboratory continues to have a strong commitment to the development and utilization of advanced electronic and optical devices to improve system capabilities.

Once a system has been designed, constructed and characterized, it is thoroughly tested, frequently in the field. Such tests may be preceded by preliminary analyses, including intensive computer-based modeling and simulations. However, simulations cannot take the place of actual field trials. In fact, field tests often provide the data necessary to extrapolate a simulation to reflect a more complex environment. The Laboratory considers a system design incomplete until its soundness has been verified by carefully planned and executed tests in the field.

Throughout the initial system study, device development, design and testing, the Laboratory requests reviews of program progress by technically qualified personnel either within the Laboratory, outside or both. Small review groups comprising individuals with a high degree of technical competence have been found to provide the most useful reviews. This technical input by peers serves as a check on the soundness of a system design and ensures that alternative approaches are considered. Both formal and informal technical reviews by Laboratory colleagues are also held whenever a staff member is planning to

make a technical presentation. These reviews are highly informative, thought provoking and critical to ensuring that the Laboratory presents high-quality work to the technical community.

The last step in the Laboratory's research and development approach is the transfer of new technologies to outside institutions and industries. Technology transfers can be accomplished through publications, seminars and field demonstrations, by Laboratory personnel temporarily or permanently transferring to outside organizations or by industry personnel residing at the Laboratory. The Laboratory hosts technical workshops, seminars on special topics and an annual series of JAC seminars covering each of the Laboratory's mission areas. Individual technical staff members also speak at symposia sponsored by professional societies, contribute to professional journals, write detailed descriptions of their research activities in technical reports and present their work to scientists and engineers in a wide range of technical disciplines through the *Lincoln Laboratory Journal*.

Unlike private industry, Lincoln Laboratory does not manufacture and sell products, and therefore it must measure the success of its work by the extent to which a new technology finds applications elsewhere. The transfer of technologies for either government or commercial use is a vital Laboratory objective and is strongly encouraged. The Laboratory frequently transfers technology to companies serving the defense sector. Mechanisms such as patent licenses, technology transfer agreements and cooperative research and development agreements now also permit the transfer of advanced technologies to nondefense commercial industries. Before a cooperative agreement is signed, it is reviewed by the Laboratory for any possible conflict of interest and by the Air Force to ensure its appropriateness.

Lincoln Laboratory provides an exceptionally supportive environment for research and development, where scientists and engineers are free to think, experiment and solve problems of national importance. Because of the quality of its technical staff and an organizational structure that fosters innovation, the Laboratory has produced research of the highest quality for more than forty years, and it will maintain this excellence as it faces new challenges.

The Lincoln Laboratory Logo

The MIT Lincoln Laboratory logo, which first appeared in February 1958 in the Lincoln Laboratory Bulletin, was conceived by Carl Overhage, the Laboratory's fourth director. Overhage drew a Lissajous figure* based on the superposition of two simple harmonic vibrations and commissioned retired Brigadier General Robert Steinle and the firm Advertising Designers of Los Angeles to transform the Lissajous figure into an artistic image.

The two *L*s rotated 180° with respect to each other stand for Lincoln Laboratory. They form a rectangle enclosing the Lissajous figure generated by the parametric equations $x = 3 \sin(8\pi t/T)$ and $y = 4 \sin(6\pi t/T)$. The figure is traced along the horizontal axis *x* and the vertical axis *y* as the variable *t* progresses from $t = 0$ to *T*.

The Lissajous figure, familiar to most physical scientists and engineers, connotes harmony, order and stability. The Lincoln Laboratory logo is an identifying symbol on Laboratory reports, presentation materials, badges and signs. Because of its distinctive and striking appearance, it was included in *The Book of American Trademarks*, a compilation of the nation's most significant trademarks, logos and corporate symbols.**

---

* Lissajous figures, named for the French mathematician Jules-Antoine Lissajous, are also known as Bowditch curves after their discoverer, Nathaniel Bowditch, the mathematician from Salem, Massachusetts.
** D.E. Carter, *The Book of American Trademarks*. Ashland, Ky.: Century Communications Unlimited, 1972.

19 Looking Forward

Before World War II, very few in the national security establishment had identified the critical relationship between the nation's security and its technological leadership.[1] The role of technology development in strengthening the national economy has been understood for an even briefer time. And yet today these facts seem self-evident: technology development is vital to both the nation's security and its economic strength. The question is how U.S. leadership in technology development will best be maintained in the future.

The Challenges to National and International Security

In the post–Cold War era, the specific challenges facing the United States have changed dramatically, but the need for advanced technology to solve problems affecting the national and international security has grown even greater. With the breakup of the Soviet Union came a widespread hope that the world would be at peace; the path to democracy for Russia, however, has been neither easy nor certain. Many now worry that Russia, consistent with much of its history, could revert to a more autocratic form of government.

The post–Cold War years have also seen the eruption of civil wars in various spots around the globe due to nationalist groups fighting for power or independence. The United States has repeatedly found itself engaged in peacekeeping operations to protect populations whose law and order have been threatened or destroyed. The Iraqi aggression in the Persian Gulf region shattered any illusion that the United States could avoid future conflicts. And added to these political realities is the actual and potential spread of theater missile technology to more aggressive, smaller nations. The rapid economic growth of some of these countries has even created the danger of the emergence of a new major military power.

The armed services must leverage their technologies to respond effectively to a wide variety of changing conflicts around the globe at a time of shrinking defense expenditures. Effective use must be made of the commercial industrial base through wider application of dual-use technologies. This will require that the process for government acquisition of dual-use high-technology equipment from industry be reformed, and that the activities of research and development laboratories be more closely coupled to technological advancements in the manufacturing sector and to operational needs in the armed services.

Among the primary tasks of the military in the post–Cold War era is to respond to contingencies involving threats against U.S. allies. Therefore, the United States must develop excellent intelligence and attack-warning systems. A wide-area combat surveillance system and the ability to communicate detailed information quickly are vitally important. In the present political climate, which tends to discourage overseas stationing of U.S. ground forces, the capability to project force rapidly over long distances from air- or sea-based weapon carriers is essential, with a strong preference for long-range stand-off precision weapons to minimize losses to U.S. forces and local civilian populations. Rapid sea transport to move ground forces quickly is also needed, as is the ability to inject ground forces into a conflict without the use of large port facilities.

A central feature of U.S. foreign policy is the encouragement of democracy, especially in countries that were formerly governed autocratically. The achievement of this goal rests primarily with diplomacy and economic support for emerging democracies, but must be supported by advanced technologies to provide high-quality intelligence on developments in the countries of interest. A major and growing activity of the U.S. armed forces in the post–Cold War world is peacekeeping in countries divided by civil war or threatened by disintegrating governments. Conventional military forces are very difficult to deploy in these situations without incurring significant casualties within the peacekeeping forces or the local civilian populations. The need to provide humanitarian aid with minimal risk to military forces from terrorist activity or local unrest calls for an approach involving the development of improved intelligence techniques and the utilization of nonlethal weapons.

Notes

1 Material for this chapter was contributed by Walter Morrow.

Nuclear, chemical and biological weapons of mass destruction have been and remain the greatest threat to international security. The primary means to counter the spread of these weapons is to develop intelligence and surveillance capabilities that can detect both weapons-development programs and the weapons themselves. An important secondary capability is to be able to destroy such weapons without creating widespread hazards. In the long term, the two great strategic threats to the United States are the development by lesser nations of long-range ballistic missiles capable of mass destruction, and the reemergence of a substantial military power with such weapons. The best response to either threat is for the United States to develop effective defenses against ballistic and aerodynamic weapons and to continue to maintain a significant strategic deterrent. Space-based surveillance and effective control of space will continue to play important roles in strategic defense, requiring cost-effective improvement of space-based assets.

The security of the United States depends as much on its economic strength as on its defense capability. Although the U.S. economy today is the largest in the world, its position is being challenged. The armed services will be called on to ensure freedom of the airways and seaways to allow U.S. commerce free access to trading partners, raw materials and energy sources. Domestically, our manufacturing, service and government sectors will need to become increasingly efficient, and our industries will need to maintain and expand their technological leadership.

The Importance of University-Related Technology Development Laboratories

In the United States the primary settings for advanced technology development are industrial research and development organizations, government laboratories, university faculty campus laboratories, independent nonprofit research institutes, and university-related technology development organizations such as Lincoln Laboratory. The primary objectives of these five types of organizations differ widely.

The goal of most industrial laboratories is the development of technologies and products that will produce profits in the relatively short term — AT&T Bell Laboratories being one of the notable exceptions. Economic conditions often make it difficult for industry to sustain

the investment needed for long-term research and development undertakings. Government laboratories, by contrast, can conduct longer-term projects, but they face other constraints. They are often unable to acquire advanced laboratory facilities expeditiously because of government regulations. In addition, they have the responsibility for procuring sponsored research from other institutions, which diverts considerable professional resources from internal research and development activities. Government laboratories have difficulty attracting and retaining the best scientists and engineers, in part because of government personnel policies, and the obstacles to performance-based personnel reductions during periods of declining funding can create long-term staffing inadequacies. Some of the best government laboratories are seeking changes in their organizational structure and policies to cope with these problems.

The innovative atmosphere of university faculty campus laboratories is conducive to scientific advances. However, these facilities tend to be small and geared to the education of graduate students carrying out research for a single professor. The work of campus laboratories can be highly creative, but they are not appropriate settings for major efforts involving large teams of scientists and engineers and requiring significant support personnel. Independent nonprofit research institutes, on the other hand, may be able to tackle larger-scale challenges but, without a relationship to a major university, they lack ready access to the diverse innovative resources of faculty and facilities available to university-related laboratories.

Large university-related laboratories such as Lincoln Laboratory provide very favorable settings for undertaking long-term, large-scale science and technology challenges. Their research priorities, unlike those of industrial organizations, can be exclusively in the national interest. They have a much more efficient organizational structure than government laboratories and are able to attract the highest-quality researchers; ultimately, the best scientists and engineers are the best source of new advanced technologies. Large university-related laboratories can also undertake complex projects that would be impossible in a small university faculty campus laboratory, and they can utilize the resources of their parent university. Thus large university-related research and development institutions have been, and will remain, an important source of forward-looking technology for the nation.

The Challenge for Lincoln Laboratory

Lincoln Laboratory is prepared to meet these challenges, and it will play a critical role in maintaining the nation's strong base in advanced technologies. Its technological directions are difficult to predict precisely, since important advancements often involve complex interactions between discoveries in several fields, and the best technical solution to a problem is not usually apparent when an investigation begins. The areas in which significant contributions are now being sought include advanced sensing systems, improved data processing and automatic recognition techniques applied to existing advanced sensors, as well as communications technologies tying sensors to data processing and distribution systems.

The new or improved sensor systems envisaged will be able to acquire data sufficient to detect and identify objects of interest that have been concealed or have had their observables reduced. These systems should be able to operate in bad weather and at night and be nearly impossible to detect and disrupt. The signal processing and recognition equipment of the future will probably be many orders of magnitude faster than present equipment. For this, completely new types of digital devices may be needed, possibly based on the use of optical signals. Other likely developments at Lincoln Laboratory in the future include advanced signal processing and recognition algorithms that can identify objects with a high degree of reliability and advanced communications technologies that permit compact equipment to support very high capacity circuits.

The first four decades of the Laboratory have witnessed the transition from the equipment developed for SAGE with limited sensing and computational capabilities to enormously powerful data processors and sensors with orders of magnitude greater capabilities netted by robust high-data-rate communications. Future technological advances are difficult to imagine today, just as they were forty years ago, and yet the security and economic strength of the nation depend on them. This is the challenge for Lincoln Laboratory as it faces the future.

Appendix

Acronyms

ABMDA	Army Ballistic Missile Defense Agency		CRT	Cathode Ray Tube
ABR	Advanced Battlefield Radar		CW	Continuous Wave
ABRES	Advanced Ballistic Reentry Systems		DABS	Discrete Address Beacon System
ACAS	Airborne Collision Avoidance System		DARPA	Defense Advanced Research Projects Agency
ACE	Atmospheric-Compensation Experiment		DCA	Direction Center Active
A/D	Analog to Digital		DDR&E	Director of Defense Research and Engineering
ADC	Air Defense Command		DEW	Distant Early Warning
ADCOM	Aerospace Defense Command		DoD	Department of Defense
ADES	Air Defense Engineering Services		DPCA	Displaced-Phase-Center Antenna
ADIS	Air Defense Integrated System		DRR	Digital Radar Relay
ADSEC	Air Defense Systems Engineering Committee		DSCS	Defense Satellite Communications System
ADTS	Advanced Detection Technology Sensor		DSNCP	Deep Space Network Control Processor
AEW	Airborne Early Warning		DSPN	Direct-Sequence Pseudonoise
AFCRL	Air Force Cambridge Research Laboratory		EHF	Extremely High Frequency
AFOAT	Air Force Office of Atomic Testing		ESD	Electronic Systems Division
AGSR	Advanced Ground Surveillance Radar		ESS	Experimental SAGE Subsector
ALCOR	ARPA-Lincoln C-Band Observables Radar		ETS	Experimental Test System
ALRI	Airborne Long-Range Input		FAA	Federal Aviation Administration
ALTAIR	ARPA Long-Range Tracking and Instrumentation Radar		FDP	Fast Digital Processor
AM	Amplitude Modulation		FEP	FLTSAT EHF Package
AMTI	Airborne Moving-Target Indicator		FET	Field-Effect Transistor
APD	Avalanche Photodiode		FFRDC	Federally Funded Research and Development Center
ARC	Average Response Computer		FFT	Fast Fourier Transform
ARPA	Advanced Research Projects Agency		FLIR	Forward-Looking Infrared
ASAMM	Advanced Surface-to-Air Missile Model		FM	Frequency Modulation
ASCA	Airplane Stability and Control Analyzer		FSK	Frequency-Shift Keying
ASDE	Airport Surface Detection Equipment		GCI	Ground Control of Intercept
ASR	Airport Surveillance Radar		GEODSS	Ground-based Electro-Optical Deep Space Surveillance
ASTA	Airport Surface Traffic Automation		GOES	Geostationary Operational Experimental Satellite
ASTB	Airborne Seeker Test Bed		GPALS	Global Protection Against Limited Strikes
ATC	Air Traffic Control		GTS	GEODSS Test Site
ATCAC	Air Traffic Control Advisory Committee		HAX	Haystack Auxiliary
ATCRBS	Air Traffic Control Radar Beacon System		HF	High Frequency
ATS	Applications Technology Satellite		HMM	Hidden Markov Model
AWACS	Airborne Warning and Control System		HOWLS	Hostile Weapons Location Systems
AWIPS	Advanced Weather Interactive Processing System		ICBM	Intercontinental Ballistic Missile
BCAS	Beacon Collision Avoidance System		IF	Intermediate Frequency
BIFF	Battlefield IFF		IFF	Identification, Friend or Foe
BMD	Ballistic Missile Defense		IMC	Instrument Meteorological Conditions
BMDO	Ballistic Missile Defense Organization		IMPATT	Impact Ionization Avalanche Transit Time
BMEWS	Ballistic Missile Early Warning System		I/O	Input/Output
BOSS	BMEWS Operational Simulation System		IPC	Intermittent Positive Control
C^3	Command, Control and Communications		IR	Infrared
C^3I	Command, Control, Communications and Intelligence		IRAR	IR Airborne Radar
CCD	Charge-Coupled Device		IRMS	IR Measurement System
CCM	Counter-Countermeasure		ISAR	Inverse Synthetic-Aperture Radar
CLASP	Closed Loop Adaptive Single Parameter		JAC	Joint Advisory Committee
CMT	Cruise Missile Technology		JSTARS	Joint Surveillance and Target Acquisition Radar System
CONUS	Continental United States		KMR	Kwajalein Missile Range
CRDA	Cooperative Research and Development Agreement		KREMS	Kiernan Reentry Measurements Site

LACE	Low-Power Atmospheric-Compensation Experiment	PPI	Plan Position Indicator
LASA	Large Aperture Seismic Array	PRESS	Pacific Range Electromagnetic Signature Studies
LCS	Lincoln Calibration Spheres	PRM	Precision Runway Monitor
LDSP	Lincoln Digital Signal Processor	RAC	Reflective Array Compressor
LDVT	Lincoln Digital Voice Terminal	RCS	Radar Cross Section
LES	Lincoln Experimental Satellite	RF	Radio Frequency
LESOC	Lincoln Experimental Satellite Operations Center	RSP	Reentry Systems Program
LET	Lincoln Experimental Terminal	RTD	Resonant-Tunneling Diode
LINC	Laboratory Instrument Computer	RV	Reentry Vehicle
LLTV	Low Light Television	SAB	Scientific Advisory Board
LPC	Linear Predictive Coding	SABLE	Scaled Atmospheric Blooming Experiment
LPE	Liquid-Phase Epitaxy	SAC	Strategic Air Command
LRIR	Long-Range Imaging Radar	SAGE	Semi-Automatic Ground Environment
LTG	Low-Temperature Grown	SAM	Surface-to-Air Missile
LTS	Lincoln Training System	SAR	Synthetic-Aperture Radar
LWIR	Long Wavelength Infrared	SATCIT	Satellite Acquisition and Tracking using Coherent Integration Techniques
MASR	Multiple Antenna Surveillance Radar		
MBA	Multiple-Beam Antenna	SATTRK	Satellite Tracking
MBE	Molecular Beam Epitaxy	SAW	Surface Acoustic Wave
MFSK	Multiple Frequency Shift Keying	SBV	Space-Based Visible
MIDYS	Millstone Dynamic Scheduler	SDI	Strategic Defense Initiative
MILSATCOM	Military Satellite Communications	SDIO	Strategic Defense Initiative Organization
MIRACL	Mid-Infrared Advanced Chemical Laser	SHF	Superhigh Frequency
MIRV	Multiple Independently Targeted Reentry Vehicles	SIT	Silicon Intensified Target
MLS	Microwave Landing System	SMTI	Shipboard Moving Target Indicator
MMS	Multistatic Measurement System	SOI	Space Object Identification
MMW	Millimeter Wave	SOT	System Operation Test
MNOS	Metal-Nitride-Oxide Semiconductor	SSB	Single Sideband
MSX	Midcourse Space Experiment	STANAG	Standardization Agreement
MTD	Moving Target Detector	STC	Sinusoidal Transform Coder
MTI	Moving Target Indicator	SWAT	Short-Wavelength Adaptive Techniques
MUSE	Matrix Update Systolic Experiment	TACCAR	Time-Averaged Clutter-Coherent Airborne Radar
NASA	National Aeronautics and Space Administration	TATCA	Terminal Air Traffic Control Automation
NATO	North American Treaty Organization	TATS	Tactical Transmission System
NCMC	NORAD Cheyenne Mountain Complex	TCAS	Traffic Advisory and Collision Avoidance System
NEROC	Northeast Radio Observatory Corporation	TDWR	Terminal Doppler Weather Radar
NFL	New Foreign Launch	TMD	Theater Missile Defense
NFLP	New Foreign Launch Processor	TOS	Transportable Optical System
NIS	NATO IFF System	TRADEX	Target Resolution and Discrimination Experiment
NOAA	National Oceanic and Atmospheric Administration	TRAPAF	Target Return Adaptive Pointing and Focus
NOMAC	Noise Modulation and Correlation	TRSB	Time-Reference Scanning-Beam
NORAD	North American Air Defense Command	UAV	Unmanned Air Vehicle
NRP	Netted Radar Program	UCT	Uncorrelated Target
OAMP	Optical Aircraft Measurements Program	UHF	Ultrahigh Frequency
OCULAR	Optical Compensation of Uniphase Laser Radiation	VERLORT	Very Long Range Tracker
OSD	Office of the Secretary of Defense	VHF	Very High Frequency
PBT	Permeable Base Transistor	VLSI	Very Large Scale Integration
PCI	Phase-Compensation Instability	VPE	Vapor-Phase Epitaxy
PMP	Parallel Microprogrammable Processor	WSMR	White Sands Missile Range
POES	Polar Operational Environmental Satellite	XD	Experimental Development

Index

Credits

The photographs and figures in this book have been supplied by the Lincoln Laboratory Publications Group except as noted below.

Page ix
Vest and Wrighton photograph taken by Dwyer Photography.

Page 2
Wiesner photograph courtesy of the MIT Museum.

Page 3
Building 20, Sloan Building and Whittemore Building photographs courtesy of the MIT Museum.

Page 6
Killian and Loomis photographs courtesy of the MIT Museum.

Page 10
Building 22 and Barta Building photographs courtesy of the MIT Museum.

Page 14
Cape Cod System direction center photograph courtesy of the MITRE Corporation Archives.

Page 38
Zacharias and Hubbard photographs courtesy of the MIT Museum.

Page 63
Texas Tower photograph courtesy of the *New York Times*.

Page 64
Atlas/Centaur launch photograph courtesy of NASA.

Page 84
Roi-Namur photograph courtesy of William Ward.

Page 86
Cobra Judy photograph courtesy of the U.S. Air Force.

Page 88
Aerial photograph courtesy of the U.S. Army.

Page 93
Gellinam photograph courtesy of the U.S. Army.

Page 96
Cobra Eye photograph courtesy of the U.S. Air Force.

Page 98
Wake Island launch photograph courtesy of the U.S. Army.

Page 117
Skylab photograph courtesy of NASA.

Page 125
Lincoln Calibration Sphere photograph courtesy of the ROHR Corporation.

Page 132
Luna See photograph courtesy of Louis Smullin.

Page 136
Firebird launch photograph courtesy of NASA.

Page 139
High-energy-laser propagation range photograph courtesy of Pratt and Whitney.

Page 139
Air Force Maui Optical Site photograph courtesy of AVCO.

Page 140
Sodium-beacon photograph courtesy of the U.S. Army.

Page 172
Mountaintop radar photograph courtesy of Jim Davis.

Page 181
ADS-18S and IDPCA photographs courtesy of Jim Davis; Kauai photograph courtesy of the U.S. Navy.

Page 187
AN/APG-70 radar photograph courtesy of the U.S. Air Force.

Page 196
Adler photograph courtesy of the MIT Museum.

Page 234
Logan International Airport photograph courtesy of Massachusetts Port Authority.

Page 245
TMA display photograph courtesy of NASA.

Page 257
GOES-7 earth image courtesy of NASA.

Page 266
Olsen photograph courtesy of Digital Equipment Corporation.

Page 267
Windfarm photograph courtesy of U.S. Windpower, Inc.

Page 268
Landsman, Lyon and Rasmussen photograph courtesy of American Power Conversion Corp.

Page 284
Loomis photograph courtesy of University Archives, University of Illinois at Urbana-Champaign; Wieser photograph courtesy of the MIT Museum; Hill photograph courtesy of the MIT News Office; Radford, Clauser, Dinneen and Morrow photographs taken by the Fabian Bachrach Studio.

Colophon

Technology in the National Interest was produced entirely on Macintosh computers. Original text was edited in Microsoft Word, line-art illustrations were created in Adobe Illustrator, and bitmapped graphics and scanned images were prepared in Adobe Photoshop. Page layout of all elements was performed in Adobe PageMaker.

Body text is set in Adobe Bembo; chapter titles, captions, sidebars, and headers are set in Adobe Helvetica Neue Heavy; footnotes are set in Adobe Helvetica Neue Light; and timeline captions are set in Adobe Helvetica Condensed Light.

Proof pages were printed on a Tektronix III PXi phase change color printer and an Apple LaserWriter IIg black-and-white laser printer.

At Nimrod Press, all color photographs were scanned on a Modular DS 757 color laser scanner, and pages were printed on a Heidelberg six-color Speedmaster press.